WORKING IN
WOOD
AN INTRODUCTION

WORKING IN
WOOD
AN INTRODUCTION

Jack Hill & Ernest Scott

First published by The Lyons Press, 2001
Working in Wood: an Introduction

First published in Great Britain in 1980 by Mitchell Beazley,
an imprint of Octopus Publishing Group Ltd,
2–4 Heron Quays, London E14 4JP
Reprinted 1984, 1988, 1992, 1993
Revised edition 1997

All enquiries should be addressed to:
The Lyons Press, 123 West 18 Street, New York, NY 10011

ISBN 1-58574-219-8

Library of Congress Cataloging-in-Publication Data
is available on file.

Set in News Gothic, Caslon and New Century

Color reproduction by Pica Colour Separation, Singapore
Produced by Toppan Printing Co, (H.K,) Ltd

Contents

Introduction & acknowledgments

'Handling wood and sensing its textures and fragrances brings to mind the pleasures of a bygone age, when the woodworking skills of master craftsmen were commonplace. In our technological age, as these traditional skills are required less and less in the pursuit of a living, they are coveted more and more for the sheer pleasure inherent in their mastery'.

Written almost two decades ago, this is the opening paragraph of the Foreword to the original version of this book by Ernest Scott, then lengthily titled *The Mitchell Beazley Illustrated Encyclopedia of Working in Wood*. That these words are still pertinent today is witnessed by the social changes that have taken place in the workplace and by the tremendous interest in working with wood that has developed in the intervening years.

I first encountered this book in the early 1980s when I reviewed it for *Woodworker* magazine. I remember my admiration for and enthusiasm about the book's content and presentation at that time – feelings that have endured to the present day and that I know are shared by many other woodworkers. When asked to carry out a revision I accepted with mixed feelings of pleasure and apprehension! For years I had revered both the book and its late author – now I was to undertake the job of reworking and updating it. A daunting task!

In the original compilation of the book, Ernest Scott and the publishers worked in close association with a team of specialist craftsmen, each skilled in his area of work. As a result *Working in Wood: an Introduction* is, in effect, a distillation of the accumulated knowledge of, literally, hundreds of years of practical experience. The craftsman best communicates his expertise by demonstrating his skills and describing his actions as he works and this is precisely how Working in Wood was created. Using clear illustrations of these craftsmen and the author at work, linked to a concise and coherent text,

the subjects of choice of materials, the variety and safe use of tools and a wide range of working methods are uniquely described.

In this revised edition this proven formula has been retained throughout and, with some modification and additional material added where required, the book has been brought fully up to date and made even more relevant to today's woodworker. The object of the book and the aim of the reviewer has been to bring the secrets of successful craftsmanship to all those who seek them and to offer the woodworker – and in particular the would-be woodworker – the opportunity to learn about and to practise the necessary skills. It's the next best thing to an apprenticeship!

Working in Wood contains five interrelated sections: Materials; Tools; Methods; Fixtures and Fittings; and Projects. Each section is linked to a comprehensive index, and technical terms are fully explained in the glossary.

The Materials section is an explanatory study of the most sympathetic of all materials – the wood with which we work. It provides a complete explanation of how wood is converted and seasoned, the differences between hardwoods and softwoods, and the considerations to be made when selecting and buying timber, manufactured boards and veneer. There is a detailed table defining the technical qualities and working properties of many of the world's major timbers, some of which are illustrated.

The Tools section is an analysis of all the hand tools and several hand-held power tools required to produce quality woodwork. These have all been brought up to date where this was considered to be necessary. The tools are grouped according to their function: measuring and marking out, holding, sawing, chiselling, planing, smoothing, drilling, woodturning and woodcarving, etc. Instructions are included on sharpening and maintaining the various tools, and their safe use is emphasized.

This is followed by the Methods section, which is a comprehensive demonstration of the most essential techniques in woodworking. All of the important woodworking joints are included: halving, mortise and tenon, dovetail, housing, dowel, etc. The making of each one is fully described and clearly illustrated. Jointing manufactured boards is also covered. Basic carcass construction and the secrets of good drawer making are .a feature of this section. Finally, surface preparation and finishing are expertly described.

Fixtures and Fittings is an exhaustive compendium of woodworking accessories, ranging from adhesives, nails and screws to a selection of hardware such as hinges, stays and handles, locks and catches. The accompanying text describes how to choose and how to use them.

The Projects section, which is entirely new to this book, was conceived as a means of providing useful items of interesting work that would allow the aspiring craftsman to practice his (or her) skills. Each project is designed to include the experience of making a specific woodworking joint as described in the Methods section.

Acknowledgments

The work of the first author, craftsman and teacher Ernest Scott, and the contribution of those members of the team who helped in the production of the original book, is acknowledged with gratitude. The latter group includes: John Barden, Bert Burrell, John Coles, Alan Dyer, Mike Farrow, Paul Ferguson, Bill Hallworth, Ernie Ives, Ernest Jones, Alan Tilbury, William Wells and Roger Woods.

This major revision and reworking of the book has, by its very nature and circumstance, also been a team effort. Special thanks are due to Judith More for another opportunity, and to Sam Ward-Dutton who oversaw the operation, Luise Roberts for efficacious art editing, Tony Truscott who dealt with the design and Cathy Lowne who worked on the words. Thanks also to Andrew Crawford whose projects occupy the final section of the book. And thanks too to those essential supernumeraries who read and sub-edit, illustrate, computerize, produce and publicize. 'By the fruits of our labours shall we be known.'

JackHill

Jack Hill, April 1997

MATERIALS

Anyone who works with wood soon becomes aware that their chosen material is a living substance and that each of the trees from which it comes imparts its own individual characteristics. Physical properties such as hardness and softness, density, durability, stiffness, strength and flexibility vary enormously and dramatically from species to species – and even within species, as do the more aesthetic qualities of colour, texture and figure. It is, above all else, this great diversity that encourages wood's use in so many different ways, from building houses and boats to making fine furniture and wooden artefacts of all kinds. And since trees grow naturally, and can be readily cultivated, wood is a renewable resource potentially capable of producing a constant supply if properly managed.

Throughout history wood has served humanity well and even today, with alternatives like metals and plastics to choose from, wood retains its position as the most versatile of materials. It is being used at a greater rate now than ever before and over-exploitation of some tree species is seriously affecting both choice and supply. We should all make the conscious decision to use only timber extracted from genuinely well-managed sources so that those who come after us can continue to enjoy this unique and beautiful material in all its varieties.

Knowing which wood is most suitable for a particular job is a most important first step in working with wood, and the following pages describe the essential properties and characteristics of many of the most commonly used timbers from around the world, together with those of a selection of manufactured boards and veneers.

Hardwoods & softwoods

Although all trees grow and produce wood in a similar way, some are of a more primitive plant type than others. Trees are therefore divided into two main classifications. The first and more primitive are the gymnosperms or conifers, which are the cone-bearing, needle-leafed trees. These are known as softwoods. The second and much greater in number are the angiosperms, which are divided into two classes: the monocotyledons, which include palms and grasses and are of little interest to the woodworker, and the dicotyledons. These are the broad-leaved, deciduous trees known as hardwoods.

The terms 'softwood' and 'hardwood' are botanical designations and do not accurately describe the physical or working properties of the wood obtained from them. The softwood yew and some pines, for example, are quite hard while the lightweight balsa wood and some varieties of lime are comparatively soft, yet they are classified as hardwoods. And while it is said that hardwoods are more difficult to work than softwoods, this can be misleading. Beech and sycamore, both hardwoods, are actually easier to work than, for example, a resinous pine or a brittle cedar wood.

Softwoods grow mainly in the northern hemisphere, abundantly across North America and Europe and at high altitude elsewhere. Relatively fast-growing, they are extensively cultivated in man-made forests, producing tall, straight trunks easily harvested, often mechanically, for conversion into useful timber. World-wide depletion of natural conifer forests has resulted in the establishment of managed softwood plantations in many countries. Softwoods are used mainly in joinery and building work, for some manufactured boards and in papermaking. High-grade or best-quality softwoods are suitable for use in furnituremaking.

Hardwoods, of which there are many different species, are widely distributed throughout the world but mainly in the temperate and tropical regions. They are mostly slow-growing, and produce a denser, more durable wood than many of the softwoods. Hardwoods provide a great variety and range of colour and figure and some are highly prized. Indiscriminate harvesting of natural forest, particularly in some tropical regions, has led to acute shortages of certain tree species and conservationists have demanded a ban on the import and export of these. More use should therefore be made of wood from trees known to be obtained from sustainable sources. Hardwoods are used in high-class joinery and furniture-making of all kinds and in the manufacture of veneers.

Wood can be identified by a number of features. These include colour, grain, texture and figure. But there can be considerable variation between wood from trees of the same species and even between different parts of the same tree. The detailed structure of the cell walls of each different species is unique, however, and it is this that is used for more positive classification. Some of the more commonly used softwoods and hardwoods are illustrated here, together with a microscopic insert showing their individual cell structure.

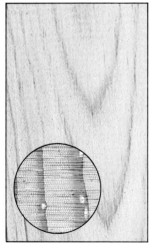

Pinus sylvestris

Pseudotsuga menziesii

Taxus baccata

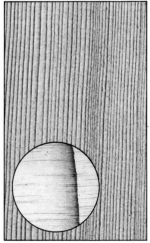

Thuja plicata

European redwood
Indigenous to Scandinavia, Scotland, northern Asia and the mountains of Europe.

Douglas fir
Indigenous to western North America

Yew
Indigenous to Asia, Europe and north Africa

Western red cedar
Indigenous to western North America

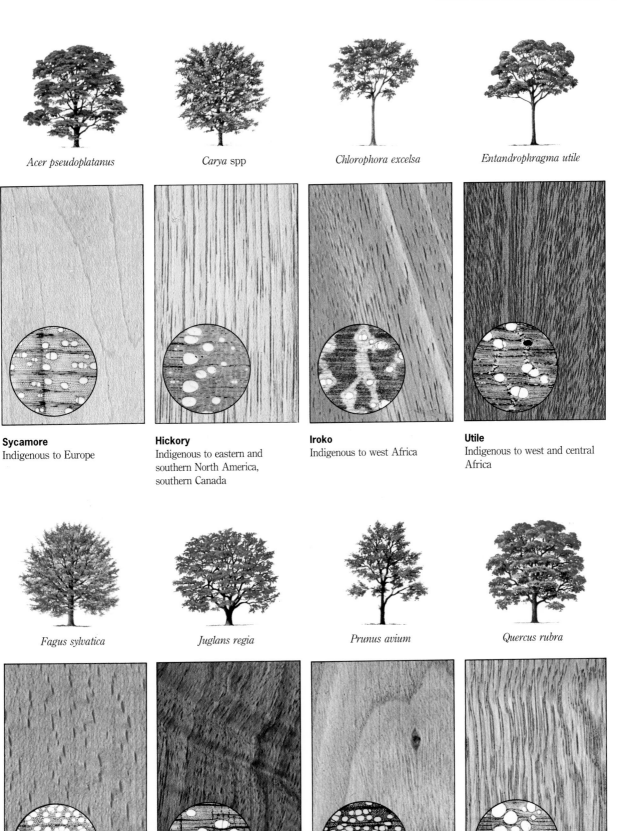

Acer pseudoplatanus

Carya spp

Chlorophora excelsa

Entandrophragma utile

Sycamore
Indigenous to Europe

Hickory
Indigenous to eastern and southern North America, southern Canada

Iroko
Indigenous to west Africa

Utile
Indigenous to west and central Africa

Fagus sylvatica

Juglans regia

Prunus avium

Quercus rubra

European beech
Indigenous to Europe

European walnut
Indigenous to Europe

European cherry
Indigenous across Europe to western and northern Asia and the mountains of north Africa

American red oak
Indigenous to North America

Selecting & buying timber

Landscape

Ray or flame

'Bird's-eye' maple

Blister

Quilt

Stripe

Ribbon

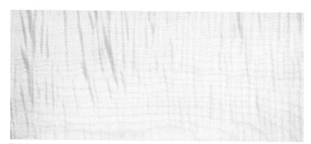

Fiddleback

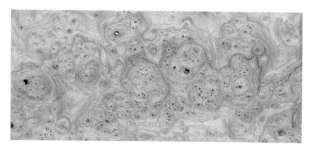

Burr

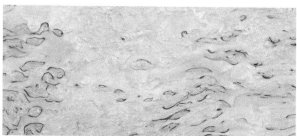

Masur birch

Mineral streaks

Gum veins

Landscape

Growth rings are one of two structural features that produce an attractive figure, depending on the method of conversion. The elongated ring pattern called landscape or cathedral figure is seen on plain-sawn surfaces. Quarter-sawn surfaces show the rings as parallel lines in the wood.

'Bird's-eye' maple

This figure is seen on tangential surfaces of only a few species, the best-known being Canadian rock maple. The pattern is caused by fungi, which attack the cambium. This retards complete formation of the annual rings, leaving conical depressions that on conversion appear as circles resembling pin knots.

Quilt

This form of blister is caused by irregularities in the growth rings. The pattern is best seen on plain-sawn surfaces, where the incident light is reflected from the irregular grain at different angles, giving wood such as African mahogany a three-dimensional appearance.

Ribbon

A growth characteristic of many tropical hardwoods is interlocked grain. This produces a striped figure on quarter-sawn surfaces. If the wood is moved in relation to the light the colour of the stripes will appear to alternate. This optical effect is not due to colour variation in the wood.

Burr

Burrs are the result of injury to trees such as common elm. The highly irregular grain, which contains many small knots, also contributes to the pattern of the figure. Burr is extremely difficult to season and convert and for this reason the wood is best utilized as a veneer rather than as solid timber.

Mineral streaks

These are localized discolorations of timber, in the form of streaks or patches that are usually darker than the natural colour of the wood, but which do not impair the strength of the piece. The streaks can vary from the dark red common in parana pine to yellow or white, as seen in red meranti and keruing.

Ray or flame

The second structural feature that plays an important role in the production of figure is rays. They occur radially throughout the tree and are best seen (if visible) on radial or quarter-sawn surfaces. Decorative figures of this type in woods such as oak and maple are used mainly as veneers.

Blister

This type of figure, in common with the 'bird's-eye' figure that is found in maple, is caused by injury to the cambium, with the result that large depressions are formed in the growth rings. The figure is seen in softwoods such as pitch pine and hardwoods such as kevazingo and American whitewood.

Stripe

This figure is most commonly seen in ebonies such as macassar. The stripes are due entirely to colour variation within the wood, caused by alternation of the pale sapwood with the darker-coloured heartwood. Where the colour is less evenly distributed the pattern is known as marblewood.

Fiddleback

A figure seen on quarter-sawn surfaces of woods such as sycamore. This particular wood is often used in violin-making, hence the name of the figure. As with ribbon figure the apparent colour changes occur because of the way in which the light is reflected from the grain.

Masur birch

This distinctive figure is found in the butt logs of birch from Finland and Norway. It is caused by the larvae of a gnat-like fly belonging to the genus *Agromyza* that tunnels into the wood. The tree heals itself by producing resin to fill the bore channels. Masur birch is used mainly in the production of treen.

Gum veins

These are caused by traumatic incidents such as wounding or forest fires. They are normally considered to be a defect, but in Italian ancona walnut they are a natural characteristic that enhances the appearance of the wood. The gum veins can show as streaks as they do in paldao or as flecks.

Wood is chosen for its structural stability and physical appearance. Grain direction is an indicator of a timber's structure and, together with characteristics that result from colouring substances, determines its appearance, which is known as figure. Marked deviation of the grain direction from the vertical axis of the tree can produce interesting figure but will also affect timber's strength. Such conflicting factors require careful consideration. Where a piece of wood is of structural importance, such as a chair or table leg, then straight grained material must be used, but where the wood is to be largely decorative, material can be chosen for its appearance.

Choosing the wood for any project can be daunting, especially for a novice. When visiting a saw mill or timber yard – or any other retail outlet – it helps everyone if you go with a clear idea of what you want and how much you want of it. It helps the seller if he has clear information and it helps you – the buyer – to buy most economically.

Make a coherent list of your requirements – a cutting list – and take it with you. Some retailers will supply material sawn and planed to your specific dimensions, otherwise it will be necessary to purchase stock sizes and cut them yourself. Remember to make an allowance for waste in this case. Whenever possible, get to see what you are buying and make your own selection.

Wood, particularly softwood, is normally sold either as 'sawn' or 'prepared'; in other words, straight off the saw, or with one or more of its surfaces machine planed. The designation PAR means 'planed all round'. Sizes quoted are usually nominal, ie, the dimensions before planing. Nominal sizes are fairly standardized throughout the timber trade. Hardwoods may be purchased with one or more edges sawn square or as waney-edged boards, ie, having irregular edges with the bark attached.

Types of grain

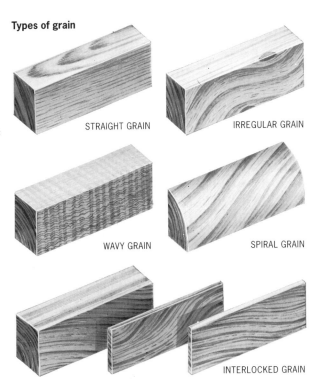

STRAIGHT GRAIN

IRREGULAR GRAIN

WAVY GRAIN

SPIRAL GRAIN

INTERLOCKED GRAIN

Defects

When buying timber check its suitability and look out for any defects that it may have. Defects can be divided into two basic categories: natural defects and those caused by incorrect or insufficient seasoning. The first includes damage caused by insect or fungal attack and internal defects and knots that occur as the tree is growing. Knots distort the grain and can affect the strength of wood. Defects that arise through poor seasoning include excessive splitting, twisting and warping. When drying is too rapid, uneven stresses are set up in the wood fibres and distortion and splitting occurs.

Remember that wood is a natural material and, as such, responds to changes in its environment. Kiln-dried wood stored in an open shed will absorb moisture from the air and must be properly dry before use; leaving it in an environment similar to where it will subsequently be used is one way of overcoming this particular problem. Check that wood shows no sign of handling or storage damage, especially if it is bought ready planed. If buying manufactured boards check these for broken corners and surface damage. Reject boards which have been badly stored and are either warped or feel wet.

CUPPING   SPRINGING   DIAMONDING

BOWING   'IN WINDING'

Defects

Wood warps as a result of too rapid drying. This defect includes cupping, springing, diamonding, where the wood goes out of square, and bowing. When a board is twisted along its length it is 'in winding'. If wet wood is dried too quickly its cells may collapse, resulting in a concave surface known as cupping. Rapid drying can also cause case hardening. Internal stresses in a growing tree and in wood being seasoned can cause splits, known as shakes. These tend to occur along the weakest tissue and on the exposed ends of boards dried too quickly. Injury to a growing tree can be the cause of internal defects. Knots are the most common defects in wood. Live knots usually stay intact, but dead knots tend to fall out and present the greater problem. Trees grown on a steep slope or in areas of strong prevailing winds develop off-centre and have uneven growth rings. This distorted growth is known as reaction or compression wood and is subject to severe shaking and warping.

SHAKES

INTERNAL DEFECTS

LIVE KNOTS

REACTION WOOD

Conversion & seasoning

The process of converting trees into marketable-sized boards takes place at a saw mill. The first stage, primary conversion, is when the log is cut by either a bandsaw or a circular saw. This is done in one of two ways: either plain sawing or quarter sawing.

Plain sawing, which is also referred to as 'through-and-through' or slash sawing, is the simplest and most common method of sawing. The logs are gripped and sliced perpendicularly. It is a fast, economical process yielding the maximum number of usable boards. Quarter sawing requires greater skill on the part of the sawyer. The logs are first cut into quarters and then sawn into boards, using radial or approximately radial cuts. Wood cut in this way is more stable in use than plain-sawn boards and is therefore more suitable for structural work. The disadvantage is cost, as a higher percentage of wood is wasted when making truly radial cuts.

Boards are usually dried or seasoned before re-sawing (secondary conversion) to specific dimensions. Before the boards are fit to use they must then be dried or seasoned to levels suitable for their required end use (*see* table right). Seasoning also minimizes subsequent shrinking and provides resistance to both insect and fungal attack. Strength properties are improved and the wood is easier to work and more able to take a surface finish.

Water in the living tree is contained in the cell walls and cavities. Once the timber has been converted into boards, it will start to lose this moisture by evaporation until a level known as fibre saturation point (about 30 per cent moisture content for most wood) is reached, in which the cell cavities are comparatively dry but the cell walls are still saturated. Subsequent moisture loss will be at a slower rate until the boards are in balance with the relative humidity of the surrounding atmosphere. At this stage the wood is at its 'equilibrium moisture content'.

The two most usual methods of seasoning wood are air drying, which uses the ambient heat from the sun, and kiln drying, which uses a combination of hot air and steam. For moisture levels below about 17 per cent (*see* table below), kiln drying is necessary.

For natural seasoning (air drying), the unseasoned boards must be stacked exactly over each other on a firm, level base of concrete or creosoted timber with 'stickers' of the same or a neutral wood, such as poplar or fir, between each board. Spacing is crucial: the boards should be wide enough apart to allow adequate circulation of air but not so far apart that the boards will sag and warp; nor should they be so close that mould and fungal attack are encouraged. The top of the stack should be weighted with waste wood and the whole stack covered with a lean-to roof to protect the boards from rain and direct heat from the sun. To dry boards to their equilibrium moisture content of 17–23 per cent takes approximately one year for every 25mm (1in) of wood thickness for hardwoods – less for softwoods.

Kiln drying has to be carefully monitored. To prevent too rapid drying, and therefore degradation in the timber, steam is injected into the kiln to temper the rate of moisture evaporation from the boards. The rate of kiln drying is controlled by many factors, such as the quality of the timber and the method of conversion. This type of drying is dependent on the skill of the operator. The advantage of kiln drying over air drying is that the drying time is reduced from years to weeks.

Moisture content of timber for various purposes		
Air drying sufficient %	27%	Appreciable shrinkage starts at about this point
	25%	Suitable moisture content for creosoting
	20%	Decay safety line (wet rots)
	18%	Exterior joinery
Kiln drying necessary %	16%	Garden furniture
	14%	Woodwork for use in places only slightly or occasionally heated
	12%	Interior woodwork with regular intermittent heating
	11%	Woodwork in continuously heated buildings
	9%	Woodwork used in close proximity to sources of heat, eg, radiator casings, mantlepieces

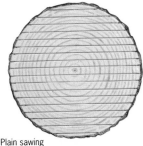

Plain sawing

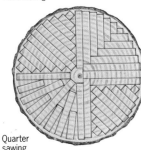

Quarter sawing

A vertical bandsaw (*above*) cuts the log to yield plain-sawn boards, which are then removed by a conveyor belt to be stacked. Quarter-sawn timber (*right*) is first cut into quarters and then converted by one of the four methods shown.

Converted boards piled in layers for air drying are said to be 'in stick'. Quarter-sawn boards may be sticked in neat stacks and plain-sawn boards in 'boules' – the order in which they were cut from the log (*above left*).

Veneers & manufactured boards

Veneering is the term given to the method of laying thin slices of wood (veneers) on a groundwork of plain, sound wood. There are two main uses for veneer: the first is as a decorative surface in traditional and fine cabinetmaking; the second is as a facing or base in the construction of manufactured boards, such as multi-ply, blockboard and laminboard. Manufactured boards can be bought ready surfaced with veneer or unsurfaced, in which case a decorative veneer can be applied separately.

Selecting trees that will yield well-figured wood is extremely difficult. Apart from external signs such as burrs and stumps, there is little to indicate in the standing tree the extent of the figure within until it is sawn. Various methods of sawing are suitable for revealing the

figures in a particular tree. The main methods are flat, quarter and half-round slicing. Rotary-cut veneers are used mainly when making three-ply and multi-ply.

Manufactured boards can be used in some instances as a substitute for solid wood. They can be categorized into plywoods (three-ply and multi-ply), blockboards, particle-boards (chipboard) and fibreboards (hardboard and medium-density fibreboard (MDF)).

One of the most utilized and versatile plywoods is obtainable in three-ply or multi-ply of up to 19 layers. Each layer is glued with the grain at right angles to the previous one. Alternating plies in this way improves strength and stability by counteracting any tendency to distort through shrinkage or swelling. Having no natural

METHODS OF OBTAINING VENEERS

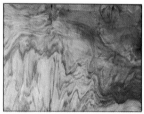

Butt veneer
A highly decorative veneer found at the swollen base of trees such as walnut. This

veneer is obtained by halving the log longitudinally and converting it by using the half-round slicing method.

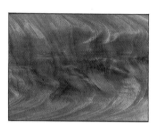

Curl veneer
This attractive veneer is found at the crown and the base of the branches. Walnut and

mahogany are highly valued for this type of figure. Other variations of curl are feather and swirl.

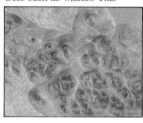
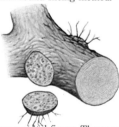

Burr veneer
Irregular outgrowths called burrs are found on many trees and often yield a highly

ornamental figure. They are caused by injury to the tree and are commonly cut from oak, ash and walnut.

Oyster veneer
The striking pattern of this veneer is achieved by cutting transversely at an angle of 45°

from the branches of trees such as kingwood and laburnum. It is used mainly on reproduction furniture.

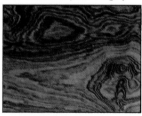

Flat-sliced veneer
This is the most common method of cutting in which the half log is sliced longitudinally,

producing landscape or cathedral figures. The rio rosewood sample shows heartwood.

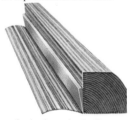

Quarter-cut veneer
A quartered log is sliced at right angles to the tree's growth rings. This is the best method

to obtain the striped effects and ray figures that are a feature of some woods. The sample is sapele.

Half-round sliced veneer
With this method, which is also known as semi-rotary, the log is mounted eccentrically on a

rotary lathe. This produces a pattern with a broad-grain figure. The sample illustrated is yew.

Rotary-cut veneer
When the log is mounted centrally on a lathe and then rotated against the blade, a

continuous sheet of veneer is produced. This method is often used to obtain the 'bird's-eye' effect in maple.

line of cleavage also eliminates the possibility of splitting along the length or the width. This is a valuable quality when nailing, screwing or fastening on the outer veneer or face, but take care not to work near the edge of the wood or the surface will delaminate. Plywood can also be cut and bent more easily than solid wood.

Blockboard differs from three- and multi-ply in having a solid core made of strips of wood combined together to form a slab, which is sandwiched between outer veneers. Blockboard has strips of wood up to 25mm (1in) wide, but when faced with veneers there may be a tendency for the line of the strips to show through the facing; so it is not normally used for high-quality work. Laminboard is of similar construction, but the strips making up the core are much narrower, between 1.5mm and 6mm ($\frac{1}{16}$ and $\frac{1}{4}$in) thick. As it is usually made of hardwood and is as a general rule used for higher-quality work, it tends to be more expensive than any other type of manufactured board.

It is important to assess the end use when selecting plywoods. Different types of adhesives are used to bond plywoods, depending on whether the materials are to be used inside or outdoors. Standard plywoods are not bonded with a waterproof adhesive, but other grades of plywoods are available that will resist not only water but extremes of weather too.

Particle-board is not as strong as plywoods, but it is still of sufficient quality for non-structural uses such as in panels, ceilings and cladding for partitions. It is made from compressed wood particles (chipboard) made from waste wood obtained from forest thinning and shavings from other wood manufacturing processes, bonded with a synthetic resin glue under heat and pressure. Various methods of processing provide the three basic types of chipboard, including a special type of furniture board that has a gradation from coarse to fine chips towards the surface, giving a smooth close-textured finish. This can then be faced with high-quality veneers. Other types of particle-board have either a single layer of chips all of a similar size, giving a uniform density and strength, or a core of coarser chips between two outer layers of finer chips (sandwich board). As with plywoods, movement is quite small compared to that which occurs in solid wood. Particle-board is very absorbent so its surfaces must be sealed if it is to be used in damp areas. It is available faced with a variety of veneers or plastic coatings.

Fibreboard is a useful and versatile manufactured board. A cheap form – known as insulation board – has no application in furnituremaking. The more common hardboard is manufactured from wet wood fibres bonded together under extreme pressure and high temperature to produce a dense finished board. MDF (medium-density fibreboard) is made from what is basically wood pulp that is bonded together under pressure with a synthetic resin adhesive. The close fibrous structure of MDF makes it a satisfactory substitute for solid wood in some situations and it is excellent as groundwork for veneer.

MANUFACTURED BOARDS

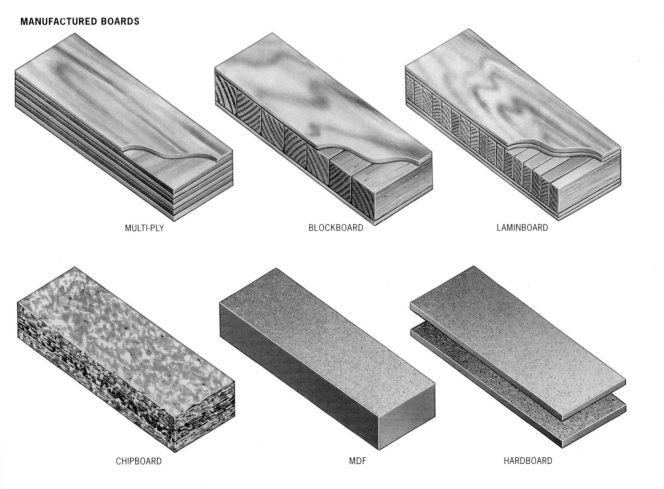

MULTI-PLY

BLOCKBOARD

LAMINBOARD

CHIPBOARD

MDF

HARDBOARD

Selected world timbers

Wood	Natural characteristics	Technical qualities	Natural durability	Reaction to preservative	Seasoning qualities
Acacia melanoxylon **Blackwood**	Medium even texture; straight to interlocked grain; fiddleback ray figure; pronounced growth ring; a natural lustre	Strong; good impact properties; pliable	Fair	Very resistant	Good; stable when dry
Acer pseudoplatanus **Sycamore**	Smooth texture; the grain may be close and wavy but is more usually straight; fiddleback ray figure; shows a satiny sheen	Quite strong; good bending strength	Poor	Resistant	Stable when dried slowly
Araucaria angustifolia **Parana pine**	Fine even texture; straight grain; fairly knot free	Varies from soft to hard	Poor	Fairly resistant	Good; but dry carefully to avoid distortion and splitting
Carya spp. **Hickory**	Coarse texture; straight grain but can be wavy; well-defined growth rings	Good steam-bending properties; very strong; hardness varies according to growth rate	Poor	Fairly resistant	Dry very slowly due to high rate of shrinkage
Castanea sativa **European chestnut**	Coarse texture; some straight but often spiral grain; growth rings prominent; tannin content	Reasonable bending strength and shear; stiff but not as good as oak; splits easily	Good	Very resistant	Dry very slowly; prone to collapse, internal cracking and distortion
Cedrus spp. **Cedar**	Fine even texture; conspicuous growth rings; aromatic when freshly sawn	Medium strength; brittle	Very good; resistant to fungi	Poor	Fair; prone to distortion
Chlorophora excelsa **Iroko**	Fairly coarse texture; interlocked grain gives typical ribbon figure on quarter-sawn surfaces; white flecks caused by calcareous deposits often present; good acid and fire resistance; Iroko is sometimes likened to teak	Good bending strength; hard; resistant to shock loading	Excellent if the grain is straight	Fairly resistant	Quite good; minimal checking and distortion
Entandrophragma cylindricum **Sapele**	Fine texture; interlocked grain; striped roe figure on quarter-sawn surfaces; growth rings pronounced on plain-sawn surfaces; cedar-like scent when freshly sawn	Good strength properties; equal to oak in bending, stiffness and shock resistance; hard; good splitting resistance	Fair	Poor	Dry carefully; seasoning needed to avoid distortion
Entandrophragma utile **Utile**	Rather coarse texture; interlocked grain shows a ribbon figure on quarter-sawn surfaces	Reasonably hard; fair shock resistance; poor bending strength	Fair	Very resistant	A tendency to check and distort; steady drying recommended
Fagus sylvatica **European beech**	Fine, even texture; straight-grained; a 'seed pip' ray figure shows on tangential surfaces; a small flecked figure on quarter-sawn surfaces	Excellent bending and impact strength; stiff; shear; resistant to splitting	Poor	Good	Fairly good; dry carefully; inclined to check and distort; high shrinkage factor
Fraxinus excelsior **European ash**	Coarse to medium-fine texture; straight grain; conspicuous growth rings	Good strength; tough; excellent bending qualities; resistant to splitting	Poor	Fairly resistant	Fairly good but inclined to distortion and end-grain splitting at high temperatures
Gonystylus bancanus **Ramin**	Moderate to fine texture; straight to slightly interlocked grain; can cause skin irritation; prone to staining	Fairly good; nearly as good as home-grown beech; good compressive strength but prone to splitting; poor bending qualities; rather weak in shear	Poor	Good	Prone to suffer from end-grain splitting but shows little distortion; care needed to prevent staining

Air-dried weight	Working qualities	Fixing qualities	Finishing qualities	Relevant uses	Wood with similar qualities	General comments
656kg/m³ 40lb/ft³	Reasonable but some hard patches; tends to crumble on the end grain	Good	Excellent	Cabinetmaking; furniture; fine interior joinery; woodwind instruments; gunstocks	Black bean	An excellent multi-purpose wood
640kg/m³ 40lb/ft³	Fair	Care needed with nails and screws; good with glue	Excellent	Fine interior joinery and veneers; string instrument backing; fine furniture; turning; flooring	Rock maple (800kgm³ (50lb/ft³) has a distinctive 'bird's-eye' figure	Susceptible to stains when being kilned; stack vertically for air drying; never put in stick formation
544kg/m³ 34lb/ft³	Good	Good	Good	Fine interior joinery; framework; drawer sides; mouldings	Western yellow pine	Prone to movement so ensure stable humidity conditions. It is also used as a general-purpose plywood
816kg/m³ 51lb/ft³	Fair; some grain pick-up; inclined to blunt tools and saws	Difficult with nails and screws; good with glue	Fair	High impact strength makes it useful for pick and hammer handles; sports equipment	European ash	Now often replaced by metals and synthetic materials
544kg/m³ 34lb/ft³	Good; tendency to bind on saws	Good	Excellent, but may need filling	Furniture; turning; kitchen ware; cleft fencing	Oak	Because of its resemblance to oak is often used as an oak substitute; stains in contact with ferrous metals
560kg/m³ 35lb/ft³	Good	Care needed with nails and screws; good with glue	Good	Fine interior joinery; non-structural parts of furniture	None	Has a decorative appearance. Cedar of Lebanon is the best-known commercial species
640kg/m³ 40lb/ft³	Good but calcareous deposits may blunt saw and tool edges	Good	Good, but needs filling	Fine interior joinery; exterior joinery; boat-building; counter and bench tops; garden seats; parquet flooring, even with underfloor heating	Afrormosia; teak	Not so attractive a wood for furniture as teak but has a good combination of properties and is comparatively inexpensive
624kg/m³ 39lb/ft³	Good; some grain pick-up when planing quarter-sawn surfaces; keep cutting angle low	Good	Excellent	Furniture, solid and veneer; fine interior joinery; flooring	African mahogany; Honduras mahogany; utile	A well-utilized, decorative and sound timber
656kg/m³ 40lb/ft³	Works well; some tendency to grain pick-up during planing due to interlocked grain	Good	Good, but needs filling	Furniture, solid and veneer; cabinetmaking; interior joinery	African mahogany; sapele	An attractive mahogany-type wood; for constructional and decorative work
720kg/m³ 45lb/ft³	Variable; some wood tends to bind and burn when sawing or drilling; usually reasonable to work	Fair with nails and screws; good with glue	Good	Furniture, especially chairs; fine interior joinery; toys; small models; small turning	Chilean beech; silver beech; Southland beech from Australasia	Good multi-purpose timber in plentiful supply
688kg/m³ 43lb/ft³	Fair; tendency to wastage when planing flat-sawn wood due to distortion	Fair with nails and screws; good with glue	Excellent; but may need filling	Furniture; fine interior joinery; tennis, squash, badminton frames; gymnasium equipment; drum frames; turning	Hickory; Japanese ash, North American ash	An excellent and and attractive general-purpose wood
656kg/m³ 40lb/ft³	Tends to tear on quarter-sawn surfaces; keep cutting angle low; wear goggles and gloves when sawing unseasoned wood	Tends to split with nails; fair with screws and glue	Good	Interior joinery; turning; mouldings; handles; toys	None	A generally good utility wood; can be quite attractive

Wood	Natural characteristics	Technical qualities	Natural durability	Reaction to preservative	Seasoning qualities
Juglans regia **European walnut**	Usually fine texture; a general naturally wavy grain; clear of knots except on burr veneers, which have pin knots	Hard, tough; good splitting and impact resistance; good bending properties and shock-loading strength	Fair	Resistant	Dries slowly but well; tendency to checking and internal cracks with thick wood
Larix decidua **European larch**	Coarse to medium texture; resinous; high contrast between early- and latewood; small knots; faintly aromatic	Strong; hard; not pliable	Fair	Fairly resistant	Good; stable when dry
Pinus sylvestris **European redwood**	Coarse texture; resinous; clear growth rings; knotty	Resilient; flexible; good bending and compressive strength	Poor; prone to insect and fungal attack	Good	Good; dries quickly
Prunus avium **European cherry**	Fine even texture; straight grain; gum marks sometimes visible on surface	A tough wood; good bending and impact strength; stiff; resistant to splitting; knots are usually small	Fair but do not use externally unless treated	Poor	Tendency to distort so care needed; reasonably stable when dry
Pseudotsuga menziesii **Douglas fir**	Coarse texture; resinous; conspicuous growth rings	Medium strength	Poor; fairly resistant to decay	Poor	Good; stable when dry
Quercus robur **European oak**	Coarse texture; straight grain; well-defined growth rings; relatively knot-free timber; quality varies according to locality; wide rays very noticeable on quarter-sawn surfaces giving a silver grain figure	Very strong, used as a yardstick for other hardwoods for this reason; bends well, but care must be taken to avoid rupture on inner face of curved wood	Fair; subject to lyctus attack	Very resistant. Do not treat with a salt chemical, which will turn the wood bluey black	Must be dried slowly; a tendency to distort; some collapse and inner checks
Quercus rubra **American red oak**	Coarse but even texture; fairly straight grain; not usually a knotty timber; fairly fire and acid resistant; pronounced growth rings	Variable according to growth conditions; good bending qualities; quite strong	Poor	Poor	Reasonable; dries slowly; prone to checking and distortion
Swietenia macrophylla **Honduras mahogany**	Reasonably fine, even texture; straight grain, but some interlocked grain shows a ribbon figure on quarter-sawn surfaces; growth rings clearly defined; natural surface lustre	Quite strong; good for bending and compression	Fair; subject to pin-hole wood borer attack	Fairly resistant	Good; dries well with little tendency to checking and distortion
Taxus baccata **Yew**	Smooth fine texture; irregular grain	High strength; very hard	Excellent	Resistant	Good
Thuja plicata **Western red cedar**	Soft texture; straight grain; prominent growth rings; subject to bruising; aromatic	Low strength	Excellent	Poor	Good; stable when dry, but thicker stock may collapse
Tilia x vulgaris **Lime**	Fine even texture, good straight grain; rather soft	Good bending and compressive strength; stiffness	Poor	Good	Good; fairly stable when dry; but some tendency to distort
Ulmus procera **European elm**	Coarse texture; often coarse grain	Good bending strength; resistant to splitting	Poor; subject to heart rot and insect attack	Poor	Variable; subject to checking and distortion

Air-dried weight	Working qualities	Fixing qualities	Finishing qualities	Relevant uses	Wood with similar qualities	General comments
640kg/m³ 40lb/ft³	Good	Good	Excellent	Furniture, solid and veneer; fine interior joinery; good for carving and turning	African walnut; American black walnut; Australian walnut; Indian laurel	A highly desirable wood, often well figured, especially ancona Italian walnut; decorative work can be done using burr veneers
592kg/m³ 37lb/ft³	Good	Care needed with nails; good with screws and glue	Good	Fencing; boat-building	All species of larch	Of limited use but excellent
528kg/m³ 33lb/ft³	Good	Good	Good	Interior joinery; furniture carcasses; flooring	Western yellow pine; pitch pine	Resinous knots can be troublesome; either pre-treat or drill out and plug. Also known as Scots pine
608kg/m³ 38lb/ft³	Very good	Good	Excellent	Furniture, solid and veneer; cabinetmaking; interior joinery	American black cherry; other fruitwoods, eg, apple, pear, plum	The European wood is used mainly for veneering; American cherry is less heavy
544kg/m³ 34lb/ft³	Good, with care	Good	Poor	Interior joinery; laminated boards	None	Prone to windblow defects
704kg/m³ 44lb/ft³	Good; some grain pick-up on lowland oak timber	Good	Good, but needs filling	Furniture, solid and veneer; fine interior joinery; flooring, both strip and block	Other oaks, especially American white, Japanese, Turkish	German slavonia considered to be the finest oak; stains occur in contact with ferrous metals in damp conditions; a well-utilized hardwood
768kg/m³ 48lb/ft³	Fair	Good	Good, but needs filling	Furniture, solid and veneer; interior joinery; flooring	American white; European; Japanese and Turkish oak	The other species listed are slightly better quality than the American red oak
544kg/m³ 34lb/ft³	Good; some grain pick-up when planing	Tends to split with nails; good with screws and glue	Excellent	Fine interior joinery; panelling; furniture, solid and veneer; cabinetmaking; turning	Honduras and Cuban mahogany are the best-quality woods but other redwoods are similar, eg, African mahogany	This wood replaced Cuban mahogany on the world market; Cuban mahogany is much darker and denser, but has been in short supply for many years
672kg/m³ 42lb/ft³	Good, but high wastage	Care needed with nails and screws; good with glue	Good	Veneers; mallet heads; long bows; objets d'art; turning	None	Has a relatively low yield; the hardest known softwood
384kg/m³ 24lb/ft³	Good	Care needed with nails and screws; good with glue	Good; an oil base is best	External cladding; wooden shingles; interior panelling; gates; sheds	None	Not a true cedar, but one of the best and most durable exterior softwoods available for non-structural work
544kg/m³ 34lb/ft³	Good	Good	Good	Brush handles; toys; models; an excellent turning and carving wood	Obeche	A very good multi-purpose wood
560kg/m³ 35lb/ft³	Fair	Variable with nails and screws; fair with glue	Good, but needs filling	Structural parts of furniture; veneers; turning; chopping blocks	Other elms, eg, American white, Dutch, rock, wych	Rock elm in particular, is noted for its strength

TOOLS

The development of tools runs parallel to human progress. The prehistoric 'ages' of stone, bronze and iron refer to the simple axes used as much as tools for shaping wood as for hunting and as weapons. Chisel-like tools first appeared in neolithic times, as did a means of drilling holes. The Romans are reputed to have introduced the first planes, which, together with saws, were further developed during the Medieval period. The 18th century – the so-called Golden Age of Woodworking – marks the zenith of this progress before machinery began to reduce the need for hand tools and led to a decline in their use.

Today that decline has been reversed – for a variety of reasons. There is currently a vast range of hand and power tools available to woodworkers and this section describes a selection of them and illustrates their use as an aid in evaluation and choice. Hand tools figure most prominently as we believe that the development of hand skills is essential to the full understanding of the principles of working with wood. Several hand-held power tools are also described, as these have become an accepted part of woodworking today, but no fixed machines are included.

Choosing the best tools is only the beginning, of course; next you must learn how to use them correctly and how to keep them in good working order. Starting properly is most important – get to understand the tools that you use, their purpose and their limitations. Then you must learn how to hold them and use them correctly and safely, as well as how to maintain them. Next, practise to acquire skill. Do not be put off by the dexterity of a skilled craftsman who is proficient through learning more about tools than the novice and has, through practice, learned to use them properly.

The tool kit

Suggesting a basic tool kit inevitably involves personal preferences that depend on the exact nature of the work; whatever the tool selected, however, always buy the top quality. Working with inferior tools is an unnecessary handicap. Equally, the best results cannot be achieved if the tool is misused or not sharpened or maintained.

The first consideration should be the purchase of a sturdy and adaptable worktop. A continental bench is preferable, as it can hold the wood at both ends.

Of those tools used for measuring and marking, the combination square is more versatile than the traditional 100mm (4in) try square. Of the gauges, a marking gauge is the most essential. A marking knife is preferable to a pencil, making a finer, clearer line for the saw to follow.

There are many ingenious holding devices available, but initially two G-clamps, one large and one small, are sufficient for general work. Two medium-length sash clamps are also indispensable for clamping frames.

Of the handsaws, a cross-cut saw is a sensible first buy. It cuts both with and across the grain. A tenon saw copes with most jointing problems and the coping saw is useful not only for its normal work of cutting curves but also for removing waste when dovetailing.

A range of top-quality bevel-edged chisels is essential. Rectangular-sectioned chisels are slightly stronger, but

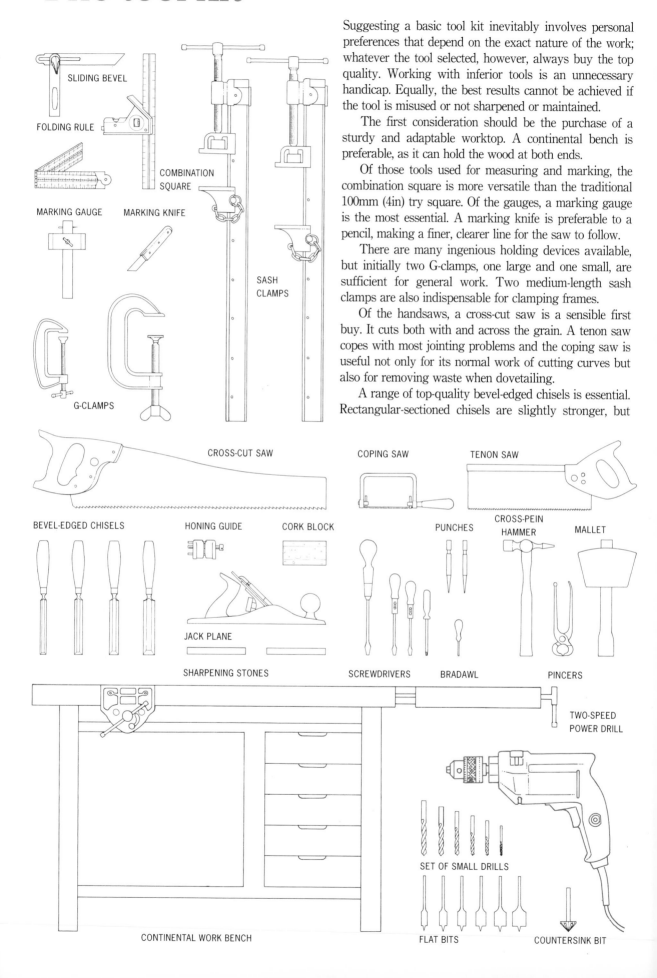

SLIDING BEVEL

FOLDING RULE

COMBINATION SQUARE

MARKING GAUGE   MARKING KNIFE

SASH CLAMPS

G-CLAMPS

CROSS-CUT SAW

COPING SAW   TENON SAW

BEVEL-EDGED CHISELS   HONING GUIDE   CORK BLOCK   PUNCHES   CROSS-PEIN HAMMER   MALLET

JACK PLANE

SHARPENING STONES   SCREWDRIVERS   BRADAWL   PINCERS

TWO-SPEED POWER DRILL

SET OF SMALL DRILLS

CONTINENTAL WORK BENCH   FLAT BITS   COUNTERSINK BIT

clumsier. A chisel bevelled on three sides gives a clear view of the area being worked; I suggest 3mm (⅛in), 6mm (¼in), 13mm (½in), 19mm (¾in) and 25mm (1in).

Most planes are designed for specific operations, but a good general choice is a jack plane. It will do the work of a jointer plane, such as planing edge joints, and in most cases that of a smoothing plane, such as cleaning up wide surfaces. For smoothing with abrasives a cork block is essential to ensure an even surface. Two sharpening stones, one medium and one fine, are needed to keep blades in prime condition, together with a honing guide for maintaining the correct bevel.

A bradawl with the blade integrated with the handle and a nail-punch are essential. Of the screwdrivers, choose a long cabinet screwdriver for heavy-gauge screws, a large and a small ratchet screwdriver for general use, and a narrow rigid screwdriver for repair work.

A cross-pein hammer and a pair of pincers cope with most nailing work. Despite the introduction of so-called unshatterable chisel handles, a wooden mallet will cause less damage than a hammer. A two-speed power drill is the best first-time buy for a basic kit. Select a set of small drills up to 6mm (¼in), a countersink bit with a round shank and a set of six flat bits. Forstner bits are better but much more expensive.

This basic tool kit as described will be quite adequate for general work. The additional tools illustrated below are probably the most useful for extending the range of the original kit. It is important, however, to realize that they are mostly specialist tools. It is therefore essential to consider whether the work justifies the additional cost.

If the intention is to make traditional joints, a mortise gauge will be necessary to set out the double lines of the mortise and tenon joint as well as two mortise chisels (3 and 6mm (⅛ and ¼in)) to lever out the waste. For dovetails, a cutting gauge makes a very fine line for accurate working. Use a dovetail saw for very fine joinery work. For large frames, a long try square is very effective for checking squareness. Two pairs of clamp heads (shown larger than other tools) will provide two extra sash clamps of variable length. A rip saw and panel saw, or a good power jigsaw, will also justify their purchase.

A smoothing plane is a good addition to a jack plane. The other planes are important, but study their specialist uses and only buy them when the need arises. Buy two spokeshaves: one with a flat sole for convex curves; the other with a curved sole for concave curves. A cabinet scraper is invaluable for finishing hardwood surfaces if used correctly. Trammel points and toothing planes are rarely used, but you might find them in an old tool kit.

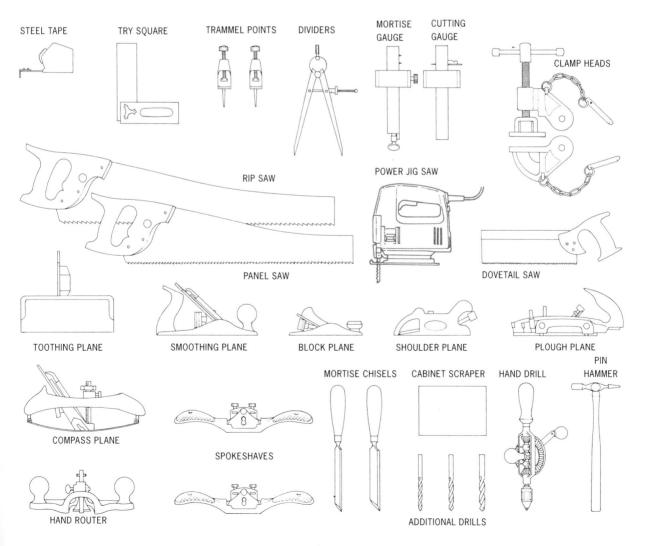

STEEL TAPE   TRY SQUARE   TRAMMEL POINTS   DIVIDERS   MORTISE GAUGE   CUTTING GAUGE   CLAMP HEADS

RIP SAW   POWER JIG SAW

PANEL SAW   DOVETAIL SAW

TOOTHING PLANE   SMOOTHING PLANE   BLOCK PLANE   SHOULDER PLANE   PLOUGH PLANE

COMPASS PLANE   SPOKESHAVES   MORTISE CHISELS   CABINET SCRAPER   HAND DRILL   PIN HAMMER

HAND ROUTER   ADDITIONAL DRILLS

The workshop should ideally be a space set permanently apart from the rest of the house. A firmly closed door will discourage any outside interference and will allow the woodworker to leave work in progress.

The workshop must be warm, well lit and have good ventilation. Windows or a corrugated vinyl transparent roof will provide natural light. Where windows cannot be opened, a ventilator must be installed to provide good air circulation. Beware of naked flames in the workshop and always keep a fire extinguisher close at hand. A basic first-aid kit should be readily available in case of injury.

Thoughtful and methodical planning of the work area will promote efficient working, especially if the workshop is kept tidy and the tools are ready to hand.

The most important item is the workbench, around which other fixtures and equipment should be arranged. The main purpose of the bench is to support the work being worked upon. To do this effectively it must be strong and sturdy, especially to withstand any diagonal stresses. The top should be absolutely flat and level, preferably made from a substantial hardwood such as beech or maple. The benchtop should be thick and supported by four solid legs and properly braced against movement. The whole bench must stand at a comfortable height for the individual worker to use; it is for this reason that many workers make their own bench or modify a proprietary one to suit their needs.

The bench vice, usually made of cast iron with jaw facings made of wood, is the main holding device. It is usually bolted to the underside of the benchtop and close to a leg for maximum stability. Some benches, such as the continental type shown here, also have an integral sliding tail vice. By using the tail vice in conjunction with metal or nylon bench dogs which drop into a row of mortises cut into the bench surface, large pieces of wood are held conveniently, securely gripped at both ends.

Drawers are useful for keeping pencils, a rule, a steel tape, small tools and other oddments. Cupboards will be used for storing tools, which should be racked separately to protect them from damage. Each tool should be considered individually when deciding the best place for storage and the method of storage such as clips and magnetic strips. Return each tool to its proper place after a working session. Planes can be laid sole downwards supported on a piece of wood to keep the blade clear of the shelf. Chisels and saws should be fitted with plastic sheaths, wherever possible, to protect their blades. Hand tools should be rubbed over with white spirit and oil occasionally to clean off resin and to prevent rust.

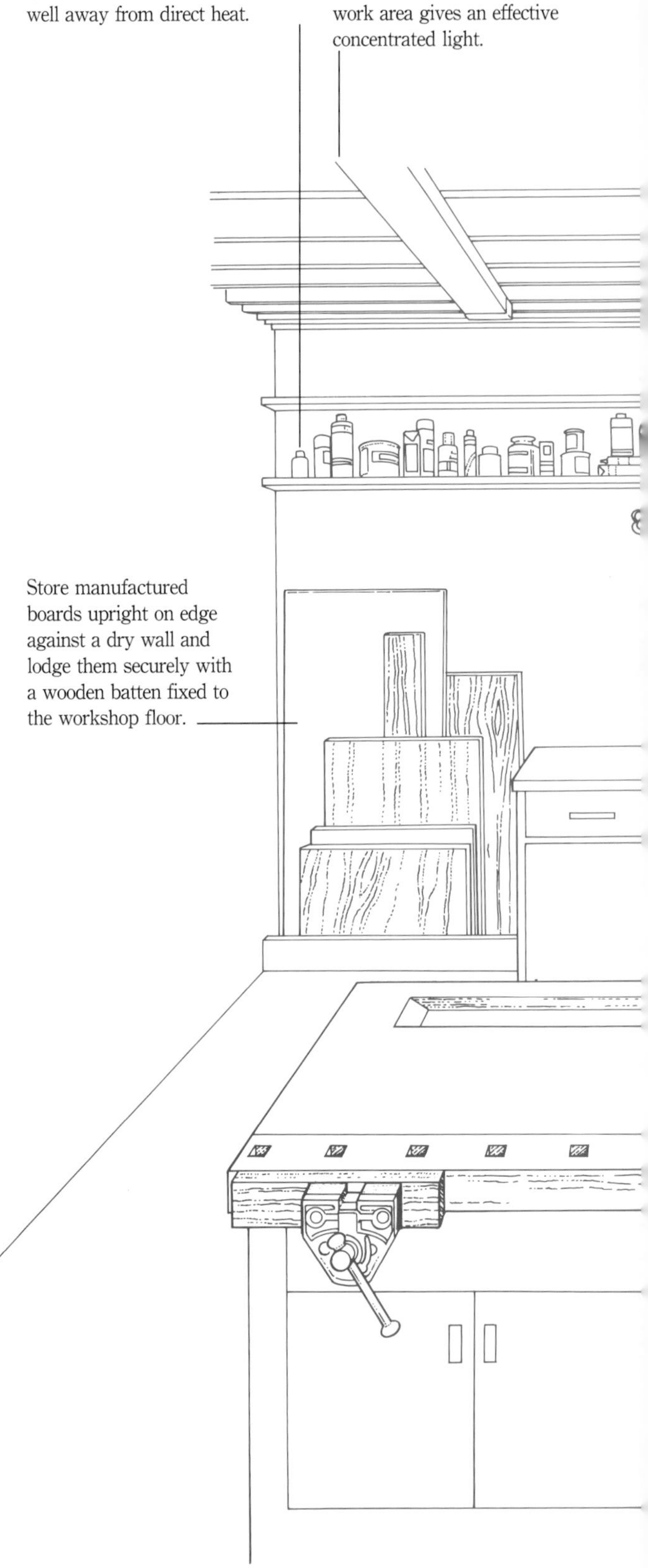

Keep all toxic materials, such as thinners and lacquers, in small quantities. Place all adhesives well away from direct heat.

Overhead fluorescent tubes give shadowless illumination and an angled spotlight over the work area gives an effective concentrated light.

Store manufactured boards upright on edge against a dry wall and lodge them securely with a wooden batten fixed to the workshop floor.

Tools placed in cupboards, drawers and under cover are protected from dust and rust. A bag of silica gel will further discourage rust.

Store nails, screws, pins, etc, in small separate containers, which must be kept dry. Label them clearly and arrange them methodically for easy access.

Many hand tools can be racked with spring clips, magnetic strips, rubber webbing, hooks, projecting dowel rods or drilled blocks.

Stout shelving provides extra storage space and is especially useful for portable power tools that are too heavy to hang on the walls.

Cover concrete floors with vinyl sheeting for warmth.

Fit power sockets above the work surfaces close to the power tools so their flexes can be short and will not trail on the workshop floor.

Measuring & marking tools

The most ancient units of measurement are those based on the human foot, outstretched arm and hand. Then, in about 2500BC, the Egyptians used calibrated wooden or stone rods based on the cubit (a forearm's length) and later the Romans used a folding foot rule

Measuring and marking tools must be treated with care: if edges, blades, surfaces, hinges, locking screws and rivets are damaged the tools lose their accuracy and are therefore of no further value.

Use a sharp HB pencil for routine marking out but always mark cutting lines, joints and anything requiring accuracy with a sharp knife or scribing point rather than a pencil. This gives a more accurate line and severs the fibres of the wood to leave a cleaner cut.

A retractable steel tape is useful when measuring long lengths but for more accuracy when laying out work the carpenter's folding rule, which can also be conveniently kept in the pocket, is more suitable. A steel rule, which is

Retractable tape
Length 900–5000mm (36–92in). Flexible steel or fibreglass tape in a case.

Folding rule
Length 300–1825mm (12–72in). For measuring and laying out.

Steel rule
Length 150–900mm (6–36in). Made of stainless steel. Can be used like a straight-edge.

Straight-edge
Length 300–1825mm (12–72in). For testing straightness and flatness. A strip of parallel-sided steel with one bevelled edge for cutting and scribing.

Spirit level
Length 75–1825mm (3–72in). Use central vial to check level of a surface and the two vials at each end to check for plumb. The bubbles should be central.

Sliding bevel
Blade length 190–323mm (7½–13in). For marking or checking angles. Set the slotted blade against a protractor or the work.

Mitre square
Blade length 150–300mm (6–12in). Set at 45° for mitres.

Try square
Blade length 150–300mm (6–12in). For checking straightness and squareness of adjacent surfaces.

Combination square
Blade length 300mm (12in). Combines the functions of the rule, try square, mitre square and spirit level. The square head slides along the steel rule.

Retractable tape

Folding rule

Steel rule

Straight-edge

Sliding bevel

Mitre square

Spirit level

Try square

Combination square

obtainable in 300 and 600 mm (12 and 24in) lengths, can be used for even greater accuracy when marking out joints, etc. The try square is essential for preparing and checking cuts square to an edge when sawing and for checking a true edge when planing. On the best-quality try squares the stock end of the blued steel blade is L-shaped and secured with three brass rivets. The 45° mitre square is used to mark or measure this fixed angle while the sliding bevel can be adjusted to any angle.

Of those tools used for marking parallel lines, the cutting gauge, with its cutting edge, is ideal for cutting across the grain of wood; the ordinary marking gauge, with its pointed spur (or point), will merely scratch the wood. However, it is most suitable for marking with or along the grain. As its name implies, the mortise gauge, which has twin spurs, is specifically designed for use in marking out mortise and tenon joints. The spurs of both marking and mortise gauges should be kept sharpened to a long point.

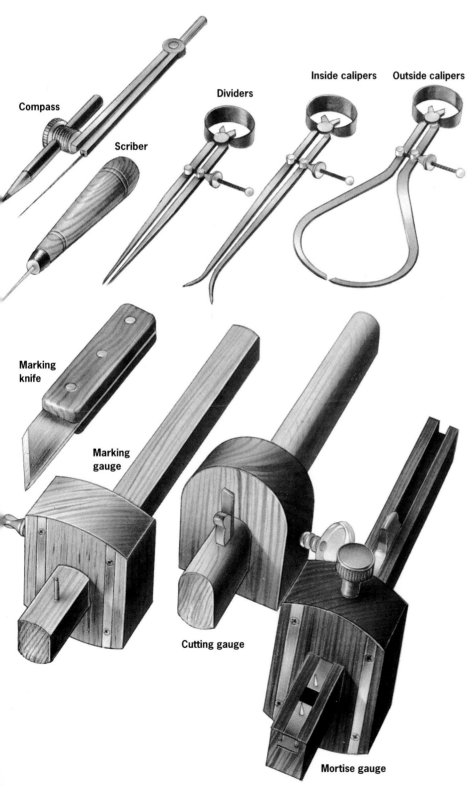

Compass

Scriber

Dividers

Inside calipers

Outside calipers

Marking knife

Marking gauge

Cutting gauge

Mortise gauge

Compass
Capacity 100–200mm (4–8in). For marking a small circle.

Scriber
Blade 100mm (4in). For marking with and across grain.

Dividers
Capacity 100–200mm (4–8in). For scribing a circle, stepping off and measuring.

Inside calipers
Capacity 100–200mm (4–8in). For measuring the inside diameter of a pipe, tube or bowl.

Outside calipers
Capacity 100–200mm (4–8in). For measuring the outside diameter of a cylinder.

Marking knife
Blade 50mm (2in). The blade is ground to a bevelled skew for marking against a rule or straight-edge.

Marking gauge
Length 160–240mm (6¼–9½in). For marking a line parallel to an edge, along the grain or on end grain. The stock, which acts as a fence and is locked by the thumb-screw, is often faced with brass to protect against wear. The spur at the end of the stem marks the line.

Cutting gauge
Length 160–240 mm (6¼–9½in). For marking across the grain parallel to an edge. The flat blade in the stem, which is secured by a wedge, can be removed and sharpened. Also cuts veneers and cardboard.

Mortise gauge
Length 225mm (9in). For marking both sides of a mortise and tenon. Two spurs, the inner one adjustable, protrude from the sliding stem to mark parallel lines.

Before marking out can begin on any piece of wood, it must have datum lines: one flat side and one edge square to it. Choose the better-looking side to be the face side. Plane it flat and level. With the straight-edge, check across the face for flatness – also along its width, its length and from corners to diagonally opposite corners. When the face is true, pencil a loop – the face mark – in the centre, extending the line to the better of the two side edges. Plane this face edge square with the face side and check it along its length with the straight-edge. To square up the remaining surfaces, set the marking gauge to the required width and, from the face edge, mark both sides. Plane to the gauge marks. Set the gauge to the required thickness and gauge both edges from the face side. Plane to the gauge marks. Accurate measuring, marking out and checking are essential. Tools must be carefully set.

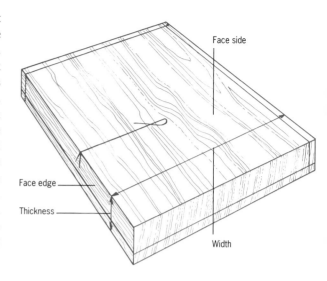

Face side

Face edge

Thickness

Width

Setting and using gauges

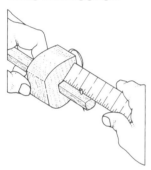

1. Set stock using a rule.

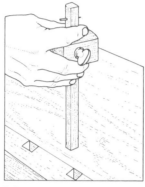

2. Tap the gauge on the bench.

3. Hold the stock firmly.

Drawing lines and outlines

Marking parallel to an edge

Finger gauging

Scribing

Making equal subdivisions

Drawing lines and outlines

To mark parallel to an edge set a combination square to the required distance. Then hold the head tightly against the edge and, with a pencil against the end of the rule, run it along the board. To draw a line close to an edge by finger gauging, hold a pencil as shown and, keeping the middle finger firmly pressed against the side of the work, run the hand along as you would a gauge. To shape a board to fit against an irregular surface first rest it at right angles to the surface, then scribe by drawing a compass along with the point running against the surface. To divide up a given width into equal subdivisions, angle a rule between the two parallel sides until the readings on the rule are easily divisible by the number of spaces required. This method is particularly helpful when marking out the socket positions for dovetail joints.

Setting and using gauges

Loosen the thumb-screw.
1. Set the required distance between stock and spur against a rule. Push the stock away from the spur with the rule or towards it with your thumb.
2. Very lightly tighten the thumb-screw and check the setting. If only slightly incorrect do not loosen the thumb screw but tap either the stock end or the spur end of the stem on the bench.
3. Recheck and, if it is correct, fully tighten the thumb-screw. When using the gauge, keep the stock tight against the work. To mark an accurate line, press the stock firmly against the face edge of the work and push, or pull, the gauge with a light but positive stroking action. The pointed spur should trail to reduce the possibility of it digging in and following the grain. The cutting gauge is set and used in the same manner; its cutting edge must be kept sharp. With the mortise gauge, the outer one of its two spurs is fixed while the other one is movable, controlled by either a raised thumb catch or by means of an adjusting screw at the end of the stem. The two spurs are first set to the required distance apart; then the stock is set at the correct distance from them and tightened. It is used in the same way as described above. Do not adjust the mortise gauge by tapping its adjusting screw on the bench edge.

Measuring and checking verticals, horizontals and planes

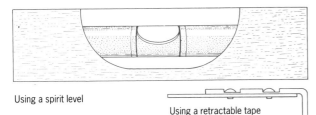

Using a spirit level

Using a retractable tape

When using a spirit level, the air bubble will be central between the datum lines when the surface is level or plumb.

Hook the end of a retractable tape over the work to take an external measurement. For an internal measurement butt the metal hook against the work.

Using pinch rods

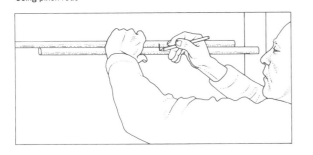

Checking for winding

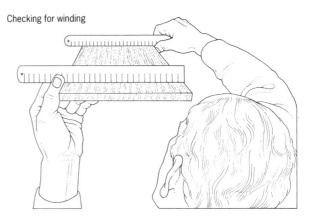

Use two overlapping battens (pinch rods) to take a longer measurement. Put coincident marks on both battens; then transfer the measurement to the wood to be cut.

To check whether a board is twisted in its length – a defect known as being 'in winding' – place a steel rule at each end and sight across the top edges to see if they are parallel. Two parallel battens can be used instead.

Measuring and checking angles

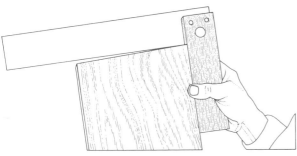

Using a try square

Measuring internal angles

Measuring and checking angles

When checking for squareness with a try square, always hold its stock tight against the work, or the tool is being used as a straight-edge and not as a square. Walls are rarely square to each other, so when checking internal angles always measure and set out the first angle with a sliding bevel.

Checking a try square

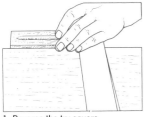

1. Reverse the try square.

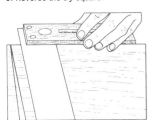

2. Draw a second line.

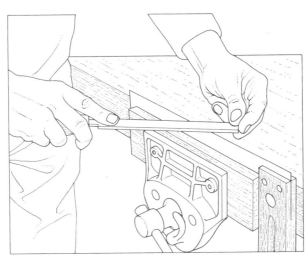

3. File blade for correction.

Checking a try square

With prolonged use or if it is dropped, a try square can become inaccurate. To check it, plane a perfectly straight edge on a board. With the stock of the try square tight against the edge, draw a line along the blade.
1. Reverse the square and check whether the blade is coincident with the line.
2. If it is not, draw another line along the blade.
3. The blade must be corrected so that it bisects these lines. File along both edges of the blade, working diagonally with a smooth file. Check the try square again. When correct, drawfile to remove the initial file marks. Smooth the edges with an oilstone.

Clamps

Clamps are used for holding materials during work and while glue dries. Originally all clamps were made of wood, but these types have mostly been superseded by metal and tough plastics. The hand-screw and cam clamp, however, have wooden jaws.

The G-clamp is the most common general-purpose clamp. It has many variations: miniature; deep-throat or long-reach; and spin-grip, which can be tightened quickly with one hand. The edge clamp, one-handed clamp and cam clamp have similar uses to the G-clamp.

The problem of clamping mitres and frames has been solved in many ingenious ways. The cast-iron mitre clamp, used in a set of four, is best for heavy-duty work, but for other work such as picture frames, various types of frame, cord and band clamp are ideal. The versatile webbing clamp can be adapted as a frame clamp by using four right-angled wooden, metal or plastic corner blocks. Modern hand-screws have wooden jaws but steel threaded spindles and are useful for angled work.

For clamping large items of work, sash or bar clamps, or similar alternatives, are required. The standard sash clamp has a simple rectangular section steel bar; the T-section bar clamp is stronger and resists bending better.

A number of bar clamps are needed when any large flat surface is being glued. Clamp heads can be fixed to a batten to make up a clamp of any length.

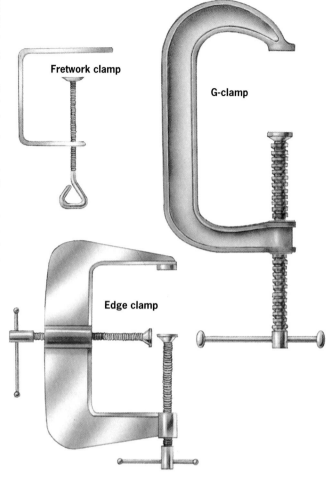

Fretwork clamp

G-clamp

Edge clamp

Fretwork clamp
Capacity 25–100mm (1–4in). A small lightweight steel clamp.

Edge clamp
Capacity 38–75mm (1½–3in). Depth 50–112mm (2–4½in). For pressure in two directions.

G-clamp
Capacity 50–300mm (2–12in). Most varieties have a swivel shoe on the screw end.

Mitre clamp
Capacity 50–100mm (2–4in). Two screw-adjusted feet set at an angle of 90° to each other hold right-angled joints, such as the two parts of a mitre joint, secure during assembly. The clamp body is drilled to allow it to be screwed down to a board or bench.

Webbing clamp
Length 3500mm (144in), width 25mm (1in). Strong canvas or nylon webbing in a steel head tensioned by a simple ratchet mechanism. For clamping large irregular, rectangular and round shapes. Also known as strap clamp and band clamp.

One-handed clamp
Capacity 150– 900mm (6–36in). Also known as the quick grip clamp, it incorporates a ratchet mechanism which advances the movable jaw forward when the trigger handle is squeezed. This allows the user to hold the work with one hand and tighten the clamp with the other. Clamping pressure is released by means of another trigger.

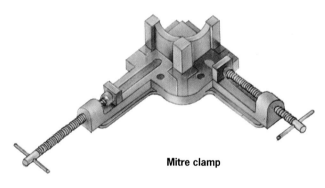

Mitre clamp

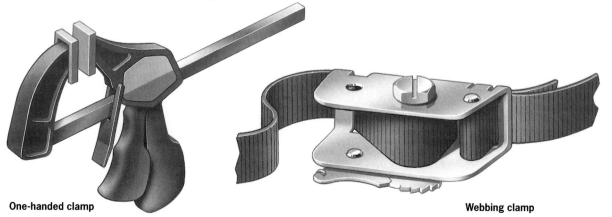

One-handed clamp

Webbing clamp

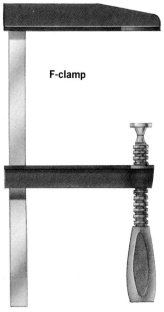

F-clamp

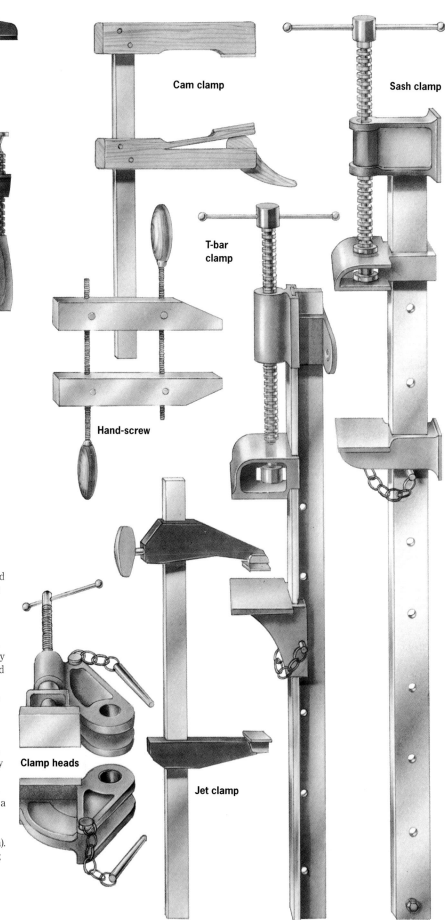

Cam clamp

Sash clamp

T-bar clamp

Hand-screw

Clamp heads

Jet clamp

F-clamp
Capacity 100–600mm (4–24in).
For clamping flat surfaces, edge
joints and the sides of carcases
and frames.

Cam clamp
Capacity 200–575mm (8–23in).
For clamping fine surfaces as its
heads are cork-faced.

Hand-screw
Capacity 50–300mm (2–12in).
Steel screws pivot in wooden
jaws, which can exert parallel
pressure or can be angled for
concentrated pressure.

Clamp heads
Can be fitted to a board of any
length over 38mm (1½in) wide and
25mm (1in) thick. Useful because
they are adaptable and easily
portable.

Jet clamp
The heads can be fitted to a steel
bar of standard section and of any
length. The heads can be reversed
to apply outward pressure for
jacking. Unlike other bar clamps,
both heads move along the steel
bar and lock by wedge action.

T-bar clamp
Capacity 760–1985mm (30–78in).
A heavy-duty joiners' clamp. Any
bar clamp over 1525mm (60in)
will usually be of T-section steel,
which resists bending. If needed, a
lengthening bar can be added.

Sash clamp
Capacity 450–13,750mm (18–54in).
For the assembly of cabinetwork;
clamping flat surfaces and edge
joints; and clamping carcases
and frames from side to side.
Two clamps can be bolted end
to end to cover a wider span.

Wood can be bruised if it is gripped too hard in the metal jaws of G-clamps and sash clamps. Clamps with wooden or plastic-capped jaws are less damaging. Place a piece of waste between the clamp and the work to spread the pressure. For odd shapes and angles, use scraps of carpet instead of waste wood. When gluing up assemblies make sure that the bar or spine of the clamp is aligned with the work, or its weight may pull the work out of square. To prevent clamps pulling the work out of alignment, alternate clamps on each side of the work when more than two are being used. For example, when clamping the sides to the top and bottom of a carcass, sash clamps should be placed alternately front and back.

Most cabinetwork requires a number of sash clamps to be used in assembly. Improvised clamps can be made from battens and waste wood.

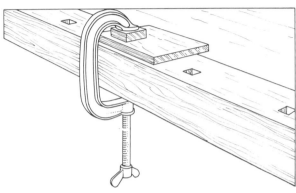

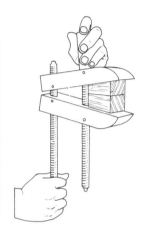

G-clamp
Always use waste wood to protect the work from the metal jaws of the G-clamp. Usually, position with the wing nut towards the ground, leaving the working area free. A swivel shoe on the screw end locates easily on slanting surfaces. The leverage exerted by the screw thread creates great pressure.

Hand-screw
To open and close a hand-screw hold a handle in each hand and revolve both handles. Tighten the inner handle; then apply final pressure with the outer handle, making the jaws parallel or angled. As long as the wooden jaws are kept clean no waste wood is needed to protect the work.

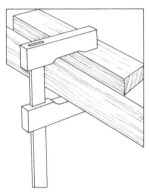

Cam clamp
Move the lower beechwood head of the cam clamp up the steel bar until it presses against the work. Lock with the lever, which is worked by cam action.

F-clamp
Slide the lower jaw of the F-clamp up the steel bar and lock it by turning the handle clockwise. Release the clamp with a single turn of the clamp handle.

Jet clamp
Move both heads of the jet clamp into position along the steel bar. The spring-loaded wedges in the heads will automatically lock themselves. Fix in position by tightening the knob on one of the heads. To apply an outward pressure for jacking work apart, remove the heads from the steel bar and reverse them.

Clamp maintenance
Clamps with threaded screws should be kept clean and lightly oiled to prevent them rusting. Stiff or damaged threads do not help the clamping process, especially if you are gluing up when speed is essential. The bars of sash clamps should likewise be absolutely clean and completely rust free; dried glue deposits will resist the movement of the sliding head.

Dried glue deposits on webbing clamps will mark any work they are in close contact with.

Webbing clamp
Slide the webbing around the work and tension it with a steel ratchet. Can be used with angled wood, metal or plastic corner blocks for clamping around corners of frames, etc.

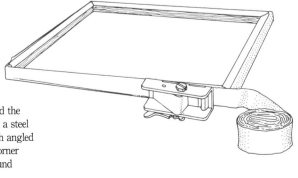

Sash clamp

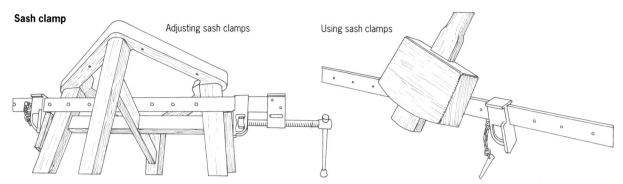

Adjusting sash clamps

Using sash clamps

Adjust the sash clamp initially by sliding the tail shoe along the steel bar and securing it with a pin through one of the holes in the bar. To move a stiff tail shoe, tap

it with a mallet. (It is made of cast iron and a hammer might shatter it.) Make final adjustments with the tightening screw at the other end of the bar. Use sash clamps

for clamping all large constructions together during assembly while the glue dries, checking the pressure is even. Ensure enough clamps of the right length are

available before beginning assembly. Use T-bar clamps in the same way as sash clamps.

Lengthening sash clamps

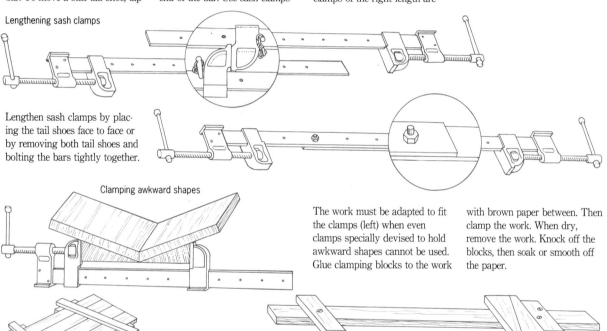

Lengthen sash clamps by placing the tail shoes face to face or by removing both tail shoes and bolting the bars tightly together.

Clamping awkward shapes

The work must be adapted to fit the clamps (left) when even clamps specially devised to hold awkward shapes cannot be used. Glue clamping blocks to the work

with brown paper between. Then clamp the work. When dry, remove the work. Knock off the blocks, then soak or smooth off the paper.

Clamping work with battens

If a number of clamps are to cover the same distance, cut battens roughly to size (*above*). Screw a pivoting cleat to each end. Put the battens in place.

Tap them so they slant, pivoting the cleats and making the battens fit tightly. Cleats rigidly screwed to each end of a batten can be used with folding wedges

tapped in to supply pressure. Bore holes in a batten to take a movable tail shoe, locked by a bolt and wing nut for rough adjustment. At the other end,

fix a cleat with one sloping side matching the slope of a wedge. Make fine adjustments by tapping in the wedge.

Mitre and frame clamps

Mitre or corner clamps of the type shown on page 32 are often used, in sets of four, for picture frame and mirror frame work. Alternatively, frames may be clamped up for gluing or nailing by means of various kinds of frame clamp. Most of these consist of four shaped corner blocks, made from wood or plastic, held in place by a nylon band or cord together with a mechanism for, or method of, applying even tension. Make a

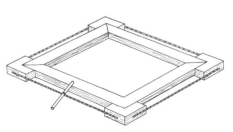

frame clamp with blocks of wood recessed at the inner corners. Apply pressure with strong cord resting in grooves on the outside. Twist the cord around a stick, rest the stick against the frame to lock the windlass.

Clamp heads

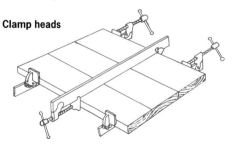

Use clamp heads in pairs on a 25mm (1in) section wooden batten. Bore holes in the batten at regular intervals. Place the clamp heads and batten over the work and lock in position with pegs placed in the holes.

Hand- & backsaws

Saws are of three main types, categorized according to their function: handsaws for rough work and conversion; backsaws for joints and fine work; and saws for curves and shapes. Handsaws have flexible tempered steel blades and, often, beechwood handles. Backsaws have a brass or steel strip folded over the top of the blade to add rigidity and weight along the line of the cut.

The basic design of the handsaw was established in the mid-17th century. The English type, incorporating an oval hand-hole and angled grip, became the standard pattern almost everywhere for both hand- and backsaws. A modern alternative is the hard-point saw the handle of which is made of polypropylene; this is usually moulded onto a PTFE-coated blade, which helps to reduce friction when cutting. Japanese saws, with thin blades and very fine teeth which cut on the backward (pull) stroke, are increasingly popular.

A saw's teeth are specifically designed to cut either along the grain, as with the rip saw, or across the grain, as with the cross-cut saw. A cross-cut saw will also cut along the grain, but less efficiently than the rip saw. The greater the number of teeth in a length of blade, the finer and slower the cut. The number of teeth is expressed as so many points per 25mm (1in). Saws also have their teeth set to prevent the blade binding in the kerf or cut.

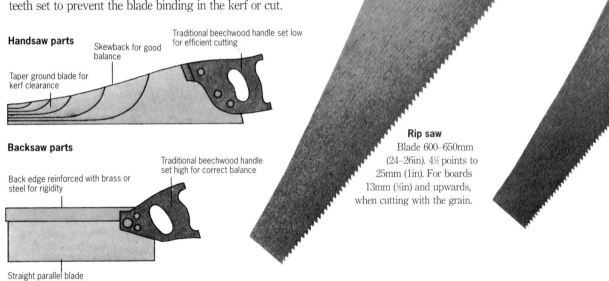

Rip saw
Blade 600–650mm (24–26in). 4½ points to 25mm (1in). For boards 13mm (½in) and upwards, when cutting with the grain.

Handsaw parts

Taper ground blade for kerf clearance

Skewback for good balance

Traditional beechwood handle set low for efficient cutting

Backsaw parts

Back edge reinforced with brass or steel for rigidity

Traditional beechwood handle set high for correct balance

Straight parallel blade

SAW TEETH

Rip saw teeth
Rip saw teeth are set as shown above, with their tips bent over in alternate directions to prevent binding in the kerf. Each tooth is filed to form a chisel edge. This enables it to cut the fibres cleanly along the grain of the wood.

Cross-cut saw teeth
The teeth on a cross-cut saw are sloped on their leading edge as well as being filed at an angle and set. Filed in this way, each tooth is sharply pointed to act as a knife to sever the fibres of the wood.

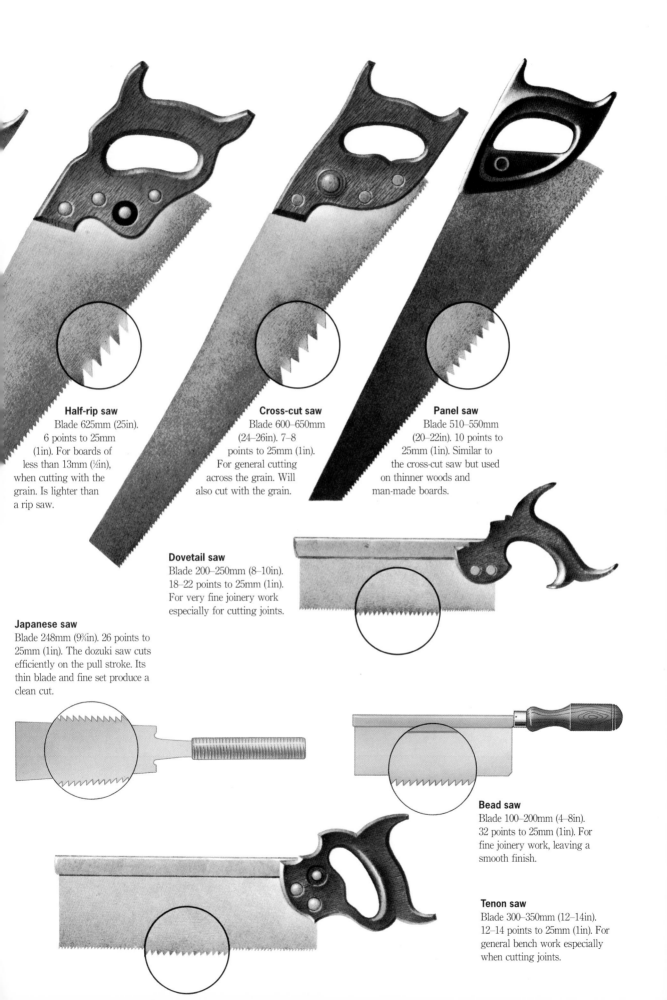

Half-rip saw
Blade 625mm (25in).
6 points to 25mm
(1in). For boards of
less than 13mm (½in),
when cutting with the
grain. Is lighter than
a rip saw.

Cross-cut saw
Blade 600–650mm
(24–26in). 7–8
points to 25mm (1in).
For general cutting
across the grain. Will
also cut with the grain.

Panel saw
Blade 510–550mm
(20–22in). 10 points to
25mm (1in). Similar to
the cross-cut saw but used
on thinner woods and
man-made boards.

Dovetail saw
Blade 200–250mm (8–10in).
18–22 points to 25mm (1in).
For very fine joinery work
especially for cutting joints.

Japanese saw
Blade 248mm (9¾in). 26 points to
25mm (1in). The dozuki saw cuts
efficiently on the pull stroke. Its
thin blade and fine set produce a
clean cut.

Bead saw
Blade 100–200mm (4–8in).
32 points to 25mm (1in). For
fine joinery work, leaving a
smooth finish.

Tenon saw
Blade 300–350mm (12–14in).
12–14 points to 25mm (1in). For
general bench work especially
when cutting joints.

Sawing is a skill; mastery is achieved only with practice, but attention to the following points will make the work easier. A blunt tool is more difficult to control than a sharp one. A sharp saw needs little pushing; force makes it more difficult to follow a line and can cause the saw to buckle. The saw should be well-balanced and should cut smoothly. For efficient cutting, saw with the blade in line with your arm and shoulder; start the cut low down and bring the saw up to the correct cutting angle. Then move the saw up and down in long steady movements.

Saw vertically wherever possible, even if the wood must be gripped out of upright in the vice to bring the cutting line to the required angle. If the saw binds in the wood, rub three drops of oil on the blade (avoid oils that stain wood). In extreme cases, drive a narrow wooden wedge into the saw-cut to hold it open. Wipe any resin off the blade, using white spirit; then wipe with oil.

If saw teeth are overset, that is alternate teeth are pushed too far over, it will be more difficult to work the saw. This can be corrected by side dressing (see pages 44–5). To bring a wandering saw back to the cutting line, twist the blade towards the line, working with the narrow front end of the saw.

Using a rip saw

Rip saw teeth are designed for cutting along the grain. If used for cross-cutting the rip saw may jump. Should ripping prove difficult, try changing to a half-rip saw or in extreme cases to a cross-cut or panel saw.

Rip short boards in the vice or on a stool. Support long work on two stools. An angle of 60° between the saw and the work is comfortable if ripping on stools, but in a vice a rip saw should be held horizontally to the work.

Controlling a blade

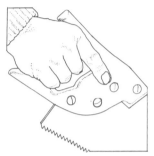 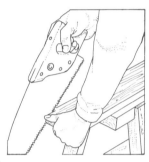

To control a handsaw accurately needs experience. A forefinger held along the handle aids control.

The saw must be guided to the cutting line. Steady the blade against the thumb. Start with a few backward cuts.

RIPPING

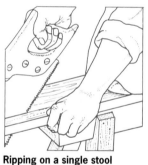 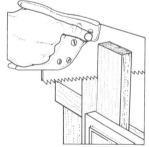

Ripping on a single stool
To saw on only a single stool overhang the board a bit at a time, steadying it with the knee. Saw halfway in from each end of the board.

Ripping short lengths
Hold short lengths in the vice. Secure the wood so that only a little bit projects at a time, or the wood will vibrate, making the cut inaccurate.

Ripping between two stools
Place the board across two stools (*right*) and start sawing at the overhang. Then lift the saw and board back and continue sawing between the stools.

Ripping on the workbench
If a level higher than the stool is more convenient for ripping, fasten the wood to the bench and hold the saw upright, using both hands (*above*).

Using a cross-cut saw

To cut a groove across the grain, the wood fibres must be cut before the waste is removed or they will splinter. This is the principle of a cross-cut saw: the knife-like points of the teeth sever the fibres.

The small teeth of a cross-cut saw make clean cuts with minimal splintering. A cross-cut saw will also rip effectively, although it is slower than the rip saw because of its smaller teeth. A panel saw is a smaller version of a cross-cut saw. It can be used for ripping, although it cuts even more slowly than a cross-cut saw does. When you are cross-cutting hold the saw blade at 45° to the work.

Using a backsaw

Backsaws are used for fine, accurate work. Their blades are thinner and teeth finer than those of handsaws. The steel or brass back enables the saw to cut under its own weight so that force is not needed to make the cut.

Both tenon saws and dovetail saws can cut along or across the grain and for bench work both are used with a bench-hook. The tenon saw is good for cutting thin plywood, giving a cleaner cut than a cross-cut saw. The back will not interfere with deep sawing if the saw is held at a shallow angle to the work. The dovetail saw is for similar but finer work to the tenon saw.

CROSS-CUTTING

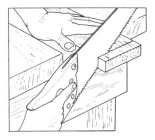

Sawing off a short end
To saw off a short end hold the board firmly against the benchwell and start cutting.

Stop before the end. To complete the cut change the direction of the saw to stop the offcut falling and splintering the board.

Alternatively place the board in the benchwell and support the offcut with the free hand while sawing.

Sawing off a long end
To saw off a long end stand at the end of the bench, rest the board along the well and support the offcut while sawing.

USING A BACKSAW

Controlling a backsaw
Begin the cut with one or two backward strokes at the far side of the cutting line. Working the blade in the cut, gradually level the saw. Then follow the vertical cutting line. Saw smoothly using the length of the blade. Hold the wood still against a bench-hook.

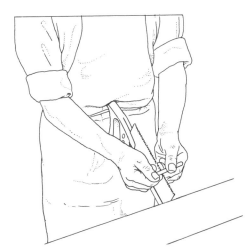

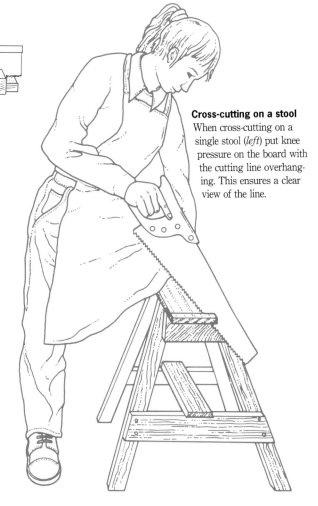

Cross-cutting on a stool
When cross-cutting on a single stool (*left*) put knee pressure on the board with the cutting line overhanging. This ensures a clear view of the line.

Cutting small pieces of wood on a backsaw
For an easier grip, and to avoid obscuring the cutting line with the blade, work small pieces of wood against the saw.

Saws for shaping

For a saw to cut round a curve the blade has to be narrow or it will bind in the wood. To cut a tight curve, the blade must be very narrow; however, the narrower the blade the weaker it becomes and this inevitably leads to compromise in the design of saws. The solution that has been used for centuries is to hold the blade in tension in some kind of frame. Frame saws with the blade in the centre of the frame were used by the Romans, and the cantilever principle of the modern bowsaw was known and in use as far back as the 13th century. The blade in the bowsaw is held between two uprights, or cheeks, that pivot on either side of a central stretcher rail. The blade is tensioned by pulling the tops of the cheeks towards each other by means of a twisted cord and toggle or, in some bowsaws, by a threaded rod tensioned by wing nuts. Coarse- and fine-toothed blades can be used in the bowsaw and the blade can be swivelled to allow the saw to cut parallel to the edge of the board.

Thick boards, 16mm (⅝in) and upwards, must be cut by a heavily framed saw such as the bowsaw; however it will not be possible to cut sharp curves. A coping saw with its narrow blade can tackle curves of very small radii, but its use is confined to wood, 16mm (⅝in) thick and below. For very thin material, such as plywood, the fretsaw is used. Both of these saws apply tension to their blades by means of a spring steel frame and their rigidity is determined by the quality of the steel in the frame, so do not buy anything less than the best.

The blades of both saws may be fitted to cut either on the pull or on the push stroke. With the blade set to cut backwards as it is pulled, ie, teeth facing towards the handle, the work is usually held flat overhanging the bench or against a 'V' block support and sawn from below. Since the saw cuts as it moves down,

the work is not lifted by the action of the saw. When using the coping saw on thicker wood set the blade with teeth facing forward and saw with the work held vertically in a vice.

Coping saw blades may be rotated through 360° to follow an intricate shape; alignment of the two blade holder pins prevents working with a twisted blade. The fretsaw has a greater capacity frame and uses a much finer blade than the coping saw, making it more suitable for small-scale work and model-making.

The two frameless saws illustrated below – the compass saw and the padsaw – have their advantages and disadvantages. Because they are frameless, they can be used in places where other saws would be restricted by their frames. Although the compass saw blade tapers, allowing it to start a fine cut, its overall width is still restricting. On a shallow curve, however, it will cut almost as quickly as a handsaw on a straight line. The compass saw shown is one of a nest of three saws fitting on a single handle with each additional blade reduced in size. The padsaw blade is narrow, but, because it has been thickened to counteract the tendency to buckle, it can become hot and hard work to use.

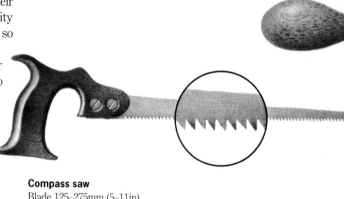

Coping saw parts

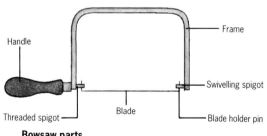

Handle

Frame

Swivelling spigot

Threaded spigot

Blade

Blade holder pin

Bowsaw parts

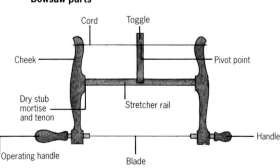

Cord

Toggle

Cheek

Pivot point

Dry stub mortise and tenon

Stretcher rail

Operating handle

Blade

Handle

Compass saw
Blade 125–275mm (5–11in).
9 points to 25mm (1in). Three interchangeable blades can be fitted according to the curvature of the cut.

Padsaw
Blades 125–375mm (5–15in).
9 points to 25mm (1in). For cutting holes away from edges; originally for making the straight cuts in keyholes.

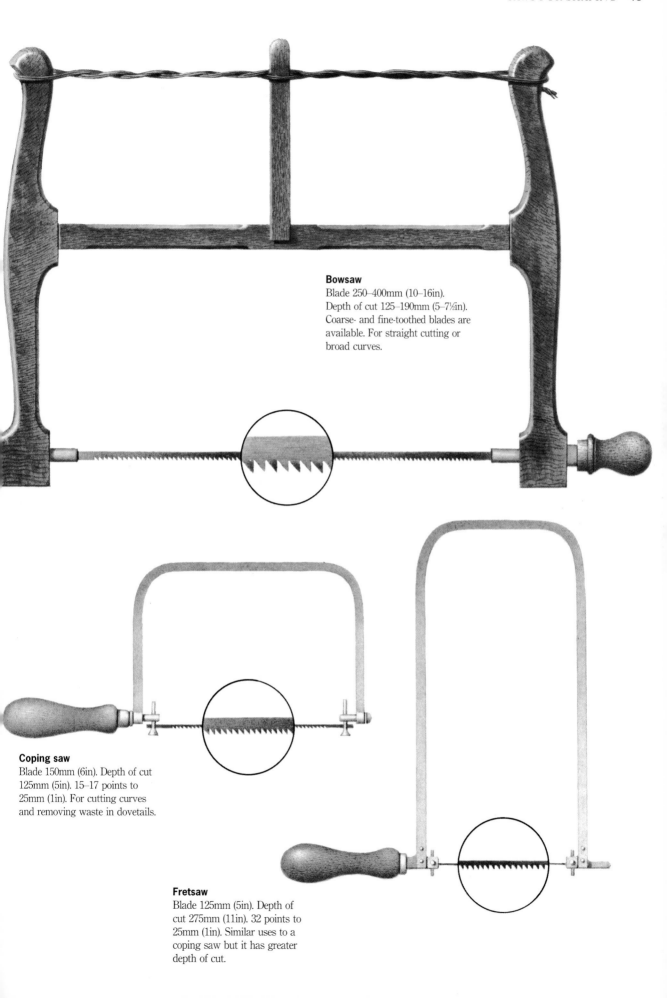

Bowsaw
Blade 250–400mm (10–16in).
Depth of cut 125–190mm (5–7½in).
Coarse- and fine-toothed blades are
available. For straight cutting or
broad curves.

Coping saw
Blade 150mm (6in). Depth of cut
125mm (5in). 15–17 points to
25mm (1in). For cutting curves
and removing waste in dovetails.

Fretsaw
Blade 125mm (5in). Depth of
cut 275mm (11in). 32 points to
25mm (1in). Similar uses to a
coping saw but it has greater
depth of cut.

When using frame saws, such as bowsaws, coping saws and fretsaws, and cutting wood held vertically in the vice, the operator should face the work directly and stand with feet apart for a well-balanced stance. The blade should be introduced at right angles to the work and the saw held in the horizontal position. For the bowsaw and coping saw a two-handed grip is recommended to control the cutting action. One hand grasps the handle with the other hand wrapped tightly around it, forefingers extended and hooked around the frame. A firm grip is always required to stop the narrow blade of these saws wandering off the marked cutting line. The bowsaw is held in this manner by the longer of its two handles.

When sawing thin material, using either the coping saw or the fretsaw, and cutting wood placed horizontally overhanging the bench or supported on a 'V' block, the operator needs to bend down to a position which brings the hands below the work. Again, the saw blade is introduced at right angles to the work with the saw held vertically. The handle is gripped with one hand while the other is used, in this case, to hold the work firmly to the bench or support.

The worker has two options while sawing shapes: to change the direction of the blade or to readjust the wood in the vice. Use these options freely, depending on the ease of working and how much support is provided by the vice. Altering the direction of the blade is quickly done on most frame saws. Place a hand on each side of the blade or the blade will twist and perhaps break.

Frequently change the position of the wood so that the point of sawing remains near the vice jaws. If this is too high the wood will vibrate and the blade may break.

With the bowsaw, cutting is on the push stroke; this comes naturally to most woodworkers. With the coping saw, where the blade can be fitted with the teeth facing either towards or away from the handle, cutting on the push stroke tends to compress the frame and loosen the blade, whereas cutting on the pull stroke conserves the blade, although the cutting line may be obscured because the fibres are raised.

The compass saw has a single-handed, pistol-grip handle and often has the facility to use interchangeable blades of different sizes. These are used to suit different situations and may be used reversed for undercutting. The teeth of these blades have a coarse set to cut quickly both with and across the grain. The padsaw has a similar cutting action but is smaller in size; it has a single-handed handle, in line with its disposable blade. To make interior cuts with either saw, first drill a hole through the work large enough to start the blade, then cut carefully to the marked line. The traditional use of the padsaw for cutting keyholes gives this saw its alternative name.

COPING SAW

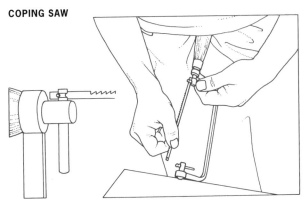

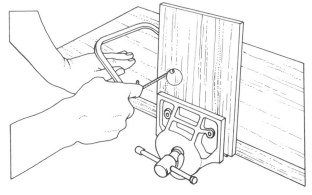

Fitting a coping saw blade
Spigot pins are split and grooved so that when a blade is slid into the split the pin will slot into the groove. To change a blade compress the frame against the bench to allow the blade pins to pass the spigots.

Making an interior cut
For an interior cut release one end of the blade. Pass it through a drilled hole, refit the blade and start sawing.

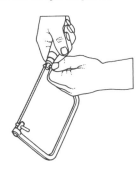

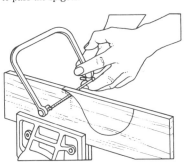

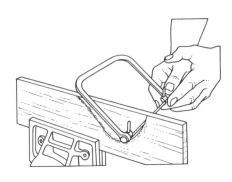

Retightening the blade handle
When retightening the handle hold the spigot to stop the blade twisting and breaking.

Controlling a coping saw
To stop the blade slipping out of line, start the cut inside the cutting line.

Finishing a cut
Finish a cut by changing the blade angle to an upward direction, or start a fresh cut at the other end.

BOWSAW

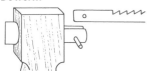

Fitting a bowsaw
To fit a bowsaw blade pass the holding pins through the handle extension into the blade and out the other side.

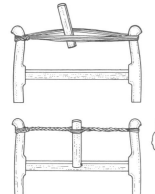

Tensioning the blade
To tension the blade turn the toggle and cord. When the blade is taut tuck the toggle against the stretcher rail.

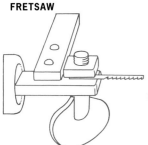

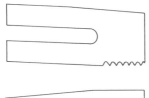

Adjusting the blade angle
To adjust the angle of a bowsaw blade hold the frame steady against the bench while turning both handles.

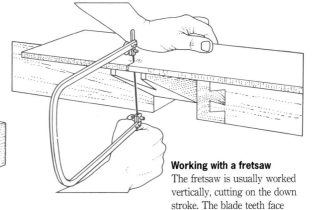

Cutting curves in thick boards
To cut curves in thick boards use a bowsaw's sturdy frame fitted with a toughened blade. Keep the blade horizontal.

FRETSAW

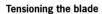

Fitting a fretsaw blade
A fretsaw blade is held, with the aid of wing nuts, by a friction grip. The frame is compressed for blade tension.

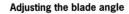

Supporting work
A 'V' block supports the work when fretsawing. Clamp the block level with the bench top and cut within the 'V'.

Working with a fretsaw
The fretsaw is usually worked vertically, cutting on the down stroke. The blade teeth face towards the handle.

COMPASS SAW AND PADSAW

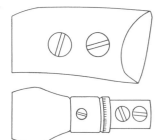

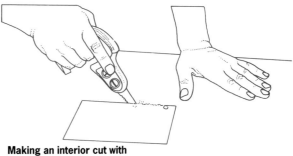

Compass saw
A compass saw blade is slotted for easy changeover. It passes around two screws in the handle, which are then secured.

Padsaw
A padsaw handle is slotted throughout its length. The blade, held by the two screws, can project to any length.

Making an interior cut with a compass saw or padsaw
To start an interior cut, first bore a hole to accommodate the blade tip.

Sharpening & maintaining saws

A sharp saw needs no forcing, but once the teeth become dulled the saw will cut slowly and inaccurately. If the blade is forced, it may wander from the cutting line, jam in the kerf, or buckle. The process of renewing the edge on saw teeth is called refitting and it involves three quite separate stages – topping, setting and sharpening. All hand- and backsaw blades can be refitted. The blades of frame saws should be discarded when blunt. Circular power-saw blades should be professionally sharpened.

During each stage of refitting the saw must be held securely along the length of the blade. A special vice for saw-sharpening is available which clamps to the bench but the traditional method is to use a purpose-made, portable saw horse which can be used where the light is best. Saws may also be sharpened in the vice, sandwiched between two wooden battens. Make the first attempt at refitting on a new saw, because the angles of the teeth will be easier to follow. If it is difficult to keep a saw to the cutting line, the teeth on one side are probably higher than those on the other. Topping is the remedy.

In topping, the teeth are filed to the same height with a smooth, flat file, held horizontally; make a topping clamp to ensure this. If the file is not held horizontally, the teeth on one side will be filed more than on the other. Each tooth touched by the file will show a bright white spot of new metal. If, after two or three strokes, some teeth are still not showing a white spot, the teeth are too uneven and should be sent to an expert for reshaping.

After topping, the teeth must be set. This involves bending the tips of the teeth alternately right and left of the blade, so that the kerf formed during cutting is wider than the thickness of the blade, giving the blade clearance and reducing friction. The width of the kerf should be no more than one and a half times the thickness of the blade. The teeth should be set to no more than half their depth and to the same side to which they were originally bent.

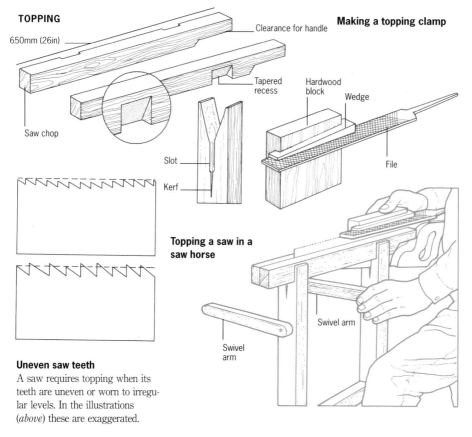

TOPPING

650mm (26in)

Clearance for handle

Tapered recess

Saw chop

Slot

Kerf

Hardwood block

Wedge

File

Making a topping clamp

Topping a saw in a saw horse

Swivel arm

Swivel arm

Uneven saw teeth

A saw requires topping when its teeth are uneven or worn to irregular levels. In the illustrations (*above*) these are exaggerated.

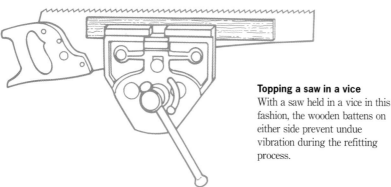

Topping a saw in a vice

With a saw held in a vice in this fashion, the wooden battens on either side prevent undue vibration during the refitting process.

Making a topping clamp

The tops of the teeth are filed with a smooth, flat file to level them. To ensure that the file is held flat, make a topping clamp from a grooved hardwood block. Taper the top of the groove. Hold the file in the groove with a wedge. Some woodworkers prefer a handsaw edge to be slightly rounded in its length to produce a more effective cut for the energy used. This can be done in stages at each topping.

Topping a saw in a saw horse

A saw horse holds the saw firmly along the length of its blade. Make the frame from two sturdy uprights, joined by through-tenoned cross rails, tall enough to bring a saw to be sharpened to a convenient height. The saw horse can be set up by propping its swinging arms against a wall; a foot resting on a lower cross rail steadies it. Cut the saw chops long enough to support the longest handsaw blades. Shape the chops at one end to provide clearance for the saw handle. Cut tapered recesses in the outside edges of the chops to fit into the uprights of the saw horse. Line the recesses with abrasive paper to increase friction. Cut the uprights to accommodate the saw chops. Cut a slot for clearance for backsaw backs. Make a kerf below the slot for handsaw blades.

To top a saw, clamp the saw blade in the saw horse, projecting above the saw chops. Hold the topping clamp against the saw blade so that the file is flat on the teeth. Run it along until a bright white spot of new metal is visible on every tooth.

The setting must be uniform on each side; the teeth on each side must do the same amount of work.

The easiest way to set a saw is to use a proprietary saw set. Professional saw doctors use the thin cross-pein of a hammer to top the teeth on an anvil. This method is quick but demands experience. Over-setting is a mistake made by amateurs; this makes the saw inefficient as more effort is needed to cut the wide kerf and more wood is wasted as sawdust. If the set is excessive, it can be remedied by side dressing. Lie the saw flat on the bench and run the edge of a lubricated oilstone lightly along the teeth for two or three strokes on each side. Subsequent sharpening without setting returns the saw to normal.

In sharpening, the cutting edge or point is renewed on each tooth. A saw can be sharpened two or three times before it needs re-setting, but it should be topped lightly before each sharpening. This process has the two-fold effect of ensuring that the teeth remain level throughout

and the white spots provide guides for sharpening. The aim in sharpening is to file away the bright white spot left on each tooth by topping. Tapered triangular files are used for sharpening. A file of the correct length must be used depending on the number of points per 25mm (1in) on the saw. The file must fit correctly in the gullet – the space between the saw teeth. Always discard files when they start losing their cutting edge. Once dulled, control of the file is lost and consequently tooth angles will be inconsistent. The teeth of rip and cross-cut saws are shaped differently and so must be sharpened accordingly. The teeth of dovetail and tenon saws are more difficult to sharpen as they are so small. Light is all-important, and this emphasizes the value of a portable saw horse.

If a saw is in very bad condition, it needs an extra stage – shaping – after topping. Shaping is necessary if the saw has been incorrectly sharpened repeatedly. It should then be given to an expert for re-cutting.

Setting

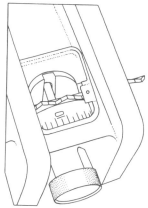

1. Adjust the dial.

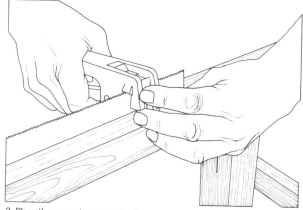

2. Place the saw set over one tooth.

Sharpening

RIP SAW TEETH

90

ANGLE OF FILING RIP SAW

CROSS-CUT TEETH

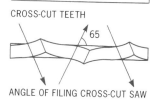
65

ANGLE OF FILING CROSS-CUT SAW

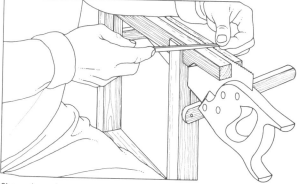

Sharpening a rip saw

Choosing the correct file for sharpening		
Type of saw	Points per 25mm (1in)	File length
Dovetail	18–22	150mm (6in)
Tenon	12–14	175mm (7in)
Panel	10–12	200mm (8in)
Cross-cut	7–8	225mm (9in)
Rip	4½–6	250mm (10in)

Setting

The easiest way to set saw teeth is with a pliers-type saw set.
1. Adjust the dial according to the number of points per 25mm (1in). This controls the amount and depth of set.
2. Place the saw set over one tooth, lining up the plunger squarely with the centre of the tooth and squeeze the handles. The plunger presses the tooth against the anvil, the bevel of which was set when the dial was adjusted. Set each alternate tooth in turn along one side of the saw, then turn the saw around and set the intermediate teeth on the other side of the blade.

Sharpening

Lower the saw in the saw chops so that the teeth and only 3mm (⅛in) of the blade are showing. Select a file. Fit a handle to it. Holding the file at each end, begin filing at the toe end of the saw. Work on every saw tooth that bends away from you. To sharpen rip saw teeth, seat the file in the gullet, holding it at right angles to the saw and horizontally. File only on the forward stroke, applying even pressure to adjoining teeth. Remove half the white spot on adjoining teeth. Turn the saw around and work back again. Sharpen cross-cut, panel and tenon saw teeth in a similar way, but hold the file at about 65° to the blade and lower the file handle slightly. Sharpen the dovetail saw teeth at right angles like rip saw teeth. After sharpening, side dress the saw very lightly to remove any wire edge, using the edge of an oilstone.

Chisels & gouges

A chisel has a long narrow blade that is used to cut deep narrow recesses for joints, such as mortises, and shallow recesses for butt hinges; it is also used for paring and chamfering. A gouge has a curved blade and is used to cut and smooth grooves and hollows. Cabinetmakers' gouges have blades with parallel sides; carvers' gouges can be parallel or fishtail.

The cutting edge of chisels and gouges is across the end of the blade, the width of which designates the size of the tool. Handles can be made of wood or plastic.

Chisels and gouges are classified by the way in which the handle is fastened to the blade: either by a tang or a socket. A tang is tapered and inserted into the handle. A socket chisel has the end of the blade formed into a conical socket, which fits over the handle. A socket chisel is generally used on heavier work than a tang chisel. A heavy-duty chisel can sometimes have a shock-absorbing leather washer between the bolster of the blade and the handle to absorb the mallet blows.

Chisel blades can be rectangular in section or bevelled to give clearance when cleaning out corners or working in undercut or acute angles, such as dovetail housings. Bevel-edged chisels are lighter and less robust than rectangular-sectioned chisels. Mortise chisels have strong but narrow blades for chopping and levering out waste. Japanese chisels are hollow ground.

TYPES OF CHISEL AND GOUGE

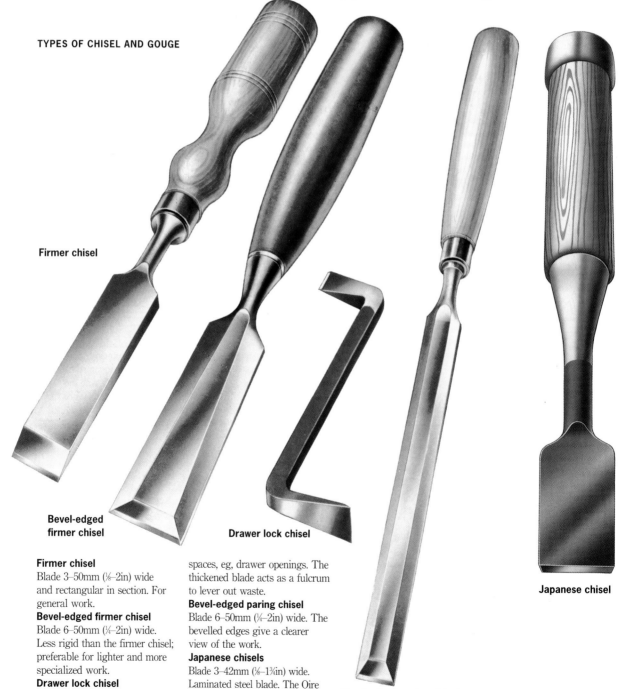

Firmer chisel

Bevel-edged firmer chisel

Drawer lock chisel

Japanese chisel

Bevel-edged paring chisel

Firmer chisel
Blade 3–50mm (⅛–2in) wide and rectangular in section. For general work.

Bevel-edged firmer chisel
Blade 6–50mm (¼–2in) wide. Less rigid than the firmer chisel; preferable for lighter and more specialized work.

Drawer lock chisel
Blade 10–16mm (⅜–⅝in) wide. Use with a hammer in close spaces, eg, drawer openings. The thickened blade acts as a fulcrum to lever out waste.

Bevel-edged paring chisel
Blade 6–50mm (¼–2in) wide. The bevelled edges give a clearer view of the work.

Japanese chisels
Blade 3–42mm (⅛–1¾in) wide. Laminated steel blade. The Oire Nomi chisel is the most common Japanese chisel for general use.

CHISEL AND GOUGE PARTS AND SHAPES

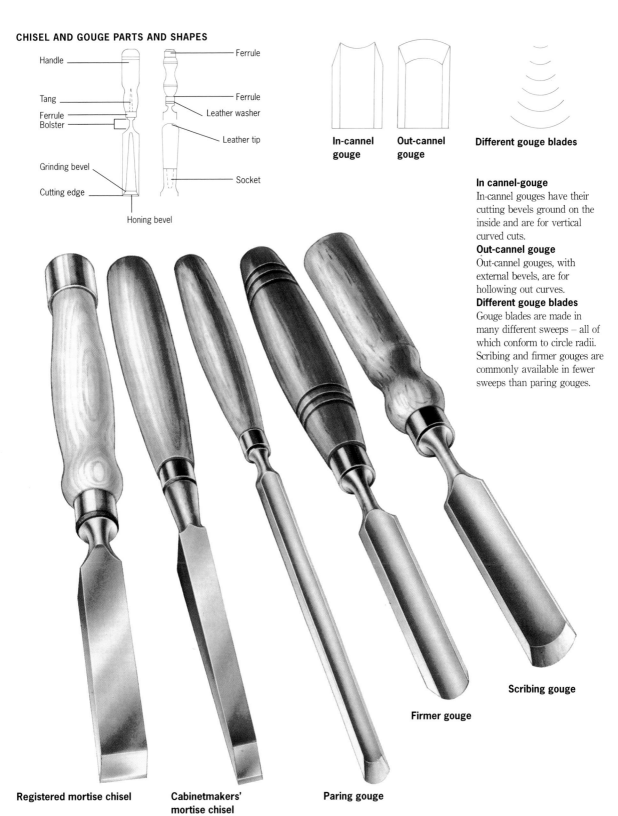

Handle
Tang
Ferrule
Bolster
Grinding bevel
Cutting edge
Honing bevel
Ferrule
Ferrule
Leather washer
Leather tip
Socket

In-cannel gouge

Out-cannel gouge

Different gouge blades

In cannel-gouge
In-cannel gouges have their cutting bevels ground on the inside and are for vertical curved cuts.

Out-cannel gouge
Out-cannel gouges, with external bevels, are for hollowing out curves.

Different gouge blades
Gouge blades are made in many different sweeps – all of which conform to circle radii. Scribing and firmer gouges are commonly available in fewer sweeps than paring gouges.

Scribing gouge

Firmer gouge

Paring gouge

Registered mortise chisel

Cabinetmakers' mortise chisel

Registered mortise chisel
Blade 6–50mm (¼–2in) wide. For heavy mortising work; the top of handle is reinforced with a steel ferrule. This chisel can be fitted with a leather washer to absorb shock when struck with a heavy mallet.

Cabinetmakers' mortise chisel
Blade 6–13mm (¼–½in) wide. Sturdy socket chisel to withstand continual blows.

Paring gouge
Blade 3–38mm (⅛–1½in) wide. Sometimes has a cranked blade for hand clearance.

Firmer gouge
Blade 3–50mm (⅛–2in) wide. An out-cannel gouge for convex curves or fluting, bevel down.

Scribing gouge
Blade 3–25mm (⅛–1in) wide. General-purpose in-cannel gouge for concave curves.

Bench planes

A plane is a cutting tool designed for removing shavings to a precisely controlled depth. A bench plane has a flat sole and a wooden or metal body; it is used for reducing the width or thickness of a piece of wood, making it straight, and for smoothing a surface. It reached an advanced stage of development in Roman times and the modern metal version can be considered a definitive tool.

Although wooden planes are still in use, metal planes have a cutting edge that is more quickly and precisely adjusted. Once a plane has been correctly set, the flat sole controls the blade and the depth of cut so that the worker's full strength can be used for the driving force. It is important therefore to know how a plane is adjusted.

The cap iron stiffens the blade and prevents the wood tearing by breaking the shaving as soon as it is raised by the blade. The closer the cap iron to the cutting edge the sooner the shaving is broken, although there is greater resistance in the cut. The size of the mouth enables cuts of varying degrees of fineness to be made; a wide mouth allows a thicker shaving to be cut with a deeper-set blade. Adjustment of the cap iron, mouth and blade should suit the grain and the required surface finish.

ADJUSTING A METAL PLANE

 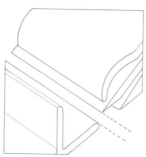  

Setting the cap iron
Set the cap iron about 1.5 mm (⅟₁₆in) back from the cutting edge for a softwood. For planing a hardwood or for a fine finish the gap should be reduced. This is done by realigning and securing the cap iron onto the back of the blade. Ensure a tight fit to prevent shavings wedging between the two.

Adjusting the mouth
The position of the frog governs the width of the mouth. For general use, line up the edge of the frog with the top edge of the mouth. For fine work the mouth should be narrower. Remove the cap iron and blade. Slacken the screws that fix the frog and move the frog using the frog adjustment screw.

Increasing the depth of cut
The depth of cut is increased by pushing the blade out. This is done by turning the adjustment nut clockwise. Check the setting by holding the plane upside-down with the sole level with your eye. The cutting edge should appear as a very narrow black line. For fine work the blade should hardly show.

Adjusting the blade angle
Use the lateral adjustment lever to ensure that the blade protrudes an equal amount across its width. Move the lever from side to side and check the alignment with the plane held upside-down. Once the blade is set, take up any slack in the adjustment nut so the blade cannot move.

Metal plane parts

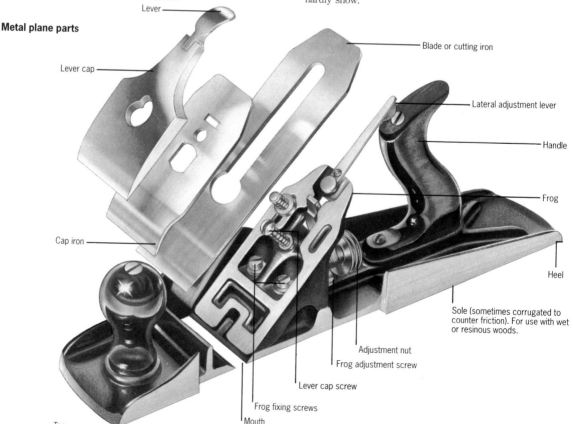

Lever

Lever cap

Blade or cutting iron

Lateral adjustment lever

Handle

Frog

Heel

Sole (sometimes corrugated to counter friction). For use with wet or resinous woods.

Cap iron

Adjustment nut

Frog adjustment screw

Lever cap screw

Frog fixing screws

Mouth

Toe

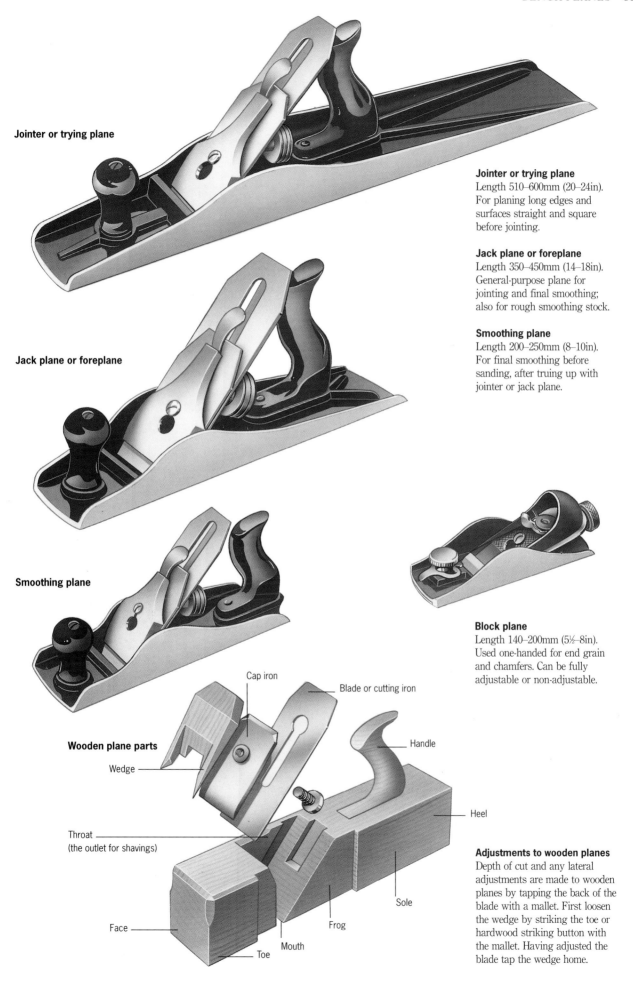

Jointer or trying plane

Jack plane or foreplane

Smoothing plane

Jointer or trying plane
Length 510–600mm (20–24in).
For planing long edges and
surfaces straight and square
before jointing.

Jack plane or foreplane
Length 350–450mm (14–18in).
General-purpose plane for
jointing and final smoothing;
also for rough smoothing stock.

Smoothing plane
Length 200–250mm (8–10in).
For final smoothing before
sanding, after truing up with
jointer or jack plane.

Block plane
Length 140–200mm (5½–8in).
Used one-handed for end grain
and chamfers. Can be fully
adjustable or non-adjustable.

Wooden plane parts

Cap iron

Blade or cutting iron

Handle

Wedge

Heel

Throat
(the outlet for shavings)

Sole

Face

Frog

Toe

Mouth

Adjustments to wooden planes
Depth of cut and any lateral
adjustments are made to wooden
planes by tapping the back of the
blade with a mallet. First loosen
the wedge by striking the toe or
hardwood striking button with
the mallet. Having adjusted the
blade tap the wedge home.

Planing smooths the wood and makes surfaces square for the accurate working out and cutting of joints. Always sharpen and adjust a plane before use. Lay the wood to be planed horizontally on the bench against a bench-stop or between bench-stops. Hold small pieces in the vice.

Keep a piece of candle and use it to lubricate the sole of the plane. Resin from wood will make planing harder so wipe any residue off the plane sole using white spirit.

To square a piece of wood, begin by planing off the high spots; then take shavings from the whole surface. When planing wide surfaces it is easy to remove too much wood from diagonally opposite corners. Therefore check the shape of the board frequently.

When planing an edge avoid the tendency to plane more off at each end by trying to plane more off in the middle to compensate. The shaving removed should, ideally, be the same width as the wood if the edge is to be kept true. The success of all construction depends upon accurate planing initially.

After using a plane, place it on its side on the bench. This will prevent the cutting edge coming into contact with other metal objects and being dulled. Store a plane on its side on a shelf or in its box. Wipe wooden planes with linseed oil occasionally to prevent drying.

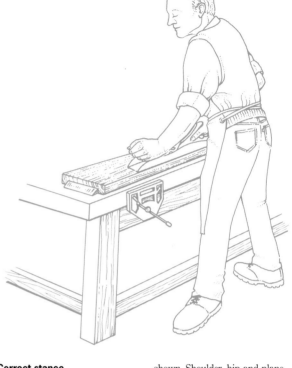

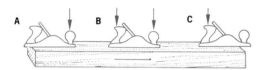

Exerting pressure on the plane
To control the plane and prevent 'dipping' at the start and finish of each stroke begin by **A** pressing firmly down on the front of the plane as it is pushed into the work. **B**. Press evenly in the middle of the stroke and then **C** transfer pressure to the back of the plane to finish.

Correct stance
A correctly-balanced position or stance is important for successful planing. Stand beside the bench and behind the work, legs slightly apart, with one foot facing forward, the other more or less at right angles to it, as shown. Shoulder, hip and plane should be in a straight line for control. To begin with, the weight of the body should be on the back foot and as the plane is pushed forward the weight should shift gradually and rhythmically to the front foot.

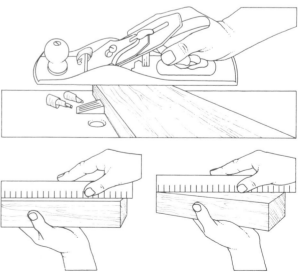

Planing a wide board
Move the plane diagonally across the wood in both directions, with and against the grain, overlapping strokes to cover the whole surface. Finish by taking fine shavings in parallel strokes down the wood in the direction of the grain. Check the smoothness of the surface by hand.

Checking a surface
To check if a surface is flat use the tilted edge of the plane as a straight-edge. Place the straight-edge diagonally to check against winding. Alternatively check a planed surface with a steel rule, along the grain, across the grain at intervals and in both directions diagonally.

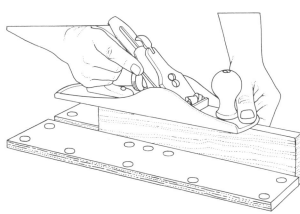

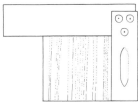

Planing square
If an edge is out of square push the plane towards the high edge. If the blade is sharpened to a slight curve it will take a thicker

shaving in the centre. To check if a face is square with one side push the stock of the try square tight against the side of the wood. Hold it against the light.

Planing a narrow edge
To keep a plane in the centre of a narrow edge place the thumb on the toe and run the fingers as a guide along the side of the wood.

A long plane rides on the high spots, levelling them out until one continuous shaving can be taken along the wood; a short plane follows the contours.

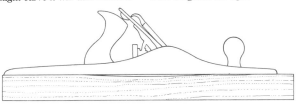

PLANING END GRAIN

Support end grain and the edges of thin boards to stop fibres on the edge breaking away. The stop on a shooting board will provide the necessary support. Hold the plane centrally at its point of balance and allow the wood to overhang slightly. Alternatively, support end grain by gluing or clamping a piece of waste wood to the work-piece before planing, so the waste wood will splinter rather than the work-piece.

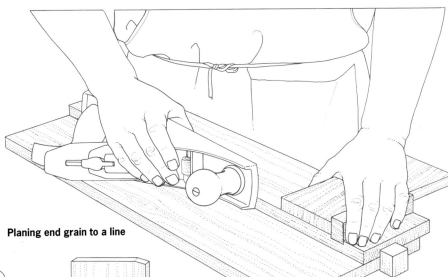

Planing end grain to a line

To plane end grain to a line first plane a chamfer at one end. Reverse the wood and plane towards the chamfer. Take care on the last strokes.

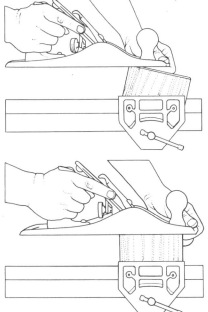

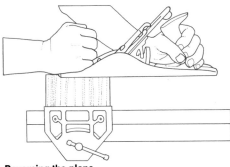

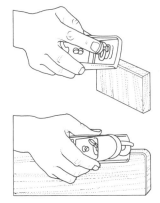

Planing wide boards
Alternatively, plane halfway from each side, especially on wide boards. The plane must be sharp, finely set and firmly under control.

Reversing the plane
Instead of reversing the wood when planing from each side reverse the plane, holding it as shown. Secure the wood firmly against juddering.

Planing chamfers
To put a light chamfer on an edge, use a block plane held at an angle; a larger plane would obscure the work.

Planes for shaping

It was once quite common for a woodworker to have two or three dozen wooden planes for the purpose of shaping or profiling wood, each one with its unique sole and matching blade. This changed with the introduction of steel-bodied planes at the end of the 19th century and the subsequent development of combination tools with their interchangeable cutters.

Planes for shaping fall roughly into two groups: those that have single blades and are used to cut and trim rebates, together with those used to trim and smooth awkward areas that bench planes cannot reach; and those planes which have interchangeable blades of different widths and profiles and are used to cut both rebates and grooves and other shapes, such as beads and mouldings.

Among the first group are the rebate and fillister planes, the shoulder and the bull-nose plane, the compass plane and the hand router. The first three have blades which extend across the full width of the plane's sole, enabling them to cut right into an inside angle, such as is found in a rebated edge. The blades of shoulder and bull-nose planes are set at a low angle, bevel up, so they cut well on end grain. The main feature of these planes, is that they have accurately machined body castings, at right angles to

their sole and correctly-set blade. This means that they can be used on their sides for trimming purposes.

Known also as the circular plane, the compass plane has a flexible, adjustable sole the curvature of which is controlled by a regulating screw and a knurled wheel. It can be used to smooth both concave and convex surfaces. This plane has the same blade assembly as is fitted to the bench smoothing plane. The name router is now more

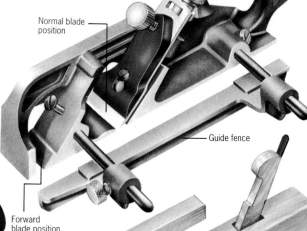

Rebate and fillister plane
Length 250mm (10in). For cutting identical rebates once the fence and depth gauge have been set. The blade has a forward position for corners.

Normal blade position

Guide fence

Forward blade position

Compass plane
Length 250mm (10in). For planing convex or concave surfaces. Metal versions have a flexible adjustable sole; on wooden ones the curve is fixed.

Sole adjustment nut

Sole locking screw

Flexible sole

Hollow

Round

Ovolo

Scratch stock
For making small mouldings and grooves for inlays. Made from a piece of saw or scraper blade ground to shape and secured in a wooden holder.

Moulding plane
Length 225mm (9in). For shaping mouldings and edges. Sole and blade have the same profile. Moulding planes can be used one after the other.

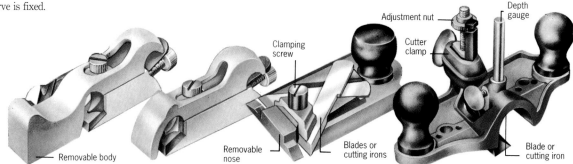

Clamping screw

Adjustment nut

Depth gauge

Cutter clamp

Removable body

Removable nose

Blades or cutting irons

Blade or cutting iron

Shoulder plane
Length 100–200mm (4–8in). For trimming shoulders and rebates. Blade extends right across the sole. This plane can also be used on its side.

Bull-nose plane
Length 75–100mm (3–4in). For working close up into corners and ends of stopped rebates. Blade is positioned at the toe of the sole.

Side rebate plane
Length 125mm (5in). For smoothing and widening side walls of grooves and rebates. Two blades enable the plane to be used in either direction.

Hand router
Width 200mm (8in). For smoothing and cutting grooves and recesses. The cutter is set at a shallow angle to work with a paring action.

commonly applied to a high-speed, portable electric tool (*see* pages 64–5) but the router plane is a much simpler affair used for cleaning up grooves and housings by hand. It may also be used to level areas of background in low-relief carving work. The cranked blade of the original wooden versions gave rise to the common nickname, 'old woman's tooth'.

The second group of shaping planes are the plough, combination and multi-planes. The plough plane is the simplest of this group, consisting of a metal body frame or stock into which is screwed a pair of support arms which carry an adjustable fence. The plough plane's main function is to cut grooves parallel to an edge at precise distances that are regulated by the setting of the fence. The plough plane can also be used to cut rebates. It is available with a range of cutters of different widths.

Combination and multi-planes have an additional body component, the sliding section, which acts as a carrier for a much wider range of cutters. In the case of the multi-plane, in excess of 50 blades are available, enabling this plane to cut a variety of moulded profiles in addition to rebating, grooving and beading.

Plough plane
Length 240mm (9½in). For cutting grooves and rebates, 3–13mm (⅛–½in) wide, with the grain. Up to 10 different blades are available.

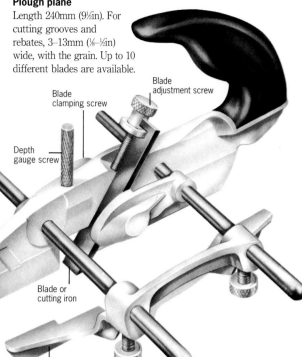

Blade clamping screw
Blade adjustment screw
Depth gauge screw
Blade or cutting iron
Guide fence

Combination plane
Length 250mm (10in). For cutting rebates, grooves and beads 3–13mm (⅛–½in) wide, and tongues 3–6mm (⅛–¼in) wide; has 18 different blades.

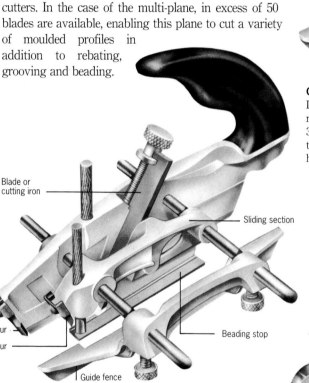

Blade or cutting iron
Sliding section
Spur
Spur
Beading stop
Guide fence

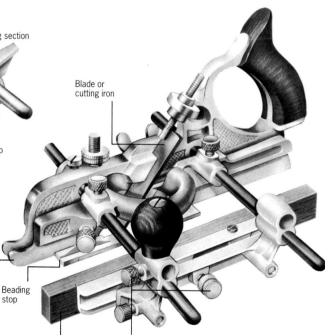

Blade or cutting iron
Sliding section
Beading stop
Guide fence
Fence adjustment screw

Multi-plane
Length 275mm (11in). For cutting mouldings; also strips from a board edge, using its slitting knife. The most versatile plane, with 55 different blades.

Plane cutters

A Sash cutter
B Tonguing cutter
C Rebate and housing cutter
D Reeding cutter
E Beading cutter
F Fluting cutter
G Ovolo cutter
H Slitting knife

To set a plough, combination or multi-plane, first fit the selected blade, adjusting it for depth of cut; then set the guide fence and the depth gauge. Blades are best set to cut thicker shavings than a smoothing plane. The sliding section holds the blade against the body of the plane. A slot at the top of the blade locates on the shoulder of the adjustment screw. Very narrow blades must be set with the adjustment nut. The guide fence can be set on either the left- or right-hand side of the body; when on the right it will cancel out the use of the depth gauge. The beading stop acts as a fence when cutting a bead on a tongued board, because the guide fence has nothing to bear against. Remove the beading stop for most operations. Always hold the plane upright and keep the guide fence tight against the wood to prevent the plane wandering. To make cuts across the grain, lower the spurs to score the grain ahead of the blade, ensuring a clean cut. Keep the spurs sharp with an oilstone. Oil all the adjustment screw threads occasionally. Rub candlewax on the fence and sole to help the plane run smoothly.

If possible always try to work a compass plane with the grain, holding it square to the wood and not at an angle. The blade is set and adjusted like a bench plane's. The blades on shoulder and bull-nose planes are set at a low angle, bevel upwards, enabling them to cut end grain. A scratch stock blade can be filed to any profile; a used hacksaw blade is ideal as the steel is tempered to just the right degree of hardness.

COMBINATION AND MULTI-PLANES

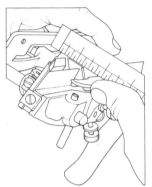

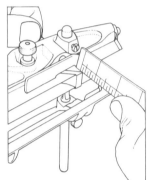

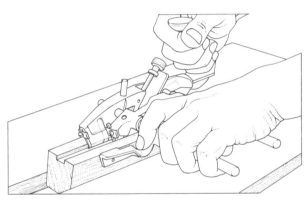

Setting the guide fence
Set the guide fence the required distance from the plane body. Finger-tighten the adjustment screws on the fence rods.

Adjusting the depth gauge
The depth gauge is a horizontal fence fitted to one side of the body. Set it to the required depth for the cut.

Cutting a groove
Start making all cuts at the far end of the work and take a few short cuts, moving a little farther back with each stroke. In this way, the plane will run in a guide groove that it has cut. Then take continuous shavings the full length of the cut until the depth gauge rests on the wood.

Cutting a wide rebate

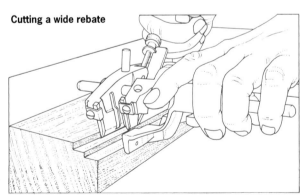

Cut a wide rebate in two stages. Make the first cut on the outside edge to the required depth. Adjust the fence and cut the inside part of the rebate. If the inner part were cut first, the depth gauge would have no support when cutting the outside edge.

Cutting a narrow rebate

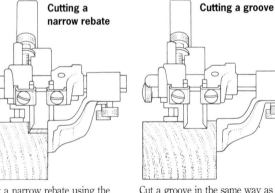

Cut a narrow rebate using the method above. Choose a blade that is very slightly wider than the rebate to cover the rebate fully.

Cutting a groove

Cut a groove in the same way as a rebate, but adjust the fence accordingly. The guide fence can be set either side of the plane body.

Cutting a housing
When cutting a housing the fence cannot be used, because it will be working against end grain, which is not smooth enough for accurate work. Pin or clamp a batten in place of the fence, making allowance for the batten when setting the depth gauge. Lower the spurs. Use the body spur alone for a cross-grain rebate.

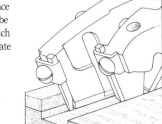

Cutting a tongue
When cutting a tongue the depth gauge is not required as the depth of cut is limited by the blade itself, which has an adjustable stop in the centre. Take extra care to set the guide fence so that the tongue will be cut exactly in the position required. Remove the beading stop from the sliding section on the plane.

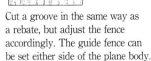

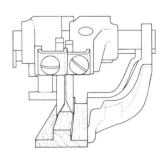

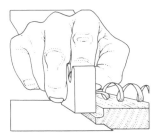

Shoulder plane
Set the blade for a fine cut. Keep the side, which is square with the base, tight against the side or bottom of the rebate.

Hand router
Insert the cutter from beneath.
1. Slacken the locking screw, raise or lower the cutter with the adjustment nut. Tighten the screw. Chisel out most of the waste. Lower the cutter onto the base of the recess. Give the nut another half turn down.
2. Lock the cutter and plane. Continue, lowering the cutter a half turn at a time until the recess is the required depth.

COMPASS PLANE

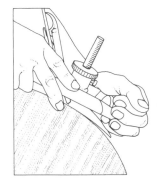

Using a compass plane
This plane is used with the grain, holding the blade square to the work, not at an angle. Set the blade when the sole is flat; then adjust the sole curvature.

Moulding plane
Use a round plane for hollows and a matching hollow plane for rounds and beads. First work a chamfer with a bench plane. Shape with the moulding plane, starting at the front and working back. Smooth with abrasive paper wrapped around a shaped block of wood. The plane has no guide fence so it requires skill to keep it at the correct angle. Hold it so the fingers of one hand act as a guide fence against the side of the work.

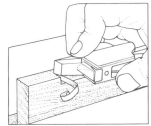

Bull-nose plane
Use a bull-nose plane for rebated corners. It can be an integral tool or, as here, a shoulder plane with the nose removed.

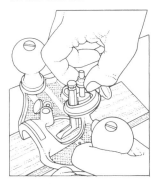

1. Adjust the cutter.

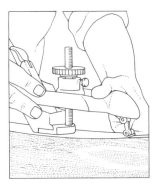

2. Plane a recess.

Planing curves
Hold the plane on the work and turn the adjustment nut until the sole is about the same shape as the work. For convex shapes, the sole should be slightly flatter

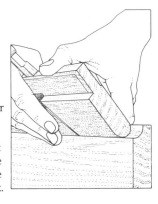

than the work. For concave shapes it should have a sharper curvature. To make a concave curve, mark the two extremities and the central depth. Hold a springy lath against the three

Scratch stock
This plane is home-made to any profile up to about 25mm (1in) wide. Slot the cutter in a thick piece of wood or between two

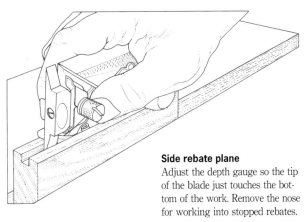

Side rebate plane
Adjust the depth gauge so the tip of the blade just touches the bottom of the work. Remove the nose for working into stopped rebates.

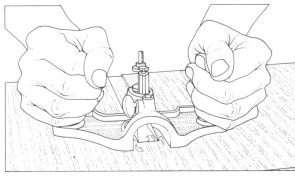

points and get someone else to draw the curve against the lath. Saw down to the line at intervals; remove most of the waste with a chisel, finish shaping to the line with the plane.

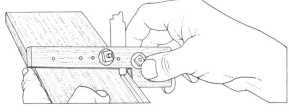

pieces screwed together. File the cutting edge square and hone it like a scraper blade. Use only with a forward scraping action with the tool tilted away.

Sharpening chisels & planes

Dull tools are unsafe and hard to use. Sight down the blade: a dull edge or one with tiny defects in it reflects the light and shows up as a white line.

New chisels, gouges, planes and shaping tools have a bevel of 25° that is ground on the cutting edge by the manufacturer. Before the tool can be used, a bevel of 30° must be honed on the edge. A smaller angle will cut wood more easily but its fragile edge will break readily; a larger angle will hold its edge longer but will create more resistance. The honing bevel of 30° can be maintained over a number of honing sessions. The grinding bevel of 25° must be restored on the tool only after repeating honing, or if the edge has become chipped. After grinding back to 25°, the edge must be honed again to 30°.

All sharpening stones work in the same way: the stone removes the softer metal particles in the tool. Coarse materials cut fast, but leave a coarse edge on the tool. Fine materials cut slowly and leave a fine, sharp edge.

Sharpening stones are used for honing. These may be oilstones, water stones or stones incorporating industrial diamond particles. All are available in different grades or grits, usually given as coarse, medium or fine.

Oilstones may be made from natural stone or be of an artificial composite material. Japanese water stones may also be of a composite material. Diamond stones have their abrasive particles embedded in a steel plate bonded to a polycarbonate substrate.

Sharpening stones should not be used dry – the pores choke with metal particles. A lubricant carries away the particles and prevents the tool becoming too hot through friction, which can draw the temper of the cutting edge, shown by the edge turning blue. If this happens, the metal must be ground back to remove all the softened metal. With oilstones, a good, thin machine oil is suitable. (Vegetable oils can clog the pores.) Paraffin can be used on artificial stones. Always soak a new oilstone in oil

GRINDING/HONING

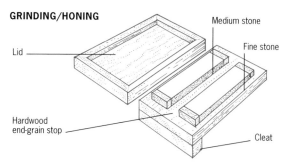

Lid

Medium stone

Fine stone

Hardwood end-grain stop

Cleat

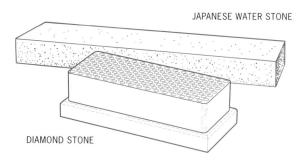

JAPANESE WATER STONE

DIAMOND STONE

Care of sharpening stones
Make a box to keep out dust. With a Forstner bit, drill out two recesses in a solid block. Fit hardwood end-grain stops at each end, level with the top of the stones. Screw a cleat to the bottom to hold the box in the vice. Then make a well-fitting lid from five-ply and 19mm (¾in) battens.

Japanese water and diamond stones
Japanese water stones are soft and easily damaged but cut very quickly and are available in much finer grades than other stones. Diamond stones are tough and durable. They are made in very fine, fine, medium, coarse and very coarse grades. They cut quickly and retain their flat surface longer than natural or other composite stones.

Slipstones

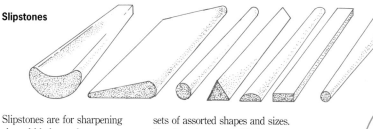

Slipstones are for sharpening shaped blades such as gouges and moulding plane blades. They can be of either natural or artificial stone and are sold in sets of assorted shapes and sizes. If a shape is not suitable, buy a larger size and rub it down on a paving stone using silver sand and water.

Double-ended bench grinder
This has interchangeable grinding wheels, the most common diameters between 126 and 200mm (5 and 8in), and aluminium oxide wheels are better. Revolving at high speed, these wheels should be used with care if tool edges are not to overheat and lose their temper.

Grinder/honing machine
Wet grinding/sharpening wheels are much safer as the large wheel revolves at a much slower speed and is constantly immersed in water which keeps edges cool during sharpening. The machine illustrated incorporates a rubberized honing wheel used to put a fine edge on a blade.

until it is saturated. Keep it in a box. Keep water stones wet with clean water – ideally, submerged when not in use. Diamond stones can be used dry but lubrication is recommended to aid the removal of metal particles.

Many woodworkers use an electric emery wheel for grinding. This has many disadvantages. It is used dry and revolves at around 3000rpm so there is danger of drawing the temper from the blade unless the tool is dipped in water to cool it. It is difficult to produce an even edge on an edge narrower than the plane blade or chisel surface, and it is dangerous as it can chip or shatter. If using one, wear goggles and work extremely carefully. Wet-grinding machines are far more suitable for grinding and honing cabinetmakers' tools. The artificial stone may be a medium 180 grit or a fine 280 grit abrasive. The stone revolves at only 150rpm and is constantly saturated with water, so it is not dangerous and the tool is kept cool. Honing is completed on a fine stone.

To hone a tool at the correct angle, hold it in the hands, place the grinding bevel flat, then raise the hands slightly. Hone on a stone with a forward and backward motion. Push forwards, keeping pressure constant; return using no pressure. Keep the wrists rigid – rocking will round the bevel. After a few strokes, check that the bevel is forming evenly. If not, adjust the pressure. Lubricate the stone and hone until a wire edge, or burr, appears. Wipe the lubricant from the tip and test with the thumb to feel if the wire edge runs across the width of the tool. To remove the wire edge, lay the blade flat and rub once on the stone. Wipe clean, and check. Finish by stropping.

The same procedure is used to sharpen all edge tools. It is vital that grooves are not worn in the stone, or blades will not be sharpened flat. Move blades about in a figure of eight to utilize the whole stone and avoid digging the corners of blades into the stone. Sharpen very narrow blades on the edge of the stone.

Using a honing guide

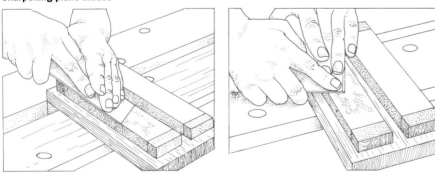

Width adjustment screw

Bed

HONING GUIDE

25°

30°

Honing and grinding bevels

Using a honing guide

Honing guides hold chisel and plane blades at the correct angle. The guide consists of a frame on wheels or rollers. The frame adjusts to take blades of varying widths and has a bevel scale to set it at the angle required. To hone, push the guide backwards and forwards along the oilstone. Woodworkers eventually dispense with guides but they are useful for beginners.

Sharpening plane blades

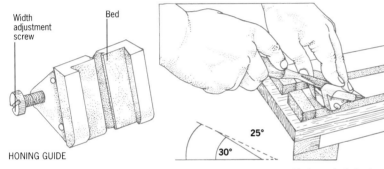

1. Hold the blade at angle.

2. Remove the wire edge.

Sharpening plane blades

1. Hold a wide blade at an angle so its whole edge is in contact with the stone.
2. Remove the wire edge when it appears on the reverse side. Hone jack plane and smoothing plane blades with a slight curvature for fast cutting. Make a few figures of eight to produce the slight curve. Hone jointer plane blades dead square; round the corners slightly to stop edges digging in. Hone rebate, block and combination plane blades dead square.

Replacing plane blades

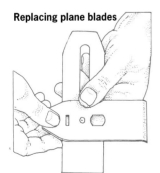

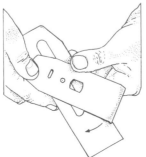

1. Position the cap iron.

2. Align the cap iron with the blade.

3. Lay them on the frog.

Replacing plane blades

1. Hold the cap iron at right angles to the blade. Insert the lever cap screw.
2. Slide the cap iron back along the slot in the blade and turn it in line with the blade. Move it forward to the right distance from the cutting edge. Hold the two together and tighten the screw.
3. Lay them on the frog. On a wooden plane replace the wedge; on a metal plane, replace the lever cap. Adjust the blade projection.

Sharpening edge-cutting tools

Edge tools, or edge-cutting tools, is a general name given to all those tools whose blades are usually maintained on a sharpening stone. It embraces planes, chisels, gouges, spokeshaves and knives of all kinds, including the drawknife, and axes. Woodcarving tools, which include a wide range of special chisels, gouges and knives, (*see* pages 88–9) are edge tools as are woodturning tools used at the lathe. The sharpening of woodturning tools has become both complex and controversial and apart from a brief outline (page 81) is not described here.

There is a distinction in the term 'sharpening' between grinding an edge tool on a revolving wheel and honing on a sharpening stone. In normal use an edge tool can be honed several times before re-grinding becomes necessary. Re-grinding need only take place when a blade's bevel becomes too short or its cutting edge is damaged.

Sharp tools are a prerequisite in producing good work safely – more cut hands result from forcing a blunt chisel to cut than from guiding a sharp one.

Sharpening chisels

1. Hone the chisel.

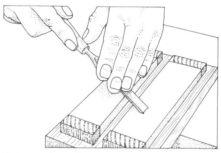

2. Remove the wire edge.

Sharpening chisels

To hone a chisel, hold it bevel down at 30° to the stone.
1. Hold the end of the handle, with the fingers of the other hand applying pressure towards the cutting edge. Chisel blades must be absolutely square across. An off-square blade will not make a true cut and is dangerous as it tends to slip sideways.
2. Turn the chisel over to remove the wire edge on the fine stone. Keep the blade flat. If not, a secondary bevel will form on the flat back of the blade and when paring vertically the cut, instead of going straight down, will follow the line of the bevel. To finish the edge, strop the chisel on a leather strop treated with a fine abrasive powder.

Sharpening gouges

Honing an in-cannel gouge

Honing an out-cannel gouge

Sharpening gouges

To hone an in-cannel gouge, first hone the inside bevel with a slipstone. Use one that matches the curve of the blade or is less curved. Hone an out-cannel gouge on a sharpening stone. Roll the blade throughout its width along the stone. Remove the wire edge from both gouges on the sharpening stone and finish on a leather strop.

Sharpening spokeshaves

1. Hold the blade by the tangs.

2. Rub the blade lengthways.

Hone on the stone.

Sharpening spokeshaves

Remove the blade from a wooden spokeshave by tapping the two tangs with a hammer. Grip the stone on its edge in a bench vice.
1. Put the blade bevel down, and hold it by the tangs. Hone it like a chisel or plane blade.
2. Remove the wire edge by rubbing the blade lengthways. Metal spokeshave blades are similar to plane blades, but being shorter are difficult to hold. Make a wooden holder with a kerf at one end to take the blade. Sharpen it in the same way as a plane blade.

Sharpening drawknives

1. Hold the tool bevel up.

2. Remove the wire edge with the stone.

Sharpening drawknives

The drawknife has such a large blade that it is more convenient to bring the stone to the blade.
1. Brace one handle against a bench-stop, holding the tool bevel up. Take a firm grip on the stone and rub it the full length of the blade, holding the stone flat against the bevel.
2. Remove the wire edge on the reverse side by turning the drawknife over, putting the stone against the flat of the blade and rubbing back and forth.

Power hand planes

Planing is a basic operation. Planing a lot of material by hand can be both time- and energy-consuming. The power plane – a compromise between the hand plane and a planing machine – can solve both problems. Power planes are at their best when planing wood which is less than the width of the plane. All power planes leave a rippled surface and work should be finished by hand.

The cutting action of the power plane is by means of a high-speed, rotating cutter block with two, occasionally three, blades which extend across the width of the plane's sole. A common cutting width is 82mm (3¼in). Blades are usually tungsten carbide, either tipped (TCT) or of solid material (TC). Most are double-sided and disposable.

The capacity of the electric motor is important. A high-rated motor will allow the tool to remove more wood with each pass than one of low rating. Motor speed is also a factor. Industrial-rated planes have motors of 800–850 watts; for lighter work, around 500 watts is common. Speed may be given as motor speed in revolutions per minute (rpm) which means that a two-blade cutter block produces double this number of cuts per minute (cpm).

Depth of cut is adjusted by lowering or raising the front part of the plane's sole by turning the depth adjustment knob, which doubles as a front handle. This is normally closely calibrated and regulates the cutting depth. The depth must not be excessive as it can overload the motor, slowing it down and resulting in damage. Some models of power plane incorporate an electronic constant power function which guards against this problem.

Most power planes may also be used for rebating. An adjustable side fence facilitates the use of this secondary option. The side fence is also useful in obtaining a right angle when edging material.

All power planes have extraction provision for the removal and containment of debris. This may be in the form of a dust bag, which is too quickly filled; connecting a vacuum hose to the tool solves this problem.

Always place a power plane on the work before switching on and remember to let the cutting block stop revolving before placing it down on the bench. Use the plane carefully on boards wider than the plane's width to minimize the grooving effect of the blades.

POWER PLANE

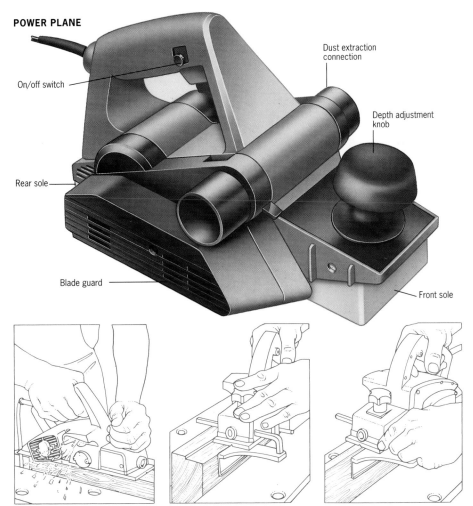

On/off switch

Dust extraction connection

Depth adjustment knob

Rear sole

Blade guard

Front sole

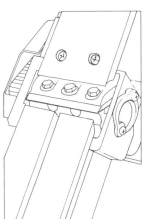

The underside
The revolving blades between the soles provide the cutting action. The groove in the front sole acts as a guide when chamfering.

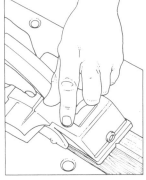

Planing a surface
To plane a surface place the tool on the work, switch it on and apply a steady, even pressure. Do not push hard through the work.

Planing a rebate
To plane a rebate adjust the fence so it limits the sole to the rebate width. Make a series of shallow cuts to the required depth.

Planing a narrow surface
For a narrow surface adjust the fence so the cutting area is in the middle of the sole, making it easier to balance the plane.

Planing a chamfer
To plane a chamfer place the groove on the front sole on to the edge of the work. Plane in several passes to the required depth.

Power routers

The power router performs a number of woodworking functions quickly and efficiently and has largely superseded such hand tools as the hand router, plough and rebate planes and moulding planes. It cuts grooves, housings, rebates and mouldings. It can also help in making tongue and groove, mortise and tenons and dovetails.

The power router is a powerful, high-speed electric motor inverted in a housing fitted with a pair of handles, which, on the majority, rise and fall on two columns attached to a rigid baseplate. A collet chuck fitted onto the motor spindle accepts a range of cutters or bits. Pressure from the user's hands causes the cutter to be 'plunged' into the wood. Return springs in the plunge mechanism retract the cutter when pressure is released.

Router cutters revolve clockwise, so the tool has a tendency to twist in that same direction. Always keep a firm grasp and feed the router into the wood against the rotation of the cutter, ie, from right to left. Router spindle speeds in excess of 20,000rpm are common but some models have variable speed control; this is particularly useful when using large cutters or when working difficult hard wood.

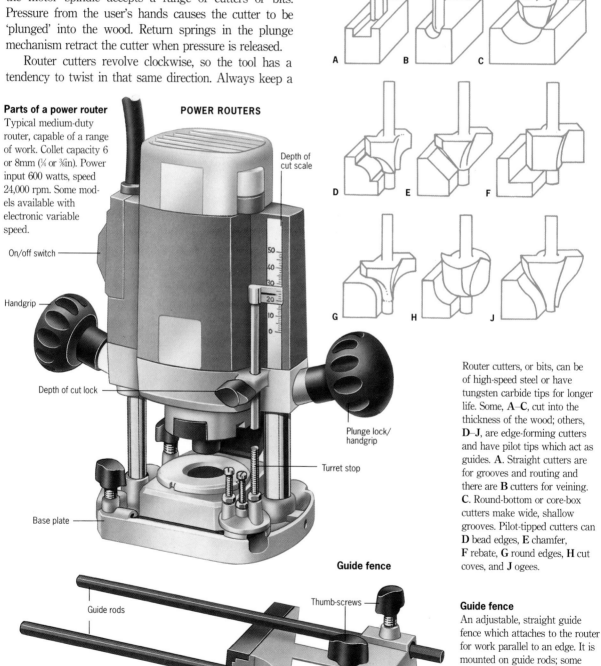

Router cutters

A B C

D E F

G H J

Parts of a power router
Typical medium-duty router, capable of a range of work. Collet capacity 6 or 8mm (¼ or ⅜in). Power input 600 watts, speed 24,000 rpm. Some models available with electronic variable speed.

POWER ROUTERS

Depth of cut scale

On/off switch

Handgrip

Depth of cut lock

Plunge lock/ handgrip

Turret stop

Base plate

Router cutters, or bits, can be of high-speed steel or have tungsten carbide tips for longer life. Some, **A–C**, cut into the thickness of the wood; others, **D–J**, are edge-forming cutters and have pilot tips which act as guides. **A**. Straight cutters are for grooves and routing and there are **B** cutters for veining. **C**. Round-bottom or core-box cutters make wide, shallow grooves. Pilot-tipped cutters can **D** bead edges, **E** chamfer, **F** rebate, **G** round edges, **H** cut coves, and **J** ogees.

Guide fence

Guide rods

Thumb-screws

Guide fence
An adjustable, straight guide fence which attaches to the router for work parallel to an edge. It is mounted on guide rods; some have a micro-adjustment for precise setting.

Fitting cutters
Work the lock nut with a spanner.
Lock the spindle with a spanner
if there is no spindle lock button.

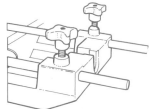

Fitting a guide fence
Fit the guide rods into slots in the
router base and set the fence to
the required position. Secure the
guide fence with the wing nuts.

ROUTER SAFETY

- Always remove the plug from the electric socket before changing
  or adjusting router cutters.
- Check that cutters are properly secure in the collet. Minimum
  12mm (½in) of cutter shank should be held in the collet.
- Wear eye protection and a dust mask, and connect to a suitable
  dust-extraction system.
- Always use both hands to operate a router.
- Ensure that the work-piece is securely held on the bench and that
  there are no obstructions.
- Rest the plunge router baseplate on the work and switch on before
  touching the cutter to the wood. Withdraw the cutter before
  switching off.
- Do not try too deep a cut and do not force the cutter into the wood.

USING ROUTERS

Freehand routing
This requires control. It is used in
removing background material in
signwriting and relief carving.

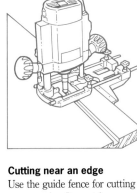

Cutting near an edge
Use the guide fence for cutting
near an edge. It must be pressed
against the edge of the work-piece.

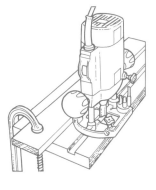

Cutting away from an edge
When cutting away from an edge
secure a straight batten to the right
of the cut to be made as a fence.

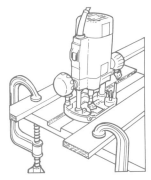

Cutting a wide housing
To cut a wide housing use two
parallel battens. Align the cutter
with right-hand batten first; then
make the second cut against the
left-hand batten.

**Using
a guide
fence**

Use a guide fence when routing
dovetails, mortise and tenons and

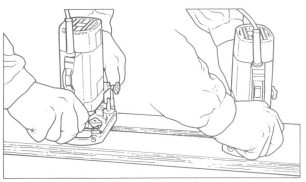
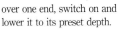

stopped grooves and housings.
For the last two place the router

over one end, switch on and
lower it to its preset depth.

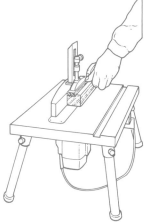

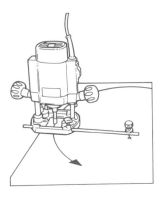

Cutting circles
Cut circles using a trammel – a
bar or arm with a central pivot.

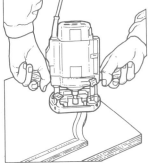

Using templates
Use templates for consistent
identical parts. Fit a guide bush.

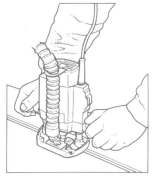

Dust extraction
Most power routers have
provision for dust extraction.

Using a router table
The router may be effectively used
mounted in the inverted position
under a router table. The cutter
protrudes through the table's
surface and work is pushed past
it against a guide fence. In this
situation the router's function is
similar to that of a spindle
moulder and it can be used to
make moulding and beading as
well as rebating and grooving.

Abrasive tools

Abrasive tools should be used only in circumstances where cutting tools are inappropriate, either because of difficulty of access, such as when shaping or smoothing small interior shapes, when a cutting tool consistently tears the surface of work with a difficult grain, or where grain changes direction, such as at the bottom of a deep concave curve. Many woodworkers feel that wood should be cut and not just worn away by the rapid abrasion of its fibres. All abrasive tools leave a rough surface that will require further smoothing if a good surface finish is to be achieved.

Rasps and files were the first abrasive tools used, the cabinetmakers' rasp being the most common. These are usually 'half-round', having one side flat and the other curved and they can be used equally well on flat, concave or convex surfaces. They are used for initial roughing out, before the file. Wood rasps and files are classified by their 'cut' – how the cutting teeth are arranged – and by their degree of coarseness. A file may be single or double cut; rasps are rasp cut. Degrees of coarseness for both rasps and files go from smooth, through medium and second cut, to bastard.

The now familiar Surform tool has a spring steel blade perforated with numerous sharp-edged holes which, as they are raised above the blade surface, provide an efficient, chisel-like cutting action. There is a variety of shapes and sizes; flat, half-round and tubular, all held under tension in appropriate holders. An advantage in their use is that the perforations in these blades allow the debris and shavings to escape without clogging the tool.

The introduction of new abrasive materials and their application to tool technology has resulted in a variety of more recent innovations. One of these involves tungsten carbide particles heat-fused to both rigid and flexible metal backing which can be used to make various shapes of abrasive tools.

File parts

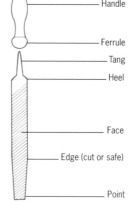

- Handle
- Ferrule
- Tang
- Heel
- Face
- Edge (cut or safe)
- Point

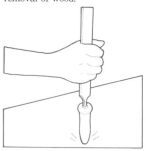

A   B   C

File teeth
B. Single cut file teeth are for precision work. **C**. Double cut and **A** rasp teeth are for fast removal of wood.

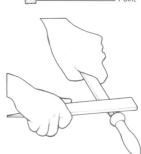

Removing a file handle
To remove a file handle strike the ferrule of the handle sharply with the 'safe' (uncut) edge of another file.

Fitting a file handle
To fix a handle on a file place the tang in the handle. Hold both vertically and strike the handle on the bench.

TYPES OF ABRASIVE TOOL

Surform plane
Length 250mm (10in).
Use as a rough plane for fast preliminary shaping of the work.

Surform round file
Length 225mm (9in).
For fast removal of wood. Can be used with or without its front handle.

Surform flat file
Length 250mm (10in).
Similar to a Surform plane but more flexible. May break fibres if worked across the grain.

File, rasp and Surform

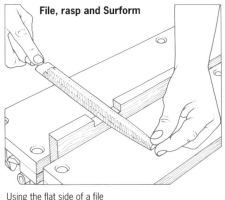

Using the flat side of a file

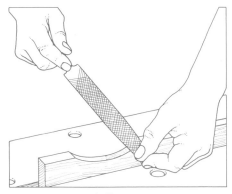

Using the round side of a file

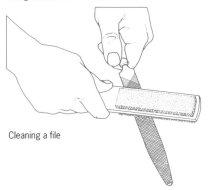

Cleaning a file

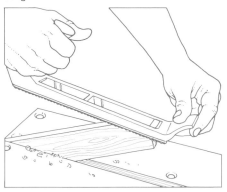

Using a Surform

File, rasp and Surform

All of these tools cut on the forward stroke only; lift the tool on the return stroke. The cabinet-makers' half-round file is the most common wood file. The flat side is handy for levelling out recesses after chiselling. Hold it diagonally across the recess and take care that the file's thin edges do not damage the sides of the recess. The flat side can be worked on convex curves. Level out concave curves with the round side of the file. Keep the file teeth clean and free of clogged-up dust by cleaning the file with a file card. Stroke the wires of the card down the file parallel to the teeth. Rasps and rasp planes, such as Surforms, rapidly remove large amounts of wood and are ideal tools for preliminary shaping before filing or planing.

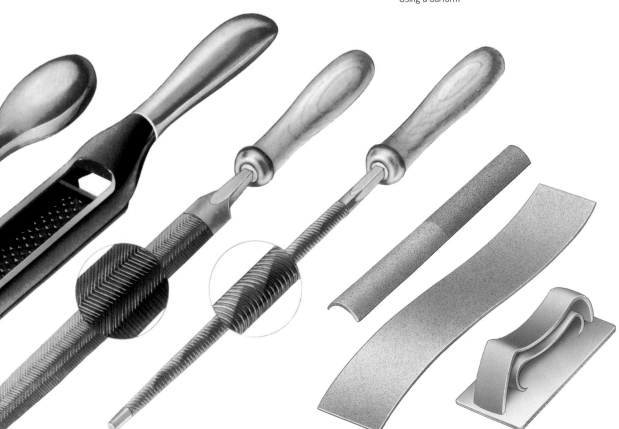

**Cabinetmakers'
half-round rasp**
Length 100–350mm (4–14in).
Combines features of both
round and flat files. Tempered
for working only on wood.

Round file
Length 100–350mm (4–14in).
Obtainable in various degrees of
coarseness. For enlarging holes.

Permagrit
Rigid and flexible tools, in
different sizes and shapes,
incorporating tungsten carbide
particles in varying degrees of
coarseness.

Shaping & smoothing tools

To work successfully with shaping and smoothing tools requires both skill and careful attention to the direction of the grain. To avoid the grain being damaged when using these tools, all of which are worked with a pushing or pulling action, it is extremely important that the work is held very securely in the vice or with clamps, or is butted against a bench-stop.

A drawknife will remove surplus wood much more quickly than a plane, but it requires both experience and an understanding of wood grain to produce good quality work. Its blade is bevelled like that of a chisel and it may be used either bevel up or bevel down. It is used with a pulling action.

Spokeshaves are normally used with a pushing action to shape and smooth narrow curved sections of wood and to make chamfered edges. The metal spokeshave cuts in a similar way to the smoothing plane; its blade is sharpened in the same way but it is adjusted by means of two threaded nuts. Two types are available: one with a flat sole for convex work, one with a curved sole for concave work. Some prefer to use the old type of wooden spokeshave; its blade is totally different and it is adjusted by tapping the blade's two tangs through the wooden stock. When using either spokeshave, hold it with both hands, thumbs on the back edge of the tool to control the cutting angle. To avoid tool judder and a rippled surface have the blade at a slight angle across the wood to make a slicing or shearing cut. Always cut with the grain – which means 'downhill' on curves.

The cabinet scraper is a flat blade of flexible saw steel with its edges turned to form a sharp hook. This hook, when it is correctly sharpened and used, enables it to give a very smooth finish to wood. Unlike an abrasive, it should produce shavings, not dust, which can clog the grain. It can also deal with awkward areas of wood such as knots, burrs and wild grain, both on solid wood and veneers, but be careful not to leave a small hollowed area as it will be evident when polished. Scrape over a wide area so that the hollow cannot be felt by the flat of the hand. Check by holding the work to the light.

The cabinet scraper must be held at the correct angle; otherwise it will not cut effectively. The area of the cut is controlled by the pressure of the thumbs, which bow out the blade, varying the curve and localizing the cut. Work in the direction of the wood grain or diagonally across it. This tool can also remove old surface finishes, without the aid of solvent. When scraping away a finish, angle the cabinet scraper so that the hook bites between the surface finish and the wood, and work the tool at an angle along the grain. The cabinet scraper is not the easiest tool to sharpen correctly (*see* opposite below). The blade edge must be made perfectly flat and square before the hook is formed. This is done with a burnishing tool – a piece of hard steel rod – and firm pressure.

A scraper plane is much easier to operate than the cabinet scraper alone, although it is not possible to achieve such a fine degree of control. It is, however, less hard on the fingers and thumbs.

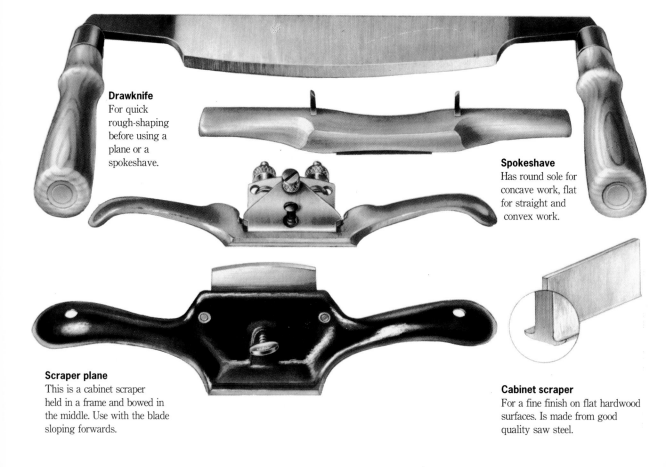

Drawknife
For quick rough-shaping before using a plane or a spokeshave.

Spokeshave
Has round sole for concave work, flat for straight and convex work.

Scraper plane
This is a cabinet scraper held in a frame and bowed in the middle. Use with the blade sloping forwards.

Cabinet scraper
For a fine finish on flat hardwood surfaces. Is made from good quality saw steel.

Using a spokeshave

Shaving concave work

Shaving convex work

Using a wooden spokeshave

Using a drawknife

Shaping convex work

Shaping concave work

Cutting a concave curve

Using a cabinet scraper

Working with a pushing action

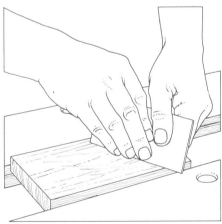

Working with a pulling action

Sharpening cabinet scrapers

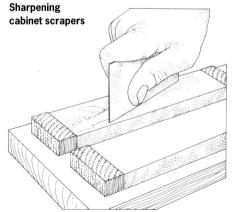

1. Hold the scraper upright across the oilstone.

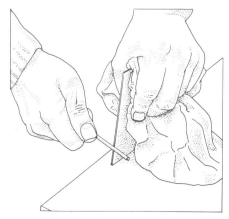

2. Form the hook.

Using a spokeshave

Use a spokeshave to smooth narrow curved pieces. All spokeshaves, whether with a round sole for concave work, a flat sole for convex work or with a wooden frame, are operated in the same way. Use with a pushing action and keep the wrists very flexible. The angle will need to be changed often. Control the angle of the tool with the thumbs pressing on the handles. Work from short to long grain, stroking the grain down.

Using a drawknife

Use with a pulling action. The depth of cut depends on the angle at which the bevelled blade is presented to the work, and all control comes from the wrists. Greater control can be exerted with the bevel down but for straight and convex cuts wood can be removed more quickly with the bevel up. Watch the grain direction and keep the blade sharp.

Using a cabinet scraper

Usually used with a pushing action, the cabinet scraper may also be pulled. Grasp the scraper in both hands and bow the centre slightly outward by pressing with the thumbs. Push and tilt it away until the hook just bites into the wood at about 70°. If dust, and not shavings, is removed the scraper needs sharpening.

Sharpening cabinet scrapers

Carefully file and then hone the edges on a stone. Rub back and forth using firm pressure. Lay the scraper flat on the oilstone and remove the burr or wire edge by rubbing both sides.
1. Lay the scraper flat on the bench and rub the edges to consolidate the metal.
2. Then form the hook with a burnisher (or use the back of a gouge). Hold the burnisher at an angle of about 5° to the blade, gradually increasing to 10°. Using firm pressure, three or four strokes should be sufficient.

Abrasives

After shaping with cutting tools, wood will normally require smoothing or sanding before it is ready for the final finish; abrasives form part of the finishing process, not the shaping process. Good woodworkers aim to reach a high standard of surface finish with cutting tools and to give a light sanding with a fine-grade abrasive.

Abrasives are backed with paper, cloth or metal and graded according to the coarseness of the grit (abrasive particles). The terms coarse, medium and fine are still used but a system related to grit size is more accurate. Coarseness increases as the number decreases.

Power sanders save work when smoothing. Switch on before lowering them on to the wood. A belt sander is heavy and will smooth rough stock quickly. An orbital sander is much lighter and can produce a very fine finish. A drum sander can be used for smoothing hollows and contoured wood. Hand sand after machine sanding.

Five abrasives are used: ground glass, crushed garnet, tungsten carbide, aluminium oxide and silicon carbide. The first two usually have paper backing, the last two may have either paper or cloth. Tungsten carbide is usually bonded to a thin metal. Grit spacing is specified: close coverage (regular or close-coat) cuts quickly but is easily clogged with dust. Widely spaced grit (open-coat) is slower-cutting but does not clog with dust so readily.

Surfaces should be sanded along the grain. Sanding across the grain will leave visible scratches. All abrasives produce scratches; always progress from coarse, through medium to fine until the scratches can no longer be felt.

Economize on paper
For economy and a fit around the block, tear a standard-sized sheet in two against the workbench.

Cleaning abrasive papers
Clear the dust on open-coat papers with a file card; rinse wet-and-dry papers under running water.

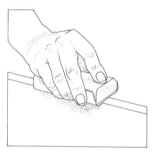

Keeping edges sharp
To maintain the sharpness on an edge hold the paper tightly around the block.

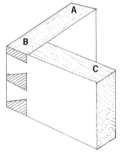

Smoothing corners
Work the abrasive between points A and B. Then work between C and B, avoiding surface AB.

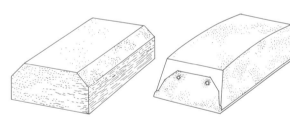

Using cork blocks
When smoothing with an abrasive use a block to produce an even surface. A cork block is firm and resilient. A metal-backed tungsten carbide abrasive lasts much longer than a conventional abrasive but is harsher.

Smoothing concave curves
To work an abrasive against a concave curve use the chamfered edge of the block.

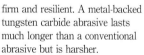

Smoothing mouldings
Smooth a moulding with a shaped sanding block with abrasive paper held tightly around it.

Type of abrasive	Glasspaper	Garnet paper	Aluminium oxide	Silicon carbide
Type of grit	powdered glass	crushed garnet	bauxite	coal and quartz
Abrasive quality	fairly soft	medium	hard	extremely hard
Suitable materials	hard- and soft-woods	hard- and softwoods	hardwoods	hardwoods, particle boards
Uses	paintwork; bare wood finishing	by hand and with machine sander	general smoothing; bare wood finishing	wet on paintwork; dry on bare wood
General comment	cuts slowly	obtainable in very fine grit size	its hard grains take fast machine smoothing	also known as carborundum paper and wet-and-dry paper

Grit size	Glass-paper	Garnet paper	Aluminium oxide	Silicon carbide
320	—	9/0 320	320	320
280	—	8/0 280	280	280
240	00 (Flour)	7/0 240	240	240
220	—	6/0 220	220	220
200	0	— —		— —
180	—	5/0 180	180	180
150	1	4/0 150	150	150
120	1½	3/0 120	120	120
100	F2	2/0 100	100	100
80	—	0 80	80	80
70	M2	— —	—	—
60	—	½ —	60	60
50	—	1 50	50	50
40	S2	1½ 40	40	40
36	2½	2 36	—	—

BELT SANDER

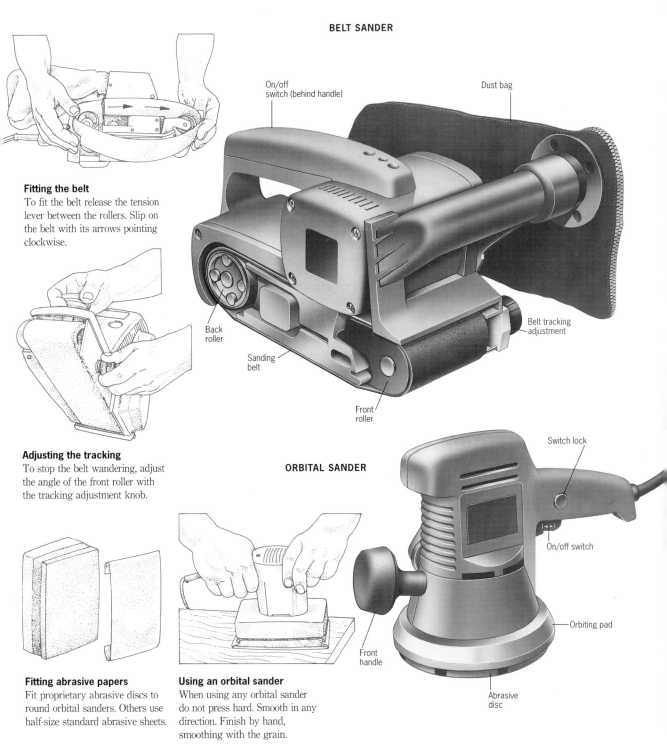

On/off switch (behind handle)

Dust bag

Belt tracking adjustment

Back roller

Sanding belt

Front roller

Fitting the belt
To fit the belt release the tension lever between the rollers. Slip on the belt with its arrows pointing clockwise.

Adjusting the tracking
To stop the belt wandering, adjust the angle of the front roller with the tracking adjustment knob.

Fitting abrasive papers
Fit proprietary abrasive discs to round orbital sanders. Others use half-size standard abrasive sheets.

ORBITAL SANDER

Switch lock

On/off switch

Orbiting pad

Front handle

Abrasive disc

Using an orbital sander
When using any orbital sander do not press hard. Smooth in any direction. Finish by hand, smoothing with the grain.

DRUM SANDER

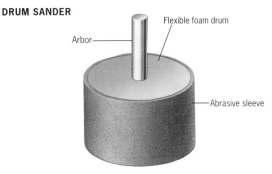

Arbor

Flexible foam drum

Abrasive sleeve

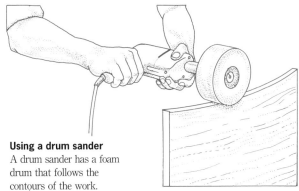

Using a drum sander
A drum sander has a foam drum that follows the contours of the work.

Drills & braces

Bits for use in braces have shanks with square taper tangs to fit the brace's two-jaw chuck. For hand drills and power drills, drill bits must have straight, round shanks to fit the standard three-jaw, self-centring chuck.

An auger bit is used in a brace. A threaded feed-screw at its tip centres the bit and pulls it into the wood. Two spurs scribe the diameter of the cut and give precise centring so that the bit remains accurate in grain of any direction. After the spurs, the cutters bite into the wood, lifting the wood chips and feeding them up the throat to the twist, which conveys them up and out of the hole.

A woodworkers' twist drill has a throat designed to clear away the wood chips on both hard- and softwood when boring at high speed. An engineers' twist drill is the drill that is in common use even though its twist is designed to clear the swarf produced when drilling metal. It is unable to clear wood chips efficiently at high speeds and is unsuitable for unseasoned softwoods.

A Forstner bit has a central point to lead the bit into the wood. The cutting is done by its circular rim and two cutters; the bit is unaffected by knots and grain direction.

The steel brace, with interchangeable bits, replaced the earlier wooden braces – which had fixed bits – some time in the mid-19th century. Many now have a ratchet chuck allowing use in confined spaces where complete rotation is restricted. The hand drill, or wheel brace, has bevelled gears driven by a cranked handle. While the brace is efficient, and still in use, especially for boring large-diameter holes in wood, and the hand drill is useful in some circumstances, most drilling is now done with one of the vast range of electric hand drills available. Single, double and multi-speed versions are obtainable, together with a wide choice of motor ratings and chuck capacities.

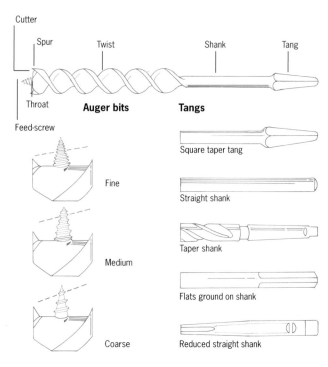

Auger bits

Tangs

Auger bits
The pitch of the feed-screw thread determines the cut made by an auger bit. Use coarse and medium threads for general work; fine for a smooth finish.

Tangs
The square taper tang fits only the brace jaw; the straight round shank fits all three-jaw, self-centring chucks. Other shank shapes are for specialized work.

Bradawl
Tip width 2–3mm (3⁄32–1⁄8in). For boring small holes and starting bits, drills, nails and screws.

Brace
Sweep 150–350mm (6–14in). Sized by the radius described by the handle. For large, deep-hole boring. Can be worked in confined spaces.

Power drill
Chuck capacity 6–16mm (1⁄4–5⁄8in). For general-purpose boring. Graded by chuck capacity, which indicates the maximum size hole the drill can make in steel; this figure can be more than doubled when drilling wood. Various speed models are available and some are fitted with keyless chucks.

Chuck key for power drill

Hand drill
Chuck capacity up to 6mm (¼in).
Accurate and convenient for
general boring.

A. Twist drill
Diameter 0.38–38mm (⅛₄–1½in) for
general drilling of wood, metal
and plastic in hand and power
drills.

B. Woodworkers' twist drill
Diameter 6–25mm (¼–1in). For
general drilling of hard- and
soft-woods in a brace.

C. Solid-centre auger bit
Diameter 5–38mm (³⁄₁₆–1½in). A
strong, fast-cutting bit for
general use.

D. Jennings-pattern auger bit
Diameter 5–38mm (³⁄₁₆–1½in). More
accurate than the solid-centre
auger bit; better for fine work
because it leaves a smooth finish.

E. Scotch auger bit
Diameter 5–38mm (³⁄₁₆–1½in). For
boring hardwoods; also end grain.

F. Centre bit
Diameter 5–56mm (³⁄₁₆–2¼in).
Fast-cutting bit for shallow,
large-diameter holes.

G. Forstner bit
Diameter 6–50mm (¼–2in). Saw
tooth version. For accurate,
flat-bottomed holes and thin
wood and three-ply.

H. Flat bit
Diameter 19–38mm (¾–1½in). For
general large-hole boring. The
lead point enables angled holes
to be started easily.

I. Expansive bit
Diameter 13–150mm (½–6in). For
fast cutting of large-diameter,
shallow holes in softwood. Has
adaptable interchangeable cutters.

J. Countersink bit
Diameter 6–25mm (¼–1in). Used
for widening the mouth of a
countersunk screw-hole, allowing
the screw-head to be set flush
with or below the surface.

K. Combination drill bit
Sized to suit common screw sizes .
For drilling, counter-sinking and
counterboring to the required
depth all in one.

L. Screwdriver bit
Blade width 6–16mm (¼–⅝in).
Used in a brace for inserting or
extracting screws.

M. Hole saw
Diameter 16–100mm (⅝–4in). For
boring large-diameter holes. A
central pilot bit is surrounded by
interchangeable saw blades.

N. Plug cutter
Diameter 10–16mm (⅜–⅝in). For
cutting wood for dowel plugs and
pellets to conceal screw-holes and
nail-heads.

O. Drill and countersink bit
Sized to suit common screw
sizes. Bores a screw-hole and
countersinks.

BRACES

Drilling vertically
When drilling by hand keep the hand brace or drill in the correct position throughout the entire operation. For vertical drilling use a try square to check if the brace or drill, is leaning backward or forward – leaning to one side or the other is easier to see and correct.

Drilling horizontally
When drilling horizontally, position is equally important. Use may be made of a spirit level to check the angle or an assistant can be used to 'sight' the drilling position at intervals. When drilling, particularly with the brace, keep the weight of the body behind the tool to assist the penetration of the bit or drill.

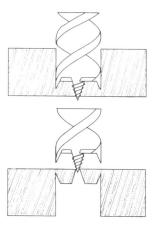

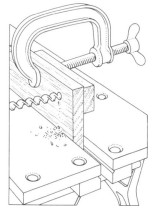

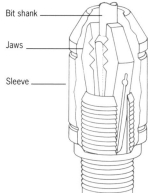

Bit shank

Jaws

Sleeve

Preventing splintering
A through hole bored with an auger bit will splinter. As soon as the feed-screw tip emerges, turn the work around and bore from the other side. Another way to prevent splintering is to clamp a piece of waste wood to the back of the work to support the fibres as the bit emerges.

Fitting a bit
To fit a bit, lock the ratchet. Holding the sleeve, swing the frame clockwise until the shank enters the jaws. Then tighten the jaws anti-clockwise. The corners of the bit shank must fit into the V-grooves in the jaws. Brace jaws can be replaced if they slacken after considerable use.

POWER DRILL

Using a drill stand
A drill stand used with a hand power drill is a useful substitute for a bench or pillar drill. In use, it ensures vertical drilling. The drill stand base should be supplemented by a wooden base bolted directly to the bench or, with a batten fixed to the base board, gripped tightly in a vice.

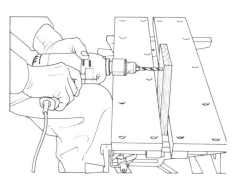

Using a power drill
Position the bit and start it while applying light pressure. Remove from the wood, then turn off.

Fitting a drill
To open the jaws turn the chuck key anti-clockwise. To secure the drill turn the key clockwise, tightening the holes in rotation.

HAND DRILL

Drilling vertically
When drilling vertically push down on the handle; apply extra force if necessary by leaning the head against the uppermost hand.

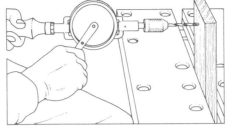

Drilling horizontally
When drilling horizontally extra pressure can be brought to bear by pushing the body weight against the hand that is holding the drill.

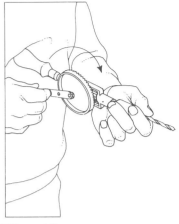

Fitting a drill
To fit a drill, hold the sleeve and turn the handle anti-clockwise. Insert the bit and turn the handle clockwise to tighten the chuck.

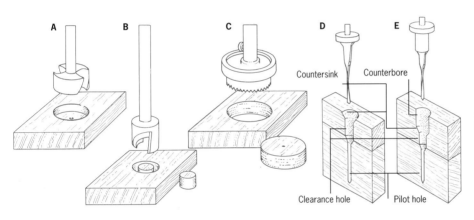

Countersink   Counterbore

Clearance hole   Pilot hole

Special bits
A. Use a Forstner bit to cut clean, flat-bottomed holes. This bit is best used in a drill stand with a depth stop, and it is ideal for removing the bulk of waste from a recess. B. A plug cutter bores to a fixed depth. After boring, break the pellet at the root with a small screwdriver. Glue and insert the pellet into the hole in line with the grain; then plane it flush. Plug cutters match standard bit sizes. C. To bore with a hole saw, secure the required size of blade to the pilot bit. The hole saw removes the waste as a complete disk. Screws require a pilot hole to take the threaded portion, a clearance hole for the threadless portion, and a countersink if the head is to be flush with the surface. D. The drill and countersink bit does all this in one. E. A combination drill bit is shaped to form a counterbore as well.

Depth stops
To drill to a fixed depth without a drill stand, fit a depth stop to the bit. This can be A a metal clamp, which locates in the flutes of an auger bit, or B a screw-on sleeve for a twist drill. C Simplest is a dowel, with a hole bored through the centre.

SHARPENING BITS

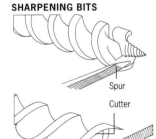

Spur

Cutter

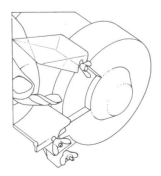

Sharpening auger bits
Sharpen the spurs from the inside not lower than the cutters, using a smooth file. Sharpen cutters on the edge facing the shank.

Sharpening twist drills
Place the cutting edge of a twist drill against the wheel; rotate the cutting edge, lifting at the same time. Repeat for the other edge. A jig will hold a twist drill at the correct angle for sharpening. Push the jig over a sheet of 180 grit abrasive paper to sharpen the drill. Twist-drill sharpeners powered by the drill itself are made to fit some drills. On some, the chuck is removed (as above); others fit into the chuck.

Hammers, mallets & screwdrivers

The first hammer was a stone held in the hand; the first mallet, a cudgel. The Romans used a hammer with a claw pein for pulling nails, while medieval pictures show a hammer with a square head that is similar in appearance to current European hammers.

Hammers are sized by the weight of their head. A hammer should be well balanced with a forged head; cast heads tend to shatter. The claw of a claw hammer should be carefully ground, tapering to a fine 'V' so it can pull nails of all sizes. Hammer handles are traditionally made from ash or hickory – which are tough, long-grained woods. Mallets should be of seasoned hardwood, such as beech. The end of the wooden shaft is impregnated with oil to prevent moisture loss and splitting. Hammers with

metal or fibreglass shafts are a modern development. The head is wedged on to a wooden handle or is forged and locked on to a metal handle. A wooden-handled claw hammer usually has an extended eye, like the eye of an adze, to prevent excessive strain on the shaft when pulling large nails.

Every workshop needs at least four screwdrivers to fit all the sizes of screw likely to be used. A traditional screwdriver has a beech- or boxwood handle that is strengthened with a metal ferrule. A modern plastic handle is moulded directly on to the blade. The bulbous end to most handles enables more torque to be applied, although some workers prefer fluted plastic handles.

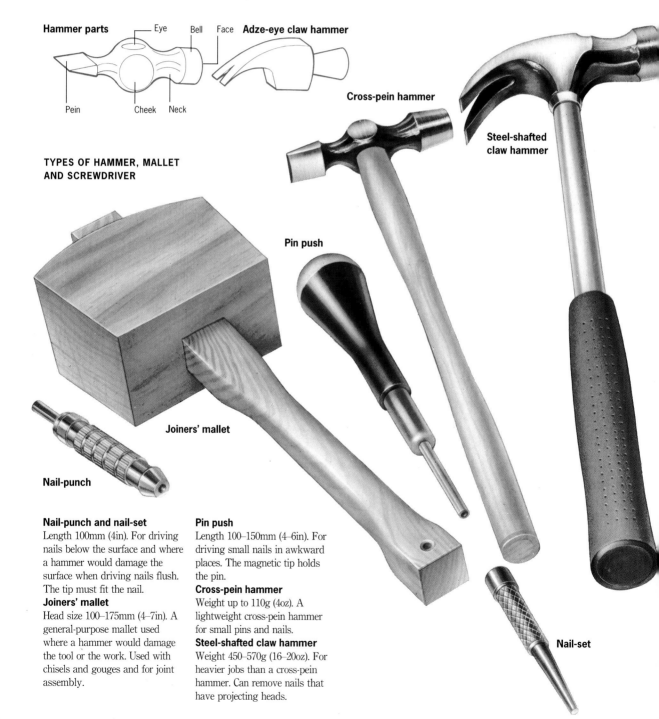

Hammer parts — Eye · Bell · Face · **Adze-eye claw hammer**

Pein · Cheek · Neck

Cross-pein hammer

Steel-shafted claw hammer

TYPES OF HAMMER, MALLET AND SCREWDRIVER

Pin push

Joiners' mallet

Nail-punch

Nail-set

Nail-punch and nail-set
Length 100mm (4in). For driving nails below the surface and where a hammer would damage the surface when driving nails flush. The tip must fit the nail.

Joiners' mallet
Head size 100–175mm (4–7in). A general-purpose mallet used where a hammer would damage the tool or the work. Used with chisels and gouges and for joint assembly.

Pin push
Length 100–150mm (4–6in). For driving small nails in awkward places. The magnetic tip holds the pin.

Cross-pein hammer
Weight up to 110g (4oz). A lightweight cross-pein hammer for small pins and nails.

Steel-shafted claw hammer
Weight 450–570g (16–20oz). For heavier jobs than a cross-pein hammer. Can remove nails that have projecting heads.

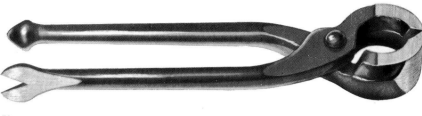

Pincers
Length 150–250mm (6–10in). For removing nails where a claw hammer cannot reach. The claw at the end of the handle is for lifting tacks.

Spiral ratchet screwdriver

Cross-head screwdriver

Ratchet screwdriver

Cabinet screwdriver

Traditional cabinet screwdriver

Cross-head screwdriver
Various types and sizes. Use only with screws slotted in the same pattern as the tip.

Ratchet screwdriver
Blade 50–300mm (2–12in). For driving screws without having to shift the grip on the tool. Ratchet can be adjusted for clockwise or anti-clockwise drive, and can be locked.

Spiral ratchet screwdriver
Blade 250–710mm (9½–28in) fully extended. Downward pressure on spiral grooves causes tip to turn.

Cabinet screwdrivers
Blade 75–250mm (3–10in). Modern style with round straight blade.
Blade 75–250mm (3–10in). Traditional screwdriver with flat blade.

Heavy-duty screwdriver
Blade 100–200mm (4–8in). Forged from solid steel; riveted wooden inserts form the handle.

Offset screwdriver
Length 75–150mm (3–6in). For awkward spaces or where extra torque is required. Can be tapped with a hammer to shift stubborn screws.

Stubby screwdriver
Blade 25–38mm (1–1½in). For confined spaces. Its thickened handle provides torque. Use tommy bar for increased torque.

Heavy-duty screwdriver

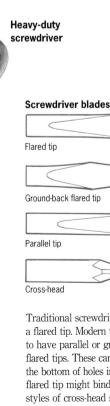

Offset screwdriver

Screwdriver blades

Flared tip

Ground-back flared tip

Parallel tip

Cross-head

Stubby screwdriver

Traditional screwdrivers have a flared tip. Modern tools tend to have parallel or ground-back flared tips. These can turn at the bottom of holes in which a flared tip might bind. Various styles of cross-head screwdriver tip are available.

Hammering nails and pins and driving screws is not that simple, and careful preparation and choice of screwdriver are necessary for flawless work. Keep the hammer-head free from grease and rub off any rust spots with a fine abrasive. When nailing near end grain, the danger of splitting is reduced if the nail tip is blunted by cutting off the tip or banging it on metal. Use clench nailing only where strength is more important than appearance.

A screwdriver blade becomes rounded through use, so restore the flat sides and tip occasionally by honing on an oilstone. Grind any sharp corners off the screwdriver blade tip to avoid damaging the wood on the last few turns when driving countersunk screws.

HAMMERS AND NAILING

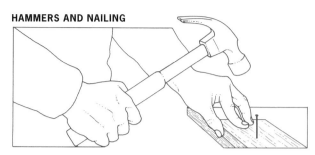

Holding the hammer correctly
Hold a hammer by the end of the handle, not in the middle. Swing the arm, pivoting from the elbow and keeping the wrist straight but flexible. Keep an eye on the nail, hitting with a firm, clean stroke so that the hammer-head meets the nail-head at right angles at the moment of impact.

Starting a nail
To start a nail in the wood tap it gently with the cross-pein. When it is able to stand unsupported, drive it in with the hammer face.

Holding short nails and pins
Short nails and pins that cannot be held in the fingers can be gripped with a small pair of pliers while they are tapped into

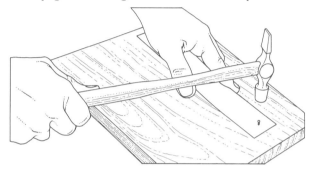

position in the wood. Short nails and pins can also be held by being pushed through a strip of card. Then hammer the nail through the card into the wood; when the nail grips, tear away the card. This method is particularly useful if the nail is to be inserted in an awkward place such as a corner or into the ceiling.

Working in confined spaces
Start a heavy nail by gripping its head against the side of the hammer and drive both in together until the nail holds.

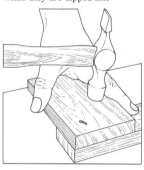

Clench nailing
Tap a long nail through both parts of the wood. Hammer the tip over and then flush, with the work resting on a firm surface.

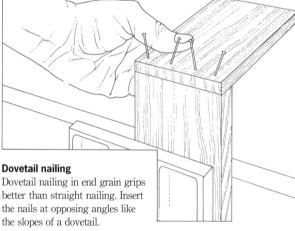

Dovetail nailing
Dovetail nailing in end grain grips better than straight nailing. Insert the nails at opposing angles like the slopes of a dovetail.

Removing nails
Remove a nail if it starts to bend. Pincers and claw hammers work by leverage so pressure on the handle is magnified at the nail

end. The force on the pivoting section can damage the work, so place a piece of metal or waste wood beneath the tool to spread pressure.

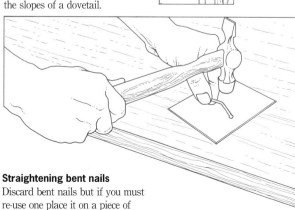

Straightening bent nails
Discard bent nails but if you must re-use one place it on a piece of scrap metal and straighten it with a few taps from a hammer.

Fitting a new hammer handle

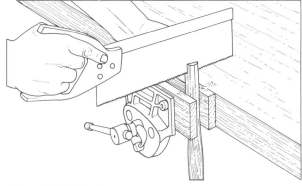

1. Plane the handle.

2. Saw a kerf in the handle.

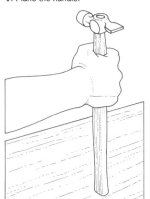

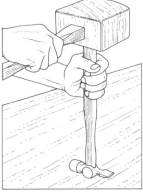

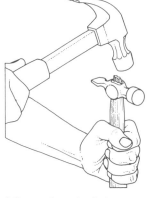

3. Tap the handle firmly.

4. Finish with a mallet.

5. Hammer the wedge flush.

Fitting a new hammer handle

If a wooden hammer handle breaks or splinters, it can be replaced with a new one secured by a metal wedge. Saw off the old handle close to the head. Drive out the remainder with a chisel or punch, working from the underside towards the top, because the eye is tapered in that direction.

1. Plane the head of the new handle to fit the hammer eye. Tap it gently partway into the eye. Remove and plane any shiny parts, which indicate where the wood is binding.

2. In the top of the handle, saw a kerf in line with the hammer-head to the depth of a metal wedge.

3. Place the head on the handle and tap firmly on the bench until the head is driven on to the shaft by its own weight.

4. Turn the hammer over and use a mallet for the final blows. If the kerf closes, open it with a chisel or screwdriver.

5. Insert the wedge and hammer it flush.

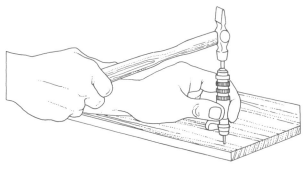

Using a nail-punch

Hold a nail-punch vertically just above the nail-head. Hit the top so the spring tip punches the nail below the surface. Fill the punched hole with stopping and smooth the surface flush for an invisible finish. The smaller the hole made by the tapered punch tip, the neater the finish will be.

Using a nail-set

Hold a nail-set just above the nail against the fleshy part of the middle finger. After impact it will automatically spring up again.

Using a pin push

Drop the nail into the sleeve – the magnetic tip will hold it even upside-down. Press down on the handle to operate.

SCREWDRIVERS

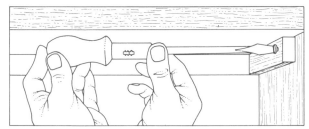

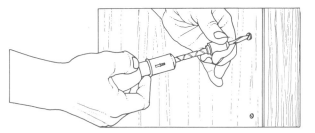

Using a ratchet screwdriver

If using a ratchet screwdriver in awkward places, it can be difficult to get sufficient pressure on the blade. For right-handed workers, in such cases, it may be easier to push on the screwdriver handle with the left hand and support the blade with the right; do this vice versa if left-handed.

Using a spiral ratchet screwdriver

Apply downward pressure on the spiral grooves to turn the tip. Small models have a mild spring that is potentially less dangerous than the strong spring in large models. If these latter slip, they can damage both the wood and the woodworker.

Woodturning tools

The hand tools that are used for woodturning are divided into those that cut and those that scrape. Gouges, chisels and parting tools cut into the wood and give a clean finish. Scraping tools are easier to use but as the name implies they scrape and this tends to give a rougher finish, so considerable sanding is necessary. Sparing use of scrapers is a useful adjunct to the craft of woodturning, but the turner should resist the temptation to follow the initially easier scraping method most of the time. Once the art of using cutting tools has been mastered, the turner will produce much better results.

Gouges have channelled or fluted blades with curved or flat cutting edges. They are used for roughing down and reducing stock to a cylindrical shape and for cutting coves, beads and sweeping curves. Gouges are bevelled on the convex side at an angle of 30–45°, depending on use. A large angle is often required when turning bowls and a smaller angle when turning work between centres.

Chisels have flat blades and straight cutting edges either at right angles or skewed at an angle of 70–80° to the edge of the blade. Skew chisels are used to make V-cuts, beads and tapers, cut down cylindrical stock and smooth shoulders. They are bevelled on both sides and sharpened to form a combined bevelled edge of 20–30°.

Gouges and chisels are held with the bevel of the tool rubbing the stock behind the cutting edge. This also gives the tool support when cutting.

Parting tools are used to cut through the stock and to make narrow recesses or grooves to a desired depth, forming a cut with parallel sides and a square bottom. The tool is bevelled on both sides to give a combined angle of 20–30°.

Scrapers are flat bladed with bluntly angled bevels and variously shaped cutting edges. They are correctly used for light finishing cuts when turning on the faceplate or between centres and for end-grain work. The cutting edge is ground at an angle of 70–80°. Never use old files as scrapers: they are brittle and therefore dangerous.

The tools illustrated will form a good basic kit for woodturning and they will enable the turner to tackle a variety of interesting work from chair legs to bowls. Always buy good-quality turning tools from a reputable manufacturer. Cheap tools will only prove a continual disappointment and they will also make it difficult to acquire the basic woodturning skills.

Tools must be sharp when turning so they will give a clean, crisp cut requiring minimal effort from the turner. During a long turning session tools will need sharpening periodically as the edges will have removed a considerable amount of wood very rapidly and will have become dull. It is not necessary to regrind the tools completely every time but, as flat bevels are so essential in woodturning, they must not be allowed to become too round. Careful use of sharpening stones will be enough to renew the cutting edges many times between grinding sessions. While grinding, the blade must be kept cool. Dip it frequently in cold water when using an emery wheel; where possible a sandstone running in water is better.

Deep fluted bowl gouge
10mm (⅜in) for general shaping inside and out when working on the faceplate.
Spindle gouge
6 and 13 mm (¼ and ½in) for coving, shaping, hollowing and rounding over.
Roughing gouge
25mm (1in) for roughing down to cylinders, waste removal and long curve shaping.

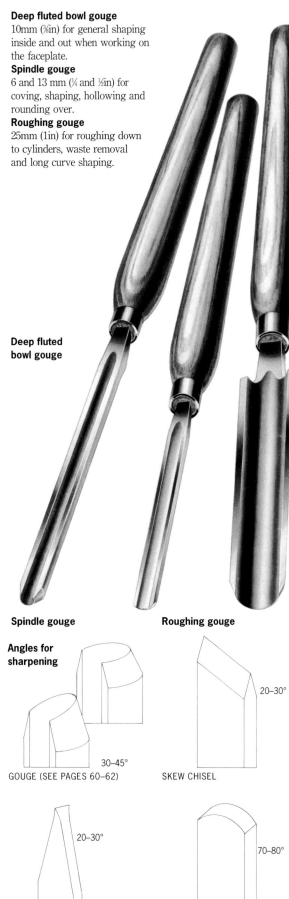

Deep fluted bowl gouge

Spindle gouge

Roughing gouge

Angles for sharpening

GOUGE (SEE PAGES 60–62)   30–45°

SKEW CHISEL   20–30°

PARTING TOOL   20–30°

ROUND-NOSED SCRAPER   70–80°

Skew chisel
19 and 25 mm (¾ and 1in) for
V-grooves, beading and
smoothing.
Round-nosed scraper
19mm (¾in) for final end-grain
shaping and smoothing
any concave surfaces in
faceplate work.

Square-nosed scraper
25mm (1in) for smoothing
convex and flat surfaces.
Parting tool
6mm (¼in) for cutting work to
length and quickly forming
narrow grooves.
Sizing tool
Used with the parting tool for
cutting grooves or for setting
out diameters.

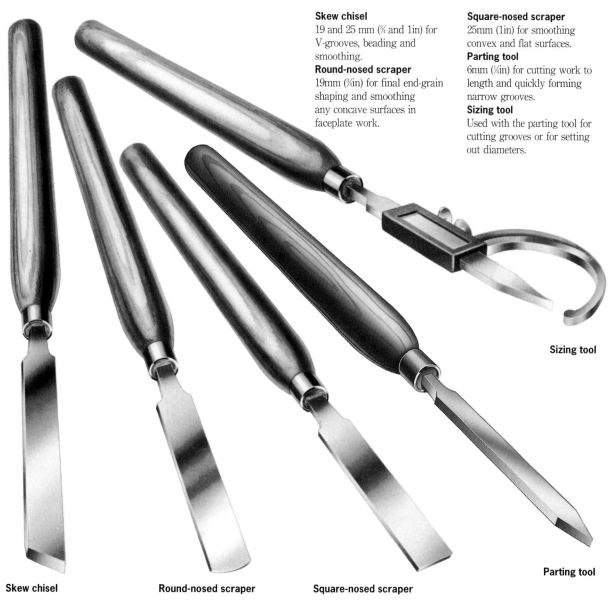

Sizing tool

Parting tool

Skew chisel

Round-nosed scraper

Square-nosed scraper

METHODS OF SHARPENING

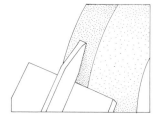
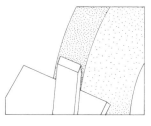
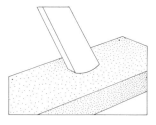
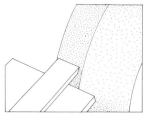

Parting tools
A parting tool needs sharpening
often. Using a tool-rest, which can
be adjusted to the bevel required,
grind the blade to a 20–30° angle
between bevels. Move the blade
across the face of the wheel while
exerting light pressure. Hone with
the bevels laid flat against the
stone and work it back and forth.
When a wire edge appears, hone
each side alternately until the
edge disappears.

Skew chisels
Sharpen a skew chisel on a
grinding wheel to an angle of
20–30° between bevels. Make the
angle of the skew between 70 and
80°. Place the centre of the bevel
against the rotating wheel. Press
until the complete bevel is ground
to the shape of the wheel. Grind
the other bevel in the same way.
Then hone each bevel alternately
on a stone, working it back and
forth to remove the wire edge.

Round-nosed scrapers
A round-nosed scraper may be
sharpened to any convex shape.
Hold its single bevel on the tool-
rest at an angle of 70–80° to the
wheel. Swing the tool from left to
right to keep the shape even until
a wire edge is produced. At the
grinding angle hone the bevel on
the stone, with a rocking motion.
Then lay the blade flat and move
it back and forth to remove the
wire edge.

Square-nosed scrapers
Sharpen a square-nosed scraper on
its single bevel at an angle of
70–80°. Using an even rhythm
move the tool from side to side
across the wheel until a wire edge
is produced. Dip the blade in cold
water at frequent intervals to stop
the steel overheating. Then hone
the bevel, back and forth, at an
angle of 70–80° to the oilstone.
Finally rub the blade flat on the
stone to remove the wire edge.

Turning between centres

When turning between centres, the wood to be turned is supported at one end by the tailstock centre and at the other by the headstock driving centre. The grain of the wood runs parallel with the lathe bed, which means that the turning tools will always be cutting across the grain. It is by using this technique that long slender items and cylindrical work with shaped profiles can be produced.

Until some confidence and skill have been acquired, it is advisable to plane the stock down to an octagon before turning it on the lathe, because turning from a square can present problems. When roughing down to a cylinder or glasspapering, the stock must be revolved at a low speed. Continually adjust the T-rest so that the gap between the stock and the T-rest is 3mm (⅛in).

When turning between centres, make a habit of keeping an eye on the general shape of the stock, especially the rear profile. Initially the temptation will be to look at the cutting edge of the tool, but this should be resisted as it will be difficult to assess whether the stock is cylindrical.

Both a scraping and a cutting method can be used in the process of turning between centres. Although the scraping method may appeal to the beginner as a more cautious approach, the finished surface will always be rougher than a surface that has been cut, and practice using the cutting method will in the long run be rewarded with more professional results. All cutting tools can scrape but not all scraping tools can cut, and therefore glasspapering will be required after scraping.

Preparing the stock and mounting it on a lathe

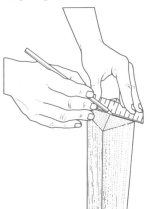

1. Draw diagonals.

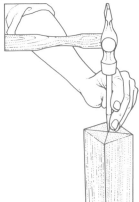

2. Punch a hole in one end.

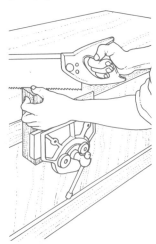

3. Make a cut in the other end.

Cutting down to a cylinder

1. Place a 25mm (1in) roughing gouge on the T-rest and move the bevel lightly against the stock so that the middle of the blade tip cuts away the waste. For quick roughing, place a hand over the gouge. For more control, place the hand under the gouge. Begin to cut at one end; gradually move the gouge along to the other end of the stock and bring it back. The cylinder is then cut down to rough size using a smooth, even rhythm.

2. Continually stop the lathe to adjust the T-rest and check the stock diameter, using calipers. Finally raise the T-rest 3mm (⅛in) above centre and smooth off the stock with a skew chisel. The cut must come from the centre of the blade and not the blade corners as this would result in the wood tearing or the chisel digging into the stock. Avoid this by starting the cut a little way in from the tailstock and work towards the headstock. Then reverse the chisel and work towards the tailstock. If the skew chisel is used correctly the stock will not require glasspapering.

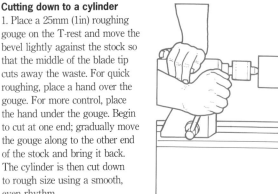

4. Mount the stock on the lathe.

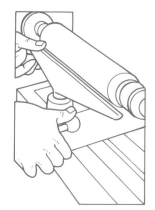

5. Adjust the T-rest.

Cutting down to a cylinder

1. Rough down the stock.

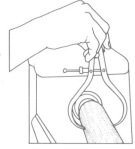

2. Check the diameter.

Preparing the stock and mounting it on a lathe

1. To locate the centre of the stock draw diagonals from corner to corner at both ends. Then, with dividers, mark out circles on both ends of the stock.

2. Make a location hole at the centre of one end, using a nail-set or bradawl.

3. At the other end make saw cuts about 3mm (⅛in) deep across one of the diagonals. These help the driving centre to bite into the stock. To relieve some of the initial stress of cutting a cylinder from a square, it is advisable to plane the stock to an octagonal section first.

4. Mount the stock on the lathe. Fasten a revolving or dead centre on to the tailstock spindle. If using a dead centre on the tailstock apply a spot of grease to the central hole in the stock to avoid friction when the work is turning. (This is unnecessary when a revolving centre is used.) Then fit a drive centre into the headstock spindle and press the centre of the kerfed end of the stock into the spurs on the drive centre. Push the tailstock up to the centre of the stock and clamp into position with the lever. Then turn the spindle feed hand wheel to drive the tailstock centre fully into the stock centre. Retract the centre a fraction to ease friction, then fix in position with the tightening screw.

5. Adjust the T-rest parallel and central to the stock, 3mm (⅛in) from the edge. Before turning, spin the stock by hand to check that there are no obstructions.

Cutting a cove

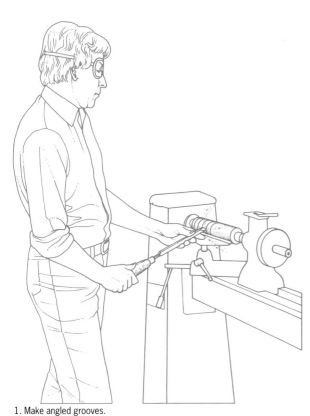

1. Make angled grooves.

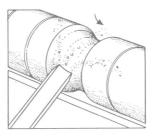

2. Start at one shoulder.

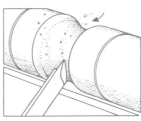

3. Cut down to the cove centre.

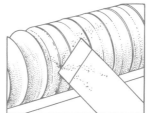

4. Cut from the other shoulder.

Cutting a cove

Mark the required cove width with a wing compass.

1. With the T-rest central to the stock make grooves at alternate angles, using a skew chisel. Then take out the waste from the centre of the cove with a spindle gouge, inclining the handle of the gouge downwards.

2. Twisting the wrist, start at one shoulder.

3. Cut from the left down to the centre.

4. Then cut from the right down to the centre.

Only cut on the down stoke, using a rhythmic movement. On the up stroke the gouge should not touch the wood but the action helps to create an even rolling motion. If a cut is made from the bottom to the top of the cove it will tear the wood. Gradually cut closer to the grooves each time, twisting the wrist from the one cove shoulder to the other. This shaping process is carried out bit by bit on each side of the cove until the required depth is achieved and the cove width stretches from angled groove to angled groove.

Cutting a bead

1. Draw lines on the stock.

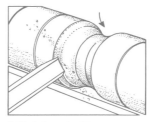

2. Cut from the pencilled line.

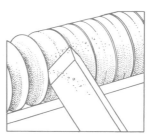

3. Roll the chisel into the groove.

4. Cut the other side.

Cutting a bead

Clamp the T-rest centrally. Scribe the stock, using a wing compass. Then make a vertical groove 3mm (⅛in) deep on each scribed line.

1. Mark the centres of the beads by holding a pencil against the revolving stock. Hold the skew chisel against the stock at 25–30° with the handle dropped to just below the T-rest. Lay the cutting edge of the chisel heel close to one of the pencilled lines.

2. Push the tool forwards so that the cutting edge of the heel is in contact with the surface of the stock, close to the bead centre. The bevel should be held flat against the stock without the heel digging into it.

3. Raise the handle slightly as the chisel is rolled slowly up and over in the direction of the groove. Push the chisel forwards in one continuous motion so that the tool finishes in an almost vertical position.

4. Cut the other half of the bead in exactly the same way with the angles reversed.

Turning on the faceplate

Circular objects can be turned on a faceplate, fixed either inside the headstock or outside when working on large-diameter stock. Successful turning requires skill, practice and a certain amount of luck because of the inherent structure of wood. As with turning between centres, the stock must be well seasoned and generally free of knots, although knots can sometimes enhance the work if they are in the base. The stock must be cut with the grain running across its diameter; or the edges of the stock will split and crack. There will be two distinct end-grain patches on the stock where the chisel or gouge is cutting into the grain and it is these areas that will cause trouble as they tend to tear out under the action of the chisel or gouge. Cutting must be done between the centre and the right-hand edge. If the tool is held elsewhere it will be lifted away. Tool sharpness is most important.

There should be minimum delay between turning the outside and inside of the stock because the wood will shrink slightly across the grain, causing the rim of the stock to become unevenly thick. Ideally, the outside should be turned and finished one day and the inside either that same day or the next.

Preparing the stock and mounting it on a faceplate

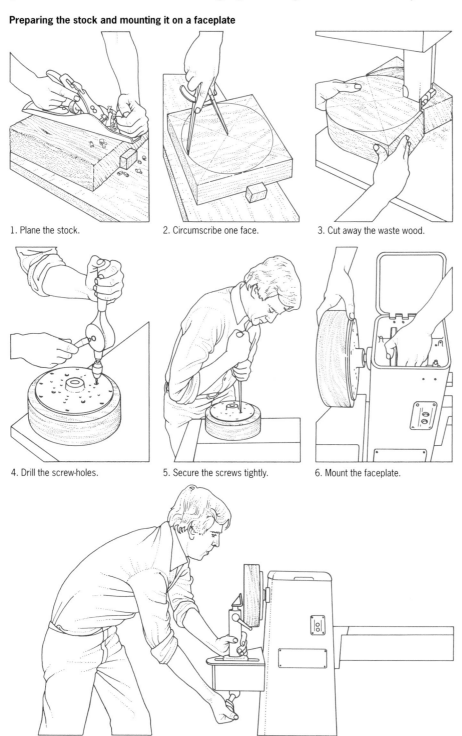

1. Plane the stock.

2. Circumscribe one face.

3. Cut away the waste wood.

4. Drill the screw-holes.

5. Secure the screws tightly.

6. Mount the faceplate.

7. Position the T-rest.

Preparing the stock and mounting it on a faceplate
1. With a jack plane, flatten one face of the stock against a bench-stop so that there are no gaps when it is placed on a faceplate. This will avoid vibration during cutting. Locate the centre by drawing diagonals across the stock, using a pencil and rule.
2. With a wing compass, mark out a circle that is slightly larger than the intended diameter of the bowl.
3. Then cut away the waste wood with a bowsaw or bandsaw. Make sure the stock is as near to round as possible to minimize the forces during roughing down. It is highly dangerous to turn a stock on the faceplate with the corners left on. Select a faceplate that is smaller in diameter than the stock. When the tools are unlikely to come into contact with the faceplate while turning, a faceplate that is larger than the stock can be used. (Or take some waste wood of larger diameter than the stock, plane both sides flat and screw it to the stock.) Place the planed side of the stock on the faceplate and visually centre it. Select at least four screws that will penetrate through the 6mm (¼in) thick faceplate so that it cannot judder or vibrate during cutting.
4. Drill the screw-holes with a hand drill, ensuring the holes are not aligned along the grain.
5. Lubricate the screws with tallow or soft soap before securing them as tightly as possible in the holes. Check that there is a leather washer on the hub of the outer faceplate spindle, giving a resilient cushion to prevent jamming.
6. Secure the faceplate to the lathe by turning the faceplate on to the spindle with one hand and pulling the pulley cone gently in the opposite direction with the other.
7. Position the T-rest so that it is central and parallel with the stock 3mm (⅛in) away.

Turning the underside

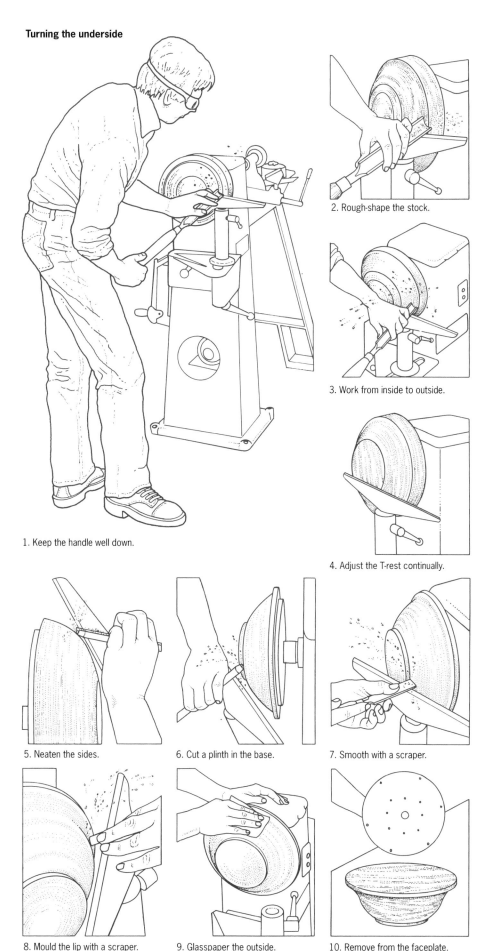

1. Keep the handle well down.

2. Rough-shape the stock.

3. Work from inside to outside.

4. Adjust the T-rest continually.

5. Neaten the sides.

6. Cut a plinth in the base.

7. Smooth with a scraper.

8. Mould the lip with a scraper.

9. Glasspaper the outside.

10. Remove from the faceplate.

Turning the underside

Spin the stock to ensure there are no hindrances. Then switch on the lathe. Initial roughing-down speed should be low. Mark the required diameter of the base with a pencil and steel rule while the stock is spinning. The work of trueing up the edge of the stock and rough shaping now begins, using a 25mm (1in) roughing gouge.

1. With forearm resting lightly on your leg, keep the handle well down and the bevel touching the stock. The other hand steadies the tool as it lies on the T-rest.

2. Rough-shape the stock by cutting a chamfer at the edge of the stock.

3. Gradually increase the chamfer towards both the rim of the stock and the diameter of the base.

4. Continually adjust the T-rest so it stays parallel with the edge of the stock 3mm (⅛in) away. Once the basic shape has been cut, speed up the lathe.

5. A 13mm (½in) deep fluted bowl gouge is then used to cut a neater, more accurate shape.

6. To form the plinth at the base, cut the stock with the gouge turned round.

7. Adjust the T-rest to just below the centre and use a very sharp square-nosed scraper to smooth the outside of the stock. Point the scraper slightly down, steadying it on the T-rest. Work outwards and inwards rhythmically.

8. Then use a round-nosed scraper to clean the lip, pivoting it round on the T-rest to make the lip more pronounced. Remove the T-rest.

9. Then glasspaper. Never use coarse glasspaper as it will cause radial scratches. Set a slow speed and allow the paper to trail in the direction of rotation. Mould across the shape of the stock, paying attention to corners and edges. Stop the lathe. The stock is ready for its surface finish. Olive oil, for example, is ideal for a salad bowl and wax suits a fruit bowl. Many other finishes, however, can be applied to the stock. Once the oil or wax finish has dried it should be lightly buffed into the grain. Switch the lathe to the slowest speed and with a clean cloth work out from the centre, supporting the wrist with the other hand. Apply a couple of coats within 2–3 hours. Leave the stock overnight to dry. Glasspaper the surface carefully.

10. Remove the stock from the lathe and take out the four screws holding it to the faceplate.

Mounting the stock base

1. Screw on the faceplate.

2. Mount on the lathe.

3. Draw a circle.

Mounting the stock base

Take a 19mm (¾in) thick piece of waste softwood larger than the diameter of the stock base. Plane the waste wood flat so that the faceplate will fit flush against it, and remove its corners.

1. Screw the waste wood to the faceplate.

2. Mount the faceplate. Position the T-rest parallel to the waste wood below its centre. Turn the waste wood by hand to ensure there are no hindrances.

3. Mark a circle the same diameter as the stock base. Remove the waste within the circle to a depth of 3mm (⅛in) with a square-nosed scraper. Stop the lathe frequently to check that the base of the stock fits closely into the recess. Remove the faceplate from the lathe. Glue the stock to the waste wood with a layer of brown paper between. Mount the faceplate, waste and stock on the lathe.

Turning the inside

1. Clamp the T-rest slightly lower than the stock centre and spin the stock by hand to check clearance.

2. Hold the handle of a deep fluted bowl gouge slightly below horizontal and cut into the middle, with the gouge at right angles to the stock. Keep the bevel touching the stock. The handle should be lifted up slightly so that the edge of the blade cuts into the stock.

3. As the cut develops, twist the handle round to an angle of about 45° to the stock. As the hollow becomes wider and deeper the twisting movement becomes more pronounced. Adjust the T-rest so that it remains close to the work. Then use a roughing gouge to cut away waste quickly.

4. Stop the lathe periodically to dust the stock and check its depth.

5. Use steel rules to sight the depth against the outside.

6. At the required depth raise the T-rest to the centre of the stock and use a round-nosed scraper to finish off the inside and smooth the rim. Hold its handle up and the blade down, lifting the bevel off the stock. Then glasspaper the stock from the centre out.

7. Apply the finish. Buff it into the grain with the lathe on its slowest speed. Remove the stock from the lathe and unscrew the faceplate.

8. Position the waste upright on the ege of the bench, with its grain vertical. Place a chisel on the edge of the waste wood, with its blade aligned along the grain. Split the grain by giving the chisel a sharp tap with a mallet.

9. Remove any glue and paper and lightly glasspaper the base.

1. Clamp the T-rest.

2. Make a cut into the middle.

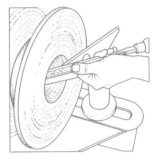

3. Twist the gouge round.

4. Measure the inside depth.

5. Sight the depth cut.

6. Finish off with a scraper.

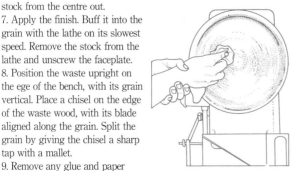

7. Buff with a clean cloth.

8. Release the stock.

9. The final product.

Combination chucks

While the faceplate has long been the standard method of mounting the work-piece in one-centre turning such as for bowls, as described, alternative methods were introduced which proved popular, especially for turning small objects like egg-cups, etc. These devices include chucks such as the cup, screw and spigot chucks, all of which screw onto the headstock spindle of the lathe.

Recently these individual mounting methods have been overtaken by combination or multi-purpose chucks. These precision-engineered chucks incorporate several of the more common independent mounting methods. Some of them form an integral part of the chuck, others can be used through the attachment of supplied or optional accessories. In addition, these chucks include expanding and contracting collets that can be used to mount bowls, etc, by means of a dovetail recess turned in the base of the workpiece, or to grip cylindrical objects firmly. A faceplate accessory is also available. A feature of these chucks is that work can be removed from the lathe and replaced without loss of concentricity.

Chuck body

Expanding jaws

Locking ring

Screw chuck

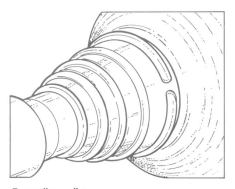

Expanding collet

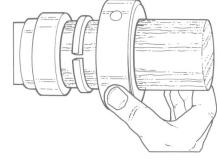

Split ring

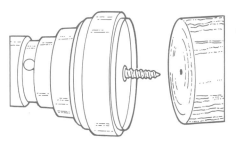

Screw chuck

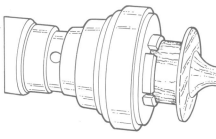

Spigot/collet chuck

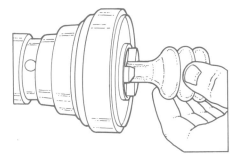

Three-jaw chuck

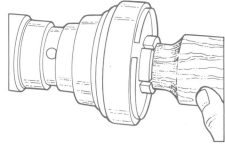

Adjustable collet chuck

Expanding collet
Has a dovetail-shaped expansion ring which grips the work-piece by expanding into a dovetail recess turned in the base of the bowl, etc.

Split ring
Serves as a flange for the threaded outer collar to tighten onto and hold the workpiece on the lathe securely. Especially useful when boring holes in turned objects.

Screw chuck
Has high tensile steel screw to give positive holding power. Screws into pilot hole drilled in base of work-piece. Useful when turning odd-shaped pieces.

Spigot/collet chuck
Provides two methods of holding small to medium-sized objects such as small bowls, etc, by means of an external dovetail or a spring steel collet.

Three-jaw chuck
Holds the work-piece by gripping a spigot turned on one end. The jaws are self-centring and this device is useful when making drawer pulls, etc.

Adjustable collet chuck
Is similar to the spigot/collet chuck but has a diameter adjustment which is essential when mounting turned objects of irregular size.

Woodcarving tools & techniques

Woodcarving gives the opportunity to combine creative ability with woodworking skill, whether used purely to embellish a piece of wood or to produce a complete work in itself. When choosing wood for carving ensure that it is free from knots, shakes and splits and is fine-textured for clean cutting. Limewood is thus particularly suited to carving, and the attractive grains of yew and various species of pine are ideal for abstract shapes.

Woodcarvers have several different names for each implement. Those illustrated below make up the basic carvers' tool kit; a selection for the more advanced wood-carver is shown opposite. Some carving tools, such as chisels and skew chisels, are beveled and sharpened on both sides. Their blades are made of tempered steel to give maximum strengh and are bought with unsharpened edges. Therefore, before use, the woodworker must always sharpen his carving tools. Bevels should be made to an approximate length of 13mm (½in). The harder the wood the shorter the bevel required. The inside face of a gouge must be honed with a slipstone (*see* page 62).

With tools that have sharp edges accidents can all too easily occur unless certain safety precautions are taken: always check the stability of the work surface and the wood itself before commencing work. One good light source is essential. The tools should be laid out on the bench with their handles towards the carver.

BASIC CUTTING TOOLS

Skew chisel
6mm (¼in). This too is useful for undercutting. The skew blade is bevelled on both sides.

Parting tool
60° 6mm (¼in) and 45° 13mm (½in). For pattern detail and outlining. It has two straight edges to form a 'V' shape of varying angles.

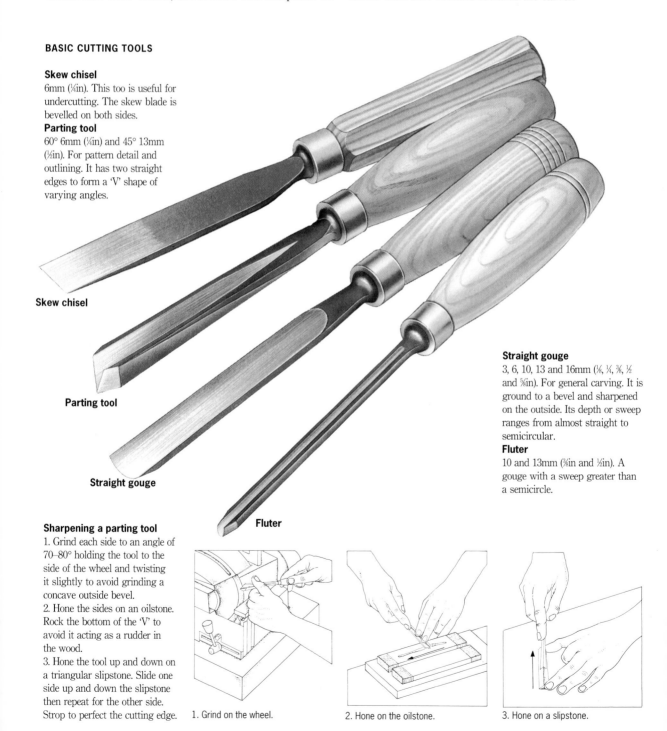

Skew chisel

Parting tool

Straight gouge

Fluter

Straight gouge
3, 6, 10, 13 and 16mm (⅛, ¼, ⅜, ½ and ⅝in). For general carving. It is ground to a bevel and sharpened on the outside. Its depth or sweep ranges from almost straight to semicircular.

Fluter
10 and 13mm (⅜in and ½in). A gouge with a sweep greater than a semicircle.

Sharpening a parting tool
1. Grind each side to an angle of 70–80° holding the tool to the side of the wheel and twisting it slightly to avoid grinding a concave outside bevel.
2. Hone the sides on an oilstone. Rock the bottom of the 'V' to avoid it acting as a rudder in the wood.
3. Hone the tool up and down on a triangular slipstone. Slide one side up and down the slipstone then repeat for the other side. Strop to perfect the cutting edge.

1. Grind on the wheel.

2. Hone on the oilstone.

3. Hone on a slipstone.

SPECIALIZED CUTTING TOOLS

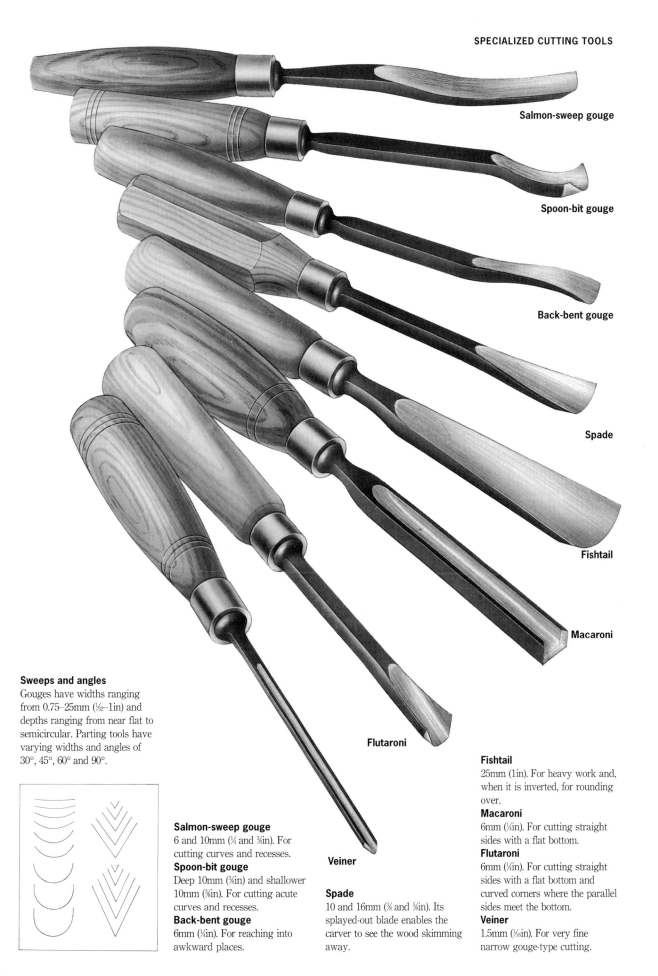

Salmon-sweep gouge

Spoon-bit gouge

Back-bent gouge

Spade

Fishtail

Macaroni

Flutaroni

Veiner

Sweeps and angles
Gouges have widths ranging
from 0.75–25mm (½–1in) and
depths ranging from near flat to
semicircular. Parting tools have
varying widths and angles of
30°, 45°, 60° and 90°.

Salmon-sweep gouge
6 and 10mm (¼ and ⅜in). For
cutting curves and recesses.

Spoon-bit gouge
Deep 10mm (⅜in) and shallower
10mm (⅜in). For cutting acute
curves and recesses.

Back-bent gouge
6mm (¼in). For reaching into
awkward places.

Spade
10 and 16mm (⅜ and ⅝in). Its
splayed-out blade enables the
carver to see the wood skimming
away.

Fishtail
25mm (1in). For heavy work and,
when it is inverted, for rounding
over.

Macaroni
6mm (¼in). For cutting straight
sides with a flat bottom.

Flutaroni
6mm (¼in). For cutting straight
sides with a flat bottom and
curved corners where the parallel
sides meet the bottom.

Veiner
1.5mm (¹⁄₁₆in). For very fine
narrow gouge-type cutting.

CARVING METHODS

For safety, work should be held securely at the bench if it is a small to medium size item, or placed vertically or horizontally if it is a large item to be carved in situ. To secure an item on the bench use a carver's bench screw or vice if it is a sculptural piece or G-clamps if is a flat, relief carving. The one-handed-clamp (page 32) is ideal.

Grain is a prime consideration. It affects how tools respond to the work, eg, much less pressure is required to drive a tool into wood when its edge is parallel with the grain than when it is cutting across it. Running cuts should be made with or across the grain and not against it. To reduce risk, several careful cuts are better than one large slice.

Holding the tool correctly contributes to the success of carving. Use both hands equally; one or the other grasps the gouge or chisel handle to provide the pushing power – when the mallet is not being used – while the other acts as a guide.

For greatest control when carving always stand up. Make sure that the workbench is at a comfortable level; work should be held securely. To control the tool, always rest an arm on the work or workbench. Never allow your body to block the path of any cut. Move the work round as each part is carved so the wood being worked is always close to hand.

A running cut

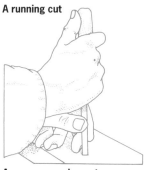

A reverse running cut

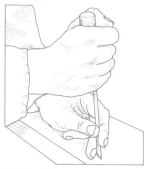

A setting-in cut

A running cut
For a running cut rest the thumb and the middle finger on the tool while the index finger exerts a backwards pressure to prevent the tool running through the wood too quickly. Push the tool forwards with the other hand and point the index finger down the shank. Gauge the depth of an incision by how much blade is showing out of the wood.

A reverse running cut
Where it is not always possible to cut away from the carver, move the body away from the direct path of the tool and let the thumb provide the backwards pressure.

Setting-in cut
For a setting-in cut stab the tool vertically into the wood. Clench the fist and place the fingers of the other hand close to the wood to ensure accurate positioning.

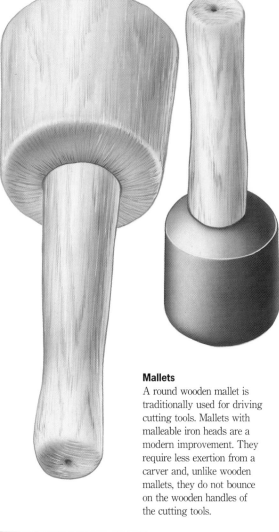

Mallets
A round wooden mallet is traditionally used for driving cutting tools. Mallets with malleable iron heads are a modern improvement. They require less exertion from a carver and, unlike wooden mallets, they do not bounce on the wooden handles of the cutting tools.

Driving a tool with a fist

Driving a tool with a mallet

Driving the tool with a fist
Where a mallet would prove too forceful and an ordinary running cut not forceful enough, tap the handle with the hard lower edge of the hand, never with the fleshy part of the palm.

Driving a tool with a mallet
For hard wood and large work wrap the fingers around the tool to provide a backwards pressure and rest the wrist against the work. Hit the tool handle with a mallet.

Carving a circle
Always cut in the direction of the wood grain where possible. When cutting a circle make four separate cuts in the directions indicated in the diagram.

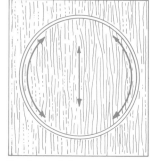

Carving a circle

Marking up with carbon paper

1. Secure the design firmly.

2. Trace on the design.

3. The design transferred.

Marking up with carbon paper

Draw the required design on a piece of paper. Lay some carbon paper face down on the selected piece of wood and, on top, place the design paper. Check that no part of the design overreaches either the edges of the wood or the carbon paper.
1. Secure both papers with tape.
2. Using a hard pencil or a ball point pen, trace around the design. Lift away both papers when complete.
3. Where necessary, touch up the design.

Marking up with a stencil

1. Secure the stencil to the wood.

2. Dab on the paint.

3. Touch up the design.

Marking up with a stencil

Draw a design on some stiff paper. Cut away the major features, using a sharp, pointed knife, to create a stencil.
1. Secure the stencil to the wood.
2. With a brush dab some paint wash through the holes. Carefully remove the stencil.
3. When the paint is dry draw in the complete design using the paint marks as a guide.

Marking up with tools

1. Transfer the measurements.

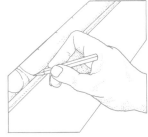

2. Fill in the design.

Marking up with tools

Set dividers against salient points on the design.
1. Move them on to the wood to be carved and transfer the measurements, using a pencil.
2. Using these datum marks, complete the rest of the design freehand.

Checking work in progress

1. Measure the model.

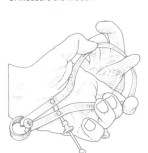

2. Measure the carving.

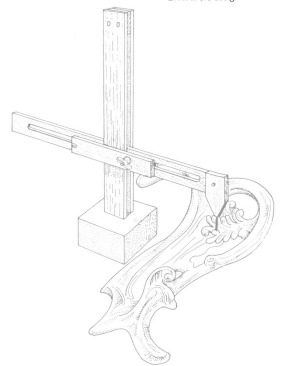

3. Using a height gauge.

Checking work in progress

1. Once a carving is under way, use dividers to check the work against the design and calipers to take measurements when high-relief carving or carving in the round. The curved legs of the calipers allow them to reach around any projection on the original model.
2. Then check the measurement against the work.
3. Make a height gauge to measure relief depths. The arm should slide vertically and horizontally and should swing through almost 180° so that depths can be checked against any model. Like the calipers and dividers, the height gauge is secured with a nut.

Repeat carving

Making an egg and dart moulding

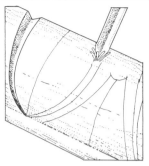

1. Make a tapered downward cut.

2. Cut down from the semicircle.

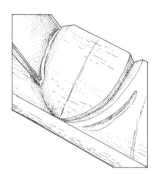

3. Set in around the egg.

4. Set in the curved line.

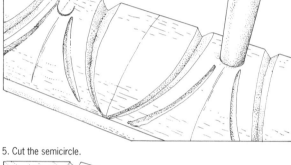

5. Cut the semicircle.

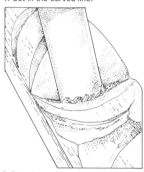

6. Round over the egg.

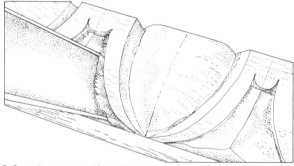

7. Carve the waste wood from either side of the dart.

8. Cut the dart.

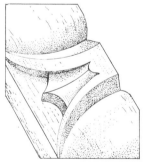

9. The finished dart.

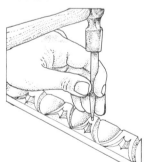

10. Punch in the decoration.

Making an egg and dart moulding

Repeat carving provides a useful introduction to the techniques required to use carving tools correctly. It most often occurs on mouldings, such as the egg and dart moulding shown here. Make each cut throughout the length of the moulding before moving on to the next. This is to reduce the time spent picking up and putting down tools.

1. With the parting tool make a tapered downward cut either side of the egg.

2. Using the same tool, cut a curved downward line from the semicircle towards the bottom centre of the egg. Remove the waste wood.

3. With a wide gouge that fits the contour of the moulding, set in around the egg.

4. Now set in the curved line.

5. With a suitably shaped gouge held vertically, cut the semicircle between the eggs.

6. Round over the egg with an inverted gouge.

7. Carve out the waste wood from either side of the dart leaving a straight vertical line down the centre.

8. Set in the point of the dart with a spade, then finish the point of the dart.

9. Clean out the waste wood, using a spade.

10. Decorate the centre of the semicircle with a punch or nail to complete the design.

Egg and dart moulding parts

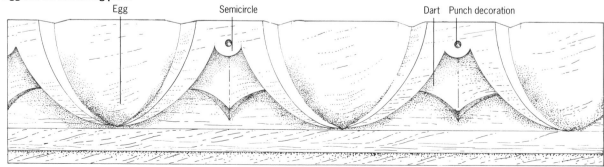

Egg   Semicircle   Dart   Punch decoration

Relief carving

Unlike incised carving where the design is sunk into the wood, in relief carving the design is raised above a cut-away surface. Low-relief carving can be simple. The outline is cut to a uniform depth and the waste removed from the background to the depth of the relief line. The design is ready for setting in and modelling.

'High relief' is in fact deep relief: the deeper the relief the greater the number of planes on which the design is carved. The techniques in high-relief work are similar to those used for carving in the round and demand skill and confidence. Undercutting gives a more three-dimensional effect. It is done by carving inwards beyond the vertical to give each feature a greater shape and to cast shadows, enhancing the three-dimensional effect. Bent gouges and chisels are used to form corners and crevices.

As with carving any mouldings each stage of relief carving should be completed across the design before moving on to the next. The background can be punched or given a tooled texture. Check the finished work for areas that may appear too deep or shallow under fixed viewing light. The Tudor rose design used to illustrate the technique is carved on a number of different planes.

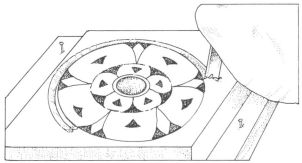

1. Cut the outer circle.

2. Remove the groundwork.

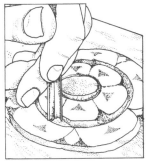

3. Mark between each petal.

Carving a Tudor rose

First transfer a design on to the wood. Then draw a line round the edges of the block to indicate the depth of the groundwork.

1. Secure the block and cut the outer, middle and inner circles around the rose with a fluter. Cut with the grain where possible.

2. With a large gouge remove the groundwork to within 3mm (⅛in) of the relief line. With a shallow tool flatten away the groundwork and smooth down to the relief line.

3. Mark the division between each petal with a vertical cut.

4. Set in with a wide gouge.

5. To carve the leaves under the outer petals, make two vertical cuts down to the groundwork.

6. Remove the waste. Cut the turnover shape on the inner and outer petals with a fluter.

7. Carve down into the centre on both inner and outer circle of petals, using a shallow gouge. With a pencil draw in the outer petal stems. Then using a small fluter take away the wood on either side of each of the stems.

8. Set in each stem with a shallow gouge or spade.

9. With an inverted gouge round over the petal edges and the central button of the flower. Soften the inner and outer turnovers. Undercut the outer petals and the little pointed leaves.

10. Use a punch and hammer to texture the ground work.

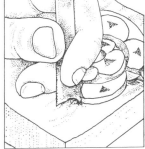

4. Set in the petals.

5. Make two vertical cuts.

6. Remove the waste wood.

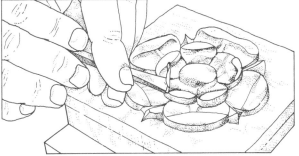

7. Carve into the petal centre.

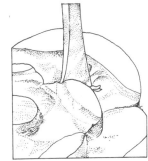

8. Set in each stem.

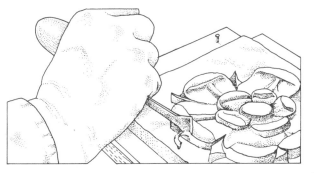

9. Round over the petal edges.

10. The final carving.

METHODS

The basic methods used when working in wood have evolved slowly over centuries and although a new technique is occasionally introduced – usually relating to innovation in design or the introduction of a new power tool – only rarely are the traditional methods improved upon. Much of what is described in the following pages has become standard practice and the processes involved are proven through experience.

The fundamental principles of joining pieces of wood together to create structures and to make furniture have had to take into account the natural movement of the material. Wood reacts to its environment: it shrinks across the grain and its growth rings tend to straighten out, which causes it to warp and twist. The joints and construction methods used today were developed with these factors in mind and we ignore them at our peril.

The emphasis here is on hand skills: the proper use of saw and chisel in making sound, tight-fitting joints – halving, housing, mortise and tenons, dovetails, and so on – is fully described and illustrated, and advice given on which of these joints is most suitable for a particular application. General frame and carcass construction and drawer-making are covered as is surface finishing. This emphasis on hand skills is not to ignore or deny the use of machinery, especially the proper use of hand-held power tools, described elsewhere in the book, for such tools can extend the range of work that the woodworker may do and remove the drudgery of repetitive such tasks as sawing and planing.

Drawing & design

Before attempting to make any article, such as a piece of furniture, from wood, the general shape and proportion, together with the dimensions and method of construction need to be established. For very simple pieces it is possible to work from a freehand sketch and a few basic measurements but more usually an accurate drawing of the whole item, together with more details of critical components and their dimensions is required. This is essential if the work is to be done by someone else.

A basic drawing can be made with relatively little equipment; for a freehand sketch a piece of paper and a pencil or pen is all that is required. For a more elaborate working drawing, a drawing pad, or preferably a drawing or draughting board on which paper may be placed, is required, together with basic drawing equipment.

Good-quality pencils will give the most satisfactory service and grades H and HB are the most suitable for this work. Mechanical and automatic pencils are now the choice of many workers. For removing pencil lines and for general cleaning up of a drawing, a rubber or plastic eraser is required. Standard set squares, 30/60° and 45°, are important items of equipment, with a protractor for drawing and measuring other angles. A spring compass is needed to draw accurate circles while a set of French curves will be useful when drawing free curved shapes.

There are basic drawing tenets, conventions and methods that help to simplify and speed up the drawing process and to avoid the problems of misreading the final result. Drawing methods relate to an understanding of basic geometric shapes, proportion and scaled drawings. In order to produce a drawing of manageable size it is necessary to reduce, in exact proportions, the intended dimensions of the object. To do this, a scale rule is ideal. Choose a scale to suit the size of the object being drawn and the amount of detail needed to be shown. Full-size drawings of such details as mouldings are often drawn alongside scaled drawings of the whole subject. The usual scale for individual pieces of furniture is 1:5 in metric or 1:4 in Imperial, and for room layouts 1:20 in metric and 1:24 in Imperial. The scale 1:5 means that 1cm on the scaled drawing represents 5cm on the object.

Third-angle projection is the best-known method of laying out a drawing; the individual face-on views usually shown are one or more of the front, side and top. By representing these views pictorially with the three surfaces adjoining each other, the projection can be more easily read and understood. The easiest pictorial projection to draw is an isometric one.

There are conventional ways to present and record dimensions, diameters, radii, sections and materials, so that they can be interpreted. For clarity, dimensions are added not to the outline itself but between extension lines, which are extensions of the object's outlines. Write the figures centrally above the dimension line, omitting the units of measurement, which can be specified in a title box. All dimensions should be placed so that they can be read from the bottom right-hand corner of the drawing.

BASIC GEOMETRIC SHAPES

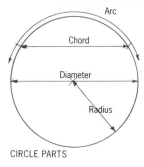

CIRCLE PARTS

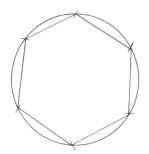

Finding the centre of a circle

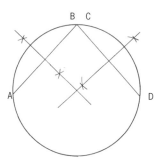

Drawing a hexagon

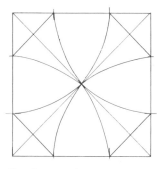

Drawing an octagon

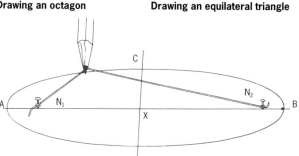

Drawing an ellipse

Finding the centre of a circle

Draw chord AB. Set a compass to over half AB. From A scribe arcs inside and outside the circle. Repeat from B, crossing the arcs. Join the intersecting points. Draw a chord CD. Repeat the process. The lines intersect at the centre.

Drawing a hexagon

Draw a circle with a radius equal to the side length of the hexagon. With the compass at this setting, step around the circumference six times. Join the points.

Drawing an octagon

To draw an octagon in a square, draw the diagonals of the square. Set a compass to half the length of a diagonal. With the compass point on a corner intersect the adjacent sides. Repeat from each corner and join up the points of intersection.

Drawing an equilateral triangle

To draw an equilateral triangle, first draw the line AB to the required length. Set a compass to the line length and describe two arcs, one from A and one from B; join up the lines from the point of intersection C.

Drawing an ellipse

Decide and draw up the major and minor axes, AB and CD, which bisect each other at right angles. Set a compass to AX. From C intersect AB to give points N_1 and N_2. Insert pins at N_1, N_2 and B. Tie string tightly from N_1 to N_2, via B. Remove pin B. Keeping the string taut, draw the ellipse.

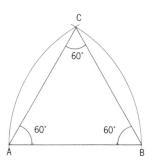

Drawing an equilateral triangle

Isometric projection

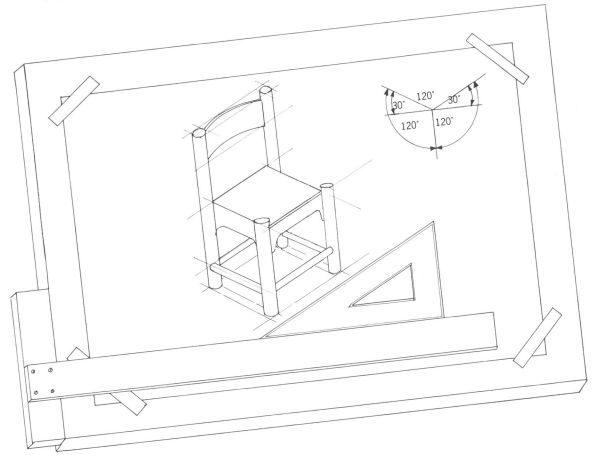

Third-angle projection

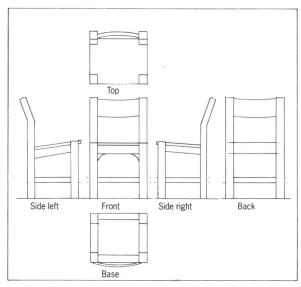

Top

Side left   Front   Side right   Back

Base

Drawing symbols

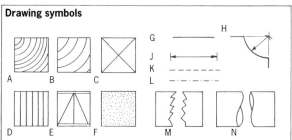

Third-angle projection

One of the simplest ways to represent a three-dimensional object is to draw the individual views from the front, side and top. The front view (front elevation) is drawn first; the view from the right (side elevation) is drawn on the right of it and the view from the left is drawn on the left; the top view (plan) is drawn above the front view. If necessary, the base (plan) is drawn below the front elevation. All views are drawn to the same scale in proportion to the intended dimensions of the object. As many as six views can be drawn; for simple objects, however, front and side elevations should convey all the necessary information.

Drawing symbols

Use symbols to show materials: **A** finished hardwood, **B** finished softwood, **C** nominal-sized timber, **D** multi-ply, **E** blockboard, **F** chipboard. Lines of different thickness are used to clarify parts of the drawing. Use the thinnest lines for initial guide-lines and **G** the thickest for the

Isometric projection

One pictorial method of present-ing a drawing is an isometric projection. Conventionally all vertical lines are drawn verti-cally and all other lines are drawn to the side of each vertical at 30° to the horizontal base line. Use a 30°/60° try square with a T-square. The three isometric axes around which all drawings are made are shown on the draw-ing (*above*). Because of this rigid geometric method, which does not follow the laws of perspec-tive, the picture will appear dis-torted. Being mechanically cor-rect, however, it can be used for taking off dimensions. This makes the projection particularly useful for complicated structures.

main outline. **H**. Make a thin line to indicate diameters and **J** radii and for dimension lines, drawn between extension lines. **K**. Use thin, short dashes for hidden details, **L** a chain line as a centre line, **M** jagged lines for rectangles and **N** wavy lines for cylinders.

Planning a project

A methodical approach to design, following the inception of an idea, is most likely to ensure the best solution to the problems of intended use and construction. This design approach can be broken down into basic stages: the brief or analysis of the idea; sketch drawings; scaled drawings; and models and rods (full-size drawings). A cutting list is then made of the required materials.

The brief identifies the intended use and function of the object within its proposed context. It can set limits on the materials and finishes and exactly how they are to be used. It can set visual guidelines; thus, for compatibility with existing furniture or room setting, the intended proportions, positioning and colour can be compared. The brief need only be a short statement clarifying the needs for the object. Even where ideas may seem very clear and the furniture simple, a brief is always useful as a written record, providing a check on progress throughout the project. In the example illustrated below, the brief would describe the following requirements: a table with fixed top to seat two people; to be used mainly with one side against a wall with seating positions either at the ends or on one side; stable hardwood supporting the structure; and a veneered top with a durable finish harmonizing with the chairs.

Sketch drawings

The designer's sketchbook will translate the written brief into a series of visual solutions. Among the general considerations that are incorporated will be the material sizes and thicknesses, with appropriate allowance made for joints. It can also include a more precise breakdown of materials required, such as any fixtures to be used and any special tools that may be required. From the various sketches and ideas, one will be selected and developed. Check that the sketch chosen conforms in all aspects with the outline on the original brief.

In the example the following are a few of the considerations that have been made: the size of the top; its height and rail width to give sufficient knee clearance; the leg structure and the method of connecting the rails with joints, knock-down fittings or dowels; the lower shape of the rail; and, finally, how to fix the top.

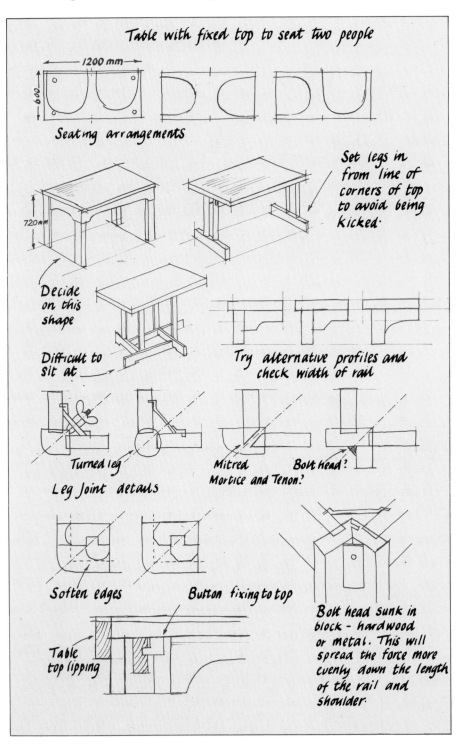

Table with fixed top to seat two people

1200 mm — 600

Seating arrangements

Set legs in from line of corners of top to avoid being kicked.

720mm

Decide on this shape

Difficult to sit at

Try alternative profiles and check width of rail

Turned leg

Leg Joint details

Mitred Mortice and Tenon?

Bolt head?

Soften edges

Button fixing to top

Table top lipping

Bolt head sunk in block - hardwood or metal. This will spread the force more evenly down the length of the rail and shoulder.

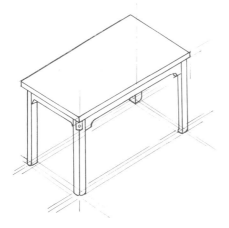

Scaled drawings

The scaled drawing is the basis for confirming the decisions taken at the sketch stage and for establishing accurate dimensions and proportions. The most straightforward drawing uses third-angle projection to show, respectively, the front, side and top views. A scale of 1:5 (metric) or 1:4 (Imperial) will usually result in an overall drawing of manageable size. An isometric drawing, showing the three views combined, is a useful aid to a fuller appreciation of the design. When designing furniture to fit a room, it may also prove helpful to apply the same principles of scaled drawing to the room itself. Cardboard cut-outs of each item of furniture can be moved around a scaled plan of the room to establish the position and suitability of the new piece. The example illustrates an isometric projection.

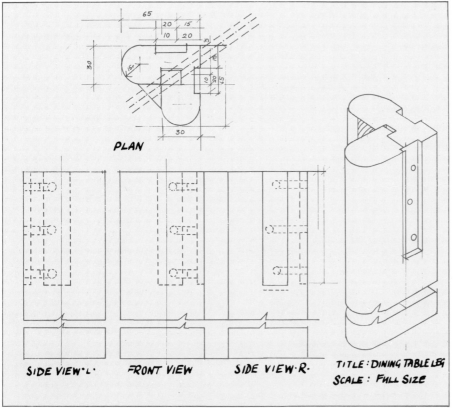

PLAN

SIDE VIEW·L·   FRONT VIEW   SIDE VIEW·R·   TITLE: DINING TABLE LEG
SCALE: FULL SIZE

Models and rods

Full-size drawings against which the work can be laid for checking are known as rods. The drawing is usually a vertical or horizontal cross-section to show the joints more clearly. It can be laid out on lining paper, a sheet of three-ply or thin board. It is especially useful when defining an intricate part of the design, such as the position of the pivot on a folding chair, and for checking the work at progressive stages. For a more complete evaluation of the appearance of the object, a scaled model, made from stiff card or balsa wood, is helpful. Balsa-model details can be taken direct from the scaled drawings; when using stiff card, take the dimensions from the scaled drawings and redraw the object, making as many surfaces as possible continuous with their adjacent sides for cutting and folding into a three-dimensional form. The example illustrates a rod for the joint in the table leg, drawn using third-angle projection and also as an isometric drawing.

The cutting list

Using scaled drawings or rods, the cutting list (such as that for the table, *left*) can be prepared for ordering the wood – either in nominal or finished sizes. Nominal is the size to which the boards are cut on the bandsaw or a circular saw. When planed the boards' thickness is reduced by at least 3mm (⅛in). Prepared wood is indicated on the cutting list either as finished sizes or PAR (planed all round). List the names of the parts, the number of pieces the same size, then, in order, the length, width and thickness, allowing 13mm (½in) of waste in length and 6mm (¼in) in width. Specify the wood required and re-check the total number of parts.

Cutting List ITEM	N° OFF	MATERIAL	LENGTH	WIDTH	THICKNESS
Leg Members	4	Pine	735	70	30
Leg Members	4	Pine	735	50	30
Rails	2	Pine	1,052	100	20
Rails	2	Pine	440	100	20
Top	1	Pine	1,212	606	23
Buttons for top	14	Pine	45	35	20
Leg inserts	4	Mahogany	102	20	20
Pellets to cover bolt heads	4	Mahogany	150	20	20
Dowels	24	Beech	40	11 (dia)	
Corner leg braces	4	Large complete with 6mm/¼" mushroom-headed bolts, washers and wing nuts.			

All finished sizes · Units in m.m.

Joints

A joint must be strong enough to resist the stresses that will be imposed on it. (For uses of joints *see* pages 131–45; for terms peculiar to each joint see under the appropriate joint.) The design of most joints has evolved slowly over the centuries to solve the problems posed by solid wood construction. Few of these joints work successfully with manufactured boards except for multi-ply (*see* page 130). All joints, except those that are dismantled or pivoted, must be glued. The greater the area on the side and edge available to be glued, the greater a joint's strength. End grain does not hold glue well.

Consider the grain direction carefully before making a joint. There should be no knots in the joint area. Decide how to arrange the pieces. Choose the best surfaces to be the face side and face edge. Cut and plane the wood to size and square it up, marking the faces (*see* page 30). Then cut the joint. The surfaces left by the saw will be quite rough; this is an advantage as it helps the glue to grip. Remove ragged edges; smooth faces that will be inaccessible when the joint is assembled, but leave pencilled reference marks on until the project has been glued and assembled. Before gluing, a joint can be tested for fit – 'dry assembly'. A well-made joint will be friction tight. Glue the inside surfaces of the joint on both pieces. Then knock the pieces home with a hammer. The hammer has the same weight as a mallet but the impact area is smaller and easier to control. Use waste wood as a buffer. Wipe off excess glue before it dries, using a damp cloth. When dry, level all surfaces with a smoothing plane and smooth with glasspaper.

Halving joints

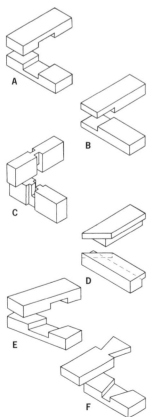

Halving joints

Halving joints provide a simple way of joining pieces that cross or meet in an L- or T-shape. They are used for small simple frames and intermediate frames and divisions within a carcass. They do not have the strength and rigidity of joints such as mortise and tenons, dovetails or housings. **A.** Cross halving joint can be cut in manufactured boards crossing in their width, making it suitable for internal dividers in boxes and small carcasses. **B.** The lap halving joint must be reinforced by screwing underneath, or by dowels or bolts. Variations on the halving joint include **C** the housed and halved joint and **D.** the mitred, rebated and halved joint – good for picture and mirror frames. Secure the mitre by dowelling or screwing from the back. **E.** The straight shoulders on the oblique halving joint give it strength and resistance to twisting. **F.** In the dovetail halving joint, the strength of a dovetail joint is added to that of a T-halving joint. Use it for jointing carcasses and frames.

Mortise and tenon joints

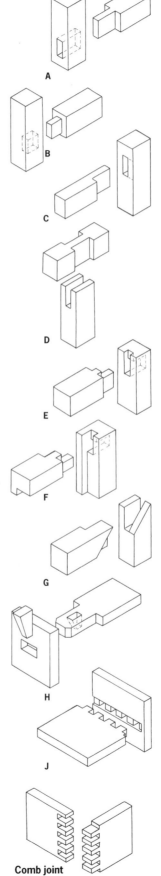

Comb joint

Mortise and tenon joints

These are the strongest of the end-to-side-edge joints and they are used in cabinetmaking for frame jointing. **A.** The through mortise and tenon joint is the basic form of this joint. The mortise is cut right through the wood showing the end grain of the tenon. Shoulders on the tenon provide stops for the tenon and a resistance to twisting. Wedges can be inserted into either tenon or mortise to give additional strength. **B.** In the stub, or blind, mortise and tenon joint, the tenon is shortened to avoid showing end grain on the outer surface. **C.** The barefaced mortise and tenon joint is used when a thin slat must be tenoned into a thicker upright to finish flush on one side. The tenon has only one shoulder. This allows the mortise to be displaced safely away from the front edge. **D.** The bridle joint is often used for leg and rail joints where a thick leg must be connected to a thinner rail. **E.** On the haunched mortise and tenon joint the width of the tenon is reduced to prevent the joint being withdrawn upwards. Instead of a complete strip of the tenon being removed, a small portion near the shoulder is left – called a haunch. The haunch helps resist any tendency to twist. The haunch can be tapered by placing it against a matching slope in the mortise piece. **F.** The long and short shoulder mortise and tenon joint is necessary when using rebated members. **G.** The mortise and tenon joint with a mitred front gives a neat appearance and is useful when working mouldings on the inside edge. **H.** The projected and wedged mortise and tenon joint forms the leg and rail connection on a table that might need to be dismantled. The tenon passes right through the leg, or truss, and is wedged on the outside. **J.** The pinned joint is extremely strong. There is a very large gluing area and the joint can resist downward and twisting pressure.

Comb joint

This joint has its main use in the volume production of boxes and drawers. The joint relies upon its large gluing area and tongues must make a tight fit in the kerfs. It is a machine-made joint and is not described here in detail.

Dovetail joints

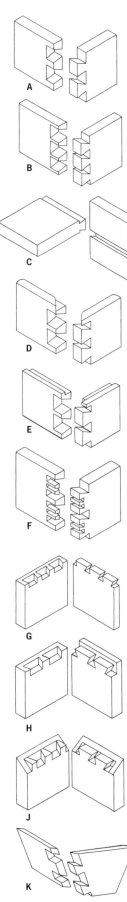

A

B

C

D

E

F

G

H

J

K

Dovetail joints

Dovetail joints are the strongest way of connecting pieces of wood together in their width. They are used to join carcasses rigidly and to make boxes and drawers. They have a comparatively large gluing area and are therefore particularly strong. Generally, the longer the tails, the better the grip. Properly made tails only fit once, so a joint should only be half entered on a dry assembly. **A.** The carpenters' through dovetail joint is the basic form of the joint. End grain shows on both pieces. When hand-made the tails are wider than the pins. **B.** The fineness of the pin is judged as a sign of quality workmanship, and in the cabinetmaker's dovetail joint the pin often comes to a point. **C.** In the dovetail housing joint, the tail is cut across the width of the wood. The joint is usually tapered on assembly to avoid excessive friction across such a wide area. This is a particularly strong joint to use for securing shelves. **D.** The through dovetail joint with mitre has the top edge mitred and usually rounded over for a neat appearance on trays and boxes. **E.** The through dovetail joint with rebate is used with a rebated frame. **F.** The decorative through dovetail joint makes a feature of the fact that end grain shows on both pieces. The small tails add to the strength of the joint by increasing the gluing area on the very large tails. **G.** The lapped dovetail joint is used when the end grain needs to be hidden on one of the pieces. The through tails are modified by shortening the tails and letting the socket piece lap over the end. The joint is often used for drawers where the end grain must not show on the front. **H.** The double lapped dovetail joint is used where tails should not show on either piece. One piece presents a flush surface while the other shows only a thin line of end grain. **J.** No end grain shows at all on the secret mitre dovetail joint, which from the outside looks like a simple butted mitre joint. **K.** The bevelled dovetail joint is used to join the sides of boxes where all four sides slope outwards; it is one of the most difficult of all joints to make. Through and lapped dovetails can be cut by machine, using a power router and jig. This is useful if many joints are to be cut.

Housing joints

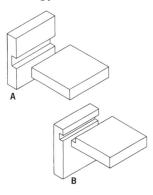

A

B

Dowel joints

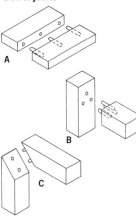

A

B

C

Edge joints

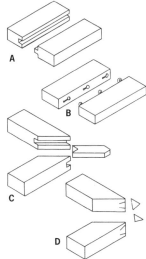

A

B

C

D

Pivoting joints

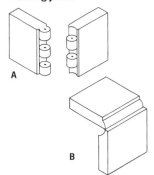

A

B

Housing joints

A. The through housing joint is used to fix shelves in carcasses and for holding intermediate rails in carcass frames. The housing can be stopped, so there is an unbroken vertical line on the carcass. **B.** In the barefaced housing joint, used for jointing a top to a side, the horizontal piece is reduced in thickness by having a tongue cut in it and only this is housed. This makes the joint better able to resist twisting.

Dowel joints

Dowels can be used to join wood **A** edge to edge or **B** at right angles edge to end. **C.** They can also be used for mitre joints and to secure solid-wood or manufactured-board shelves. In traditional work they were rarely used as the dowels had to be cut by hand. Dowel joints are now often substituted for mortise and tenon joints, as they are easier to make and almost as strong. They are especially suitable when awkwardly shaped or angled pieces of wood meet as, for instance, in canted or round table legs joining a rail.

Edge joints

To build up a wide surface in solid wood two or more boards can be joined edge to edge. The most basic joint is the rubbed glue joint. It is a perfectly strong joint if the mating edges are planed and glued together correctly. **A.** The tongued and grooved joint has a large gluing area. The tongue can be cut in one operation using a tonguing cutter or be formed by cutting a rebate on both edges. Both pieces can be grooved and a loose tongue glued in. **B.** Alternatively, the slot-screwed joint may be used. A mitre joint can be strengthened with **C** a loose tongue glued in grooves or **D** by keys inserted after assembly.

Pivoting joints

A. The knuckle joint is cut when a pivoting joint is required. It is usually formed on the brackets supporting the flaps on Pembroke tables. **B.** The rule joint is traditionally used for fall flaps such as on a gateleg table. It looks neat when the flap is both up and down and adds strength as pressure on the flap is transmitted to the main top when the flap is up. It must be used with a special rule joint hinge (*see* page 156).

Halving

A CROSS HALVING JOINT

Edge

Side

THE FINISHED JOINT

Length

Depth

Width

Thickness

Length

THE JOINT PULLED APART

Top piece

Thickness

Squared line

Gauged line

Bottom piece

THE WOOD MARKED UP

Making a cross halving joint

1. Mark the width of the top.

2. Square down both edges.

3. Gauge half the thickness.

4. Saw to the gauged line.

5. Check the marked lines.

6. Chisel out the waste.

7. Saw the wood fibres.

8. Check with a straight-edge.

9. Check the joint for fit.

Variations on the cross halving joint

LAP HALVING
JOINT

VIEW OF THE
UNDERSIDE

HOUSED AND
HALVED JOINT

MITRED,
REBATED AND
HALVED JOINT

Making a cross halving joint

Both pieces of wood must be of equal thickness.

1. Place the top piece on the bottom piece, face sides uppermost, and mark the width of the top piece on the bottom piece.

2. Square the marks across the bottom piece and halfway down both edges. Place the pieces in their original position and mark the width of the bottom piece on to the underside of the top piece.

3. Set the marking gauge to half the thickness of the wood. Gauge between the marks on the edges of both pieces from the face sides.

4. Hold one piece in the bench-hook and saw across the grain just inside the squared line, down to the gauged line.

5. Put the two pieces together and check that they will make a tight fit when the second cut is made to the marked line. Move the saw in relation to the squared line if necessary. Make one or two kerfs in the waste to remove it more easily. Secure the piece in the vice.

6. With a bevel-edged chisel and mallet, chisel out the waste from the housing in stages. Work halfway in from each edge.

7. With a saw, remove the fibres that do not come away cleanly.

8. Check the flatness of the housing with a straight-edge. Level out any unevenness, chiselling with hand pressure only. Cut the second housing.

9. Check the joint by putting the end of one piece into the housing on the other and vice versa. The joint should be tight enough for you to lift the second piece up.

Variations on the cross halving joint

The lap halving joint is one of the easiest joints to make for frames. It needs reinforcing either with a through dowel or by gluing and screwing from the underside. The housed and halved joint is another variation on the cross halving joint and is similar to the bridle joint. Although more wood is removed than in the cross halving joint, the variation is stronger because of the two housings, which eliminate lateral movement. The mitred, rebated and halved joint is suitable for picture and mirror frames and it is stronger than the plain mitre joint. The lap allows a screw to be inserted from the underside. Drill the screw-hole near the mitre shoulder for additional strength.

AN OBLIQUE HALVING JOINT

Side

Edge

THE FINISHED JOINT

Length

Depth

Width

Thickness

THE JOINT PULLED APART

Top piece

Squared line

Gauged line

Bottom piece

THE WOOD MARKED UP

Making an oblique halving joint

1. Place the sliding bevel on the rod.

2. Mark the length of the housing.

3. Mark in the housing.

4. Make the saw cuts.

5. Chisel away the waste.

A DOVETAIL HALVING JOINT

Side

End

Thickness

THE FINISHED JOINT

Edge

Length

Tail piece

Width

Depth

Housing piece

Length

THE JOINT PULLED APART

Squared line

Gauged line

Thickness

Gauged line

THE WOOD MARKED UP

Making a dovetail halving joint

1. Gauge the wood.

2. Saw across the grain.

3. Mark in the tail slope.

4. Remove the waste.

5. Mark the housing.

6. Chisel out the waste.

Making an oblique halving joint

Both pieces must be of equal thickness. Take the oblique angle from the rod of the whole project. Hold the top piece in position on the rod, face side up.
1. Place a sliding bevel against the edge, aligning the stock with the marks for the bottom piece. Set the bevel blade to this angle.
2. Mark the width and position of the oblique housing on the edges of the top piece.
3. Check the marks against the sliding bevel and use it to draw the oblique housing on the underside of the top piece. Square the marks halfway down the edges. Mark the housing on the face side of the bottom piece. Gauge the depth of the housing on both pieces from the face sides. Remove the waste at the centre of each housing, where it is squared across, using a saw and bevel-edged chisel. To make the oblique saw-cuts, use a bench-hook and clamp the wood where necessary so that the cut can be made at the easiest angle.
4. Make two straight saw cuts.
5. Then chisel away the waste in the oblique corner pieces.

Making a dovetail halving joint

Mark the housing piece width on the tail piece. Square the marks across the underside and down both edges.
1. Set the marking gauge to half the thickness of the wood and gauge along both edges and around the end. Remove half the thickness of the dovetail piece from the underside; saw a 3mm (⅛in) kerf with the wood upright in the vice. Clamp the wood at an angle and saw down the line gauged along one edge. Turn the wood around and repeat. Put the wood upright in the vice again and complete the cut to the squared line.
2. Put the wood on the bench-hook and saw across the grain. Square the line of the cut edges across the face of the tail piece.
3. Pencil in the angle of the tail slope by eye, or with a rule measuring 1 in 6 or 1 in 8 units. Repeat the slope on the other side. Saw the tail shoulders across the grain to the pencil marks.
4. Chisel out the waste, working along the grain to the saw cut.
5. Mark the housing from the tail.
6. Saw and chisel out the waste.

Mortise & tenon

A THROUGH MORTISE AND TENON JOINT

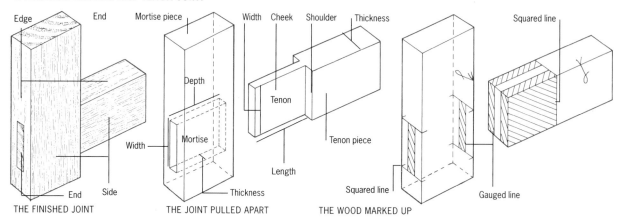

Edge · End · Mortise piece · Width · Cheek · Shoulder · Thickness · Squared line · Depth · Tenon · Mortise · Width · Tenon piece · Length · Thickness · Squared line · Gauged line

THE FINISHED JOINT · THE JOINT PULLED APART · THE WOOD MARKED UP

End · Side

Marking up a through mortise and tenon

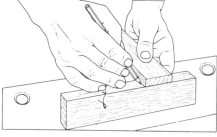

1. Mark the length of the tenon.

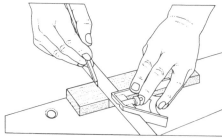

2. Square all around the lines for the tenon.

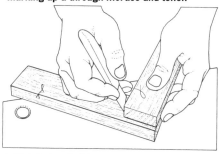

3. Mark the mortise width from the tenon.

4. Square around the lines for the mortise.

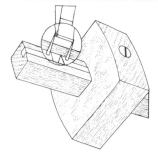

5. Set the spurs of the gauge.

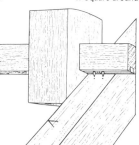

6. Set the gauge stock

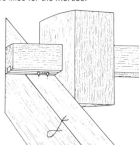

7. Check from the other side.

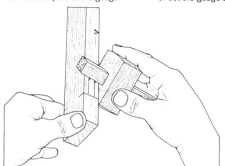

8. Gauge from the face side.

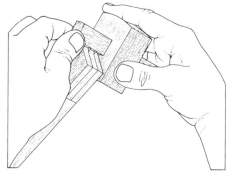

9. Gauge around the tenon end.

Marking up a through mortise and tenon

A tenon should generally be one-third the thickness of the tenon piece. The grain of the mortise piece should run along the width of the mortise so that the mortise can be chopped out against the grain. This will ensure a clean cut that is the exact width of the chisel being used.

1. Mark the length of the tenon from the mortise piece, using a marking knife.

2. Square the line around the tenon piece.

3. Mark the width of the mortise from the width of the tenon piece.

4. Square the line around to both edges.

5. To mark the mortise thickness set the spurs of the mortise gauge to the width of the chisel to be used for chopping out the mortise.

6. Set the gauge by eye so the marks are in the centre of the mortise piece.

7. Check by placing the stock against the other side to see if the spur marks coincide. If they do not coincide, readjust the stock.

8. When the mortise gauge is correctly set, gauge the mortise on both edges from the face side. To set out the tenon leave the gauge at the same setting but adjust the stock if joining woods of different thicknesses.

9. Grip the tenon piece in the vice and gauge around one edge and the end from the face side. Then turn the wood around and gauge the other edge from the face side. Cut the mortise first.

Chopping out a mortise

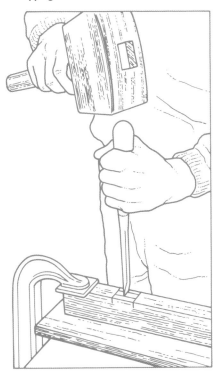

1. Chop from the middle of the mortise.

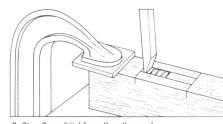

2. Stop 3mm (⅛in) from the other end.

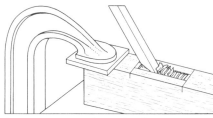

3. Lever out the waste from each end.

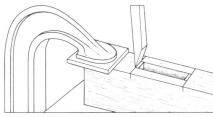

4. Chisel vertically, bevel inwards.

Sawing a tenon

1. Make a level cut.

2. Saw into tilted wood.

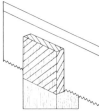

3. Saw to the line.

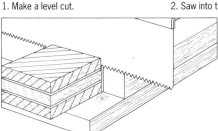

4. Saw off each shoulder.

5. Check the corners for fit.

Wedging a through mortise and tenon

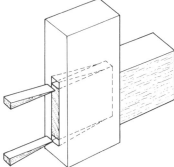

OUTSIDE WEDGES

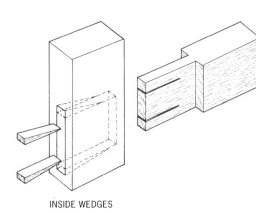

INSIDE WEDGES

Chopping out a mortise

Place the mortise piece on a piece of waste and clamp to the bench. To prevent the wood splitting, the mortise must be chopped halfway through from each side.

1. Make an upright cut in the middle of the mortise, then move the chisel backwards about 3mm (⅛in) at a time with the bevel towards the middle.

2. Stop 3mm (⅛in) from the squared line to allow for compression when levering out the waste. Reverse the chisel and continue from the middle to within 3mm (⅛in) of the other end.

3. Turn the chisel round and lever out the waste from each end towards the centre.

4. Finish by chiselling vertically on the end lines, bevel inwards. Unclamp the mortise piece and shake out any chips. Placing the uncut edge uppermost, reclamp the mortise piece to the bench. Repeat the chiselling and waste removal process to meet the previous cut from the other side of the mortise piece.

Sawing a tenon

Grip the tenon piece upright in the vice. At each stage work on both gauged lines each side of the tenon. Position the saw against the waste side of the gauged line. Tilting it so it bites into the edge of the wood, saw down about 3mm (⅛in).

1. Level out the saw and cut about 3mm (⅛in) down.

2. Regrip the tenon piece at 45°. Saw to the squared line. Turn the tenon piece around and saw the other edge, again at 45°.

3. Grip the tenon piece upright in the vice and saw straight down to the gauged line.

4. With the tenon piece flat, saw off the waste at each shoulder.

5. To check the fit, try each corner of the tenon in the mortise.

Wedging a through mortise and tenon

Wedges give the joint extra strength. They can be inserted outside the tenon or into saw-cuts in the tenon. Extend the mortise on the outside edge by chiselling at an angle 3mm (⅛in) from the squared line to half the mortise depth. If the tenon is tight, grip the mortise piece in the vice so it does not split. Glue and insert the tenon and tap in the wedges alternately. Saw off the excess and plane flush.

A STUB MORTISE AND TENON JOINT

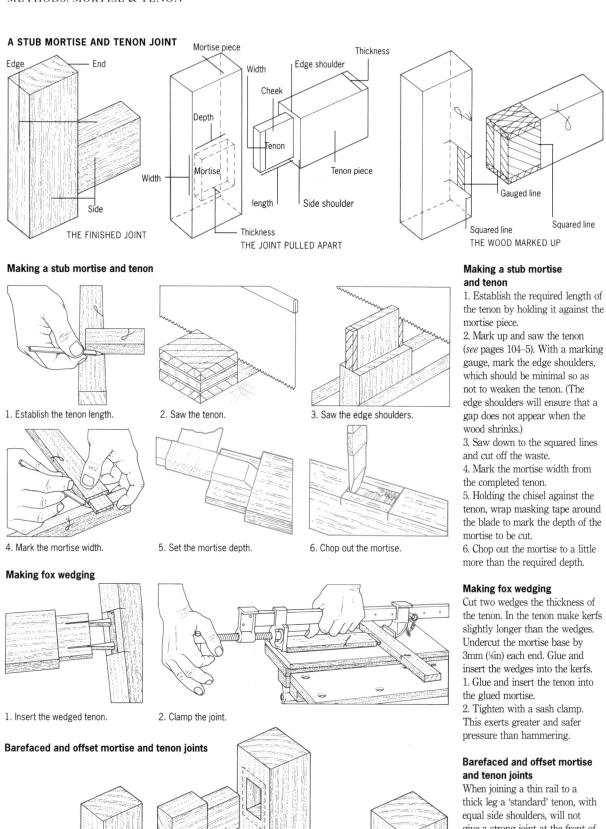

Edge — End
Side

THE FINISHED JOINT

Mortise piece
Width
Depth
Width
Mortise
length
Thickness

THE JOINT PULLED APART

Edge shoulder
Thickness
Cheek
Tenon
Tenon piece
Side shoulder

Gauged line
Squared line
Squared line

THE WOOD MARKED UP

Making a stub mortise and tenon

1. Establish the tenon length.

2. Saw the tenon.

3. Saw the edge shoulders.

4. Mark the mortise width.

5. Set the mortise depth.

6. Chop out the mortise.

Making fox wedging

1. Insert the wedged tenon.

2. Clamp the joint.

Barefaced and offset mortise and tenon joints

TENON WITH ONE SIDE SHOULDER

TENON WITH TWO EDGE SHOULDERS

OFFSET TENON

Making a stub mortise and tenon

1. Establish the required length of the tenon by holding it against the mortise piece.

2. Mark up and saw the tenon (*see* pages 104–5). With a marking gauge, mark the edge shoulders, which should be minimal so as not to weaken the tenon. (The edge shoulders will ensure that a gap does not appear when the wood shrinks.)

3. Saw down to the squared lines and cut off the waste.

4. Mark the mortise width from the completed tenon.

5. Holding the chisel against the tenon, wrap masking tape around the blade to mark the depth of the mortise to be cut.

6. Chop out the mortise to a little more than the required depth.

Making fox wedging

Cut two wedges the thickness of the tenon. In the tenon make kerfs slightly longer than the wedges. Undercut the mortise base by 3mm (⅛in) each end. Glue and insert the wedges into the kerfs.

1. Glue and insert the tenon into the glued mortise.

2. Tighten with a sash clamp. This exerts greater and safer pressure than hammering.

Barefaced and offset mortise and tenon joints

When joining a thin rail to a thick leg a 'standard' tenon, with equal side shoulders, will not give a strong joint at the front of the leg if the rail and leg finish flush. Therefore a barefaced mortise and tenon with only one side shoulder on the tenon is used. If the rail is to finish in the middle of the leg the tenon can have two edge shoulders. If the rail is to be inset from the front of the leg a slightly offset 'standard' tenon can be used.

A BRIDLE JOINT

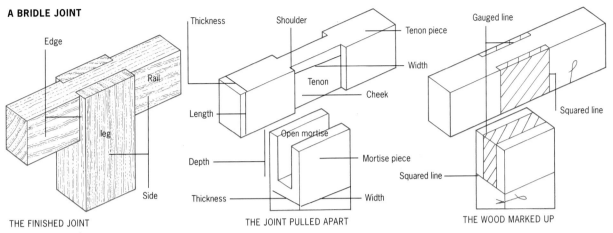

THE FINISHED JOINT THE JOINT PULLED APART THE WOOD MARKED UP

Making a bridle joint

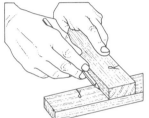
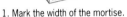
1. Mark the width of the mortise.

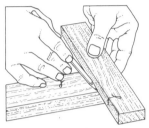
2. Mark the length of the tenon.

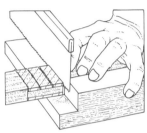
3. Saw down to gauged line.

4. Chisel the waste from the tenon.

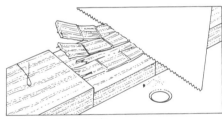
5. Sever the fibres cleanly.

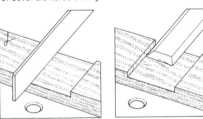
6. Check for flatness.   7. Level out

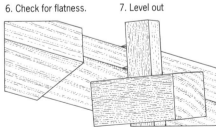
8. Set the mortise gauge for the mortise.

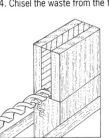
9. Bore out the base.

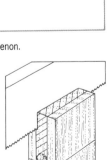
10. Saw to the hole.

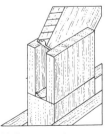
11. Remove waste.

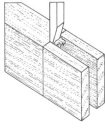
12. Square up.

Making a bridle joint

A bridle joint is a reversed mortise and tenon used where the leg is thicker than the rail.
1. Mark in pencil the width of the mortise on to the tenon. To ensure a tight fit, square all around with a marking knife inside the lines.
2. Mark the length of the tenon on to the top end of the mortise. Square all around the mortise piece. To form the tenon, mark a 5mm (⅜in) recess either side of the tenon piece.
3. Hold the tenon piece on the bench-hook and saw to the gauged line on the waste side. Make one or two saw cuts in the centre of the waste and remove it. Secure the tenon piece in the vice. With a bevel-edged firmer chisel and a mallet begin removing the waste wood. Rest the elbow on the bench and hold the chisel bevel upwards with the hand near the cutting edge. Hold the mallet just below its head.
4. Chisel away a bit at a time halfway across: chiselling directly at the gauged lines may make the wood break away along the grain to a greater depth than required.
5. If the fibres do not come away cleanly, saw slightly deeper into the waste wood to sever them.
6. Check the tenon for flatness.
7. Level out any unevenness, chiselling with hand pressure only, not a mallet.
8. Set the mortise gauge to the thickness of the tenon. Adjust the stock on top of the mortise piece and gauge around for the open mortise.
9. Start cutting the mortise by boring a hole at the base, drilling into the middle from both sides.
10. Saw along each gauged line down to the hole.
11. Remove the waste wood.
12. Square up the bottom of the mortise with a mortise chisel.

A HAUNCHED MORTISE AND TENON JOINT

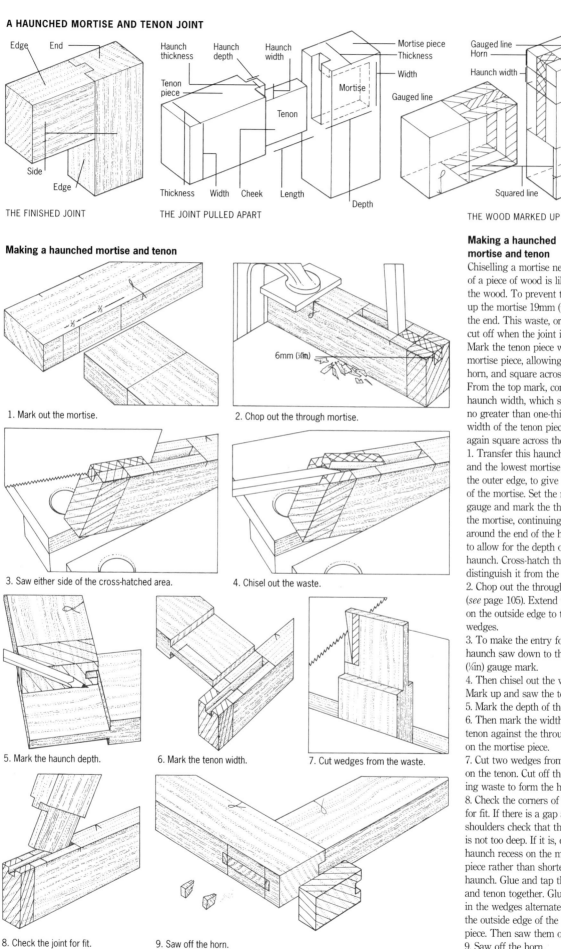

Edge End

Side

Edge

THE FINISHED JOINT

Haunch thickness
Haunch depth
Haunch width
Tenon piece
Thickness   Width   Cheek   Length
Tenon
Depth

THE JOINT PULLED APART

Mortise piece
Thickness
Width
Mortise
Gauged line

Gauged line
Horn
Haunch width
Squared line

THE WOOD MARKED UP

Making a haunched mortise and tenon

1. Mark out the mortise.

2. Chop out the through mortise.

6mm (¼in)

3. Saw either side of the cross-hatched area.

4. Chisel out the waste.

5. Mark the haunch depth.

6. Mark the tenon width.

7. Cut wedges from the waste.

8. Check the joint for fit.

9. Saw off the horn.

Making a haunched mortise and tenon

Chiselling a mortise near the end of a piece of wood is likely to split the wood. To prevent this, mark up the mortise 19mm (¾in) from the end. This waste, or horn, is cut off when the joint is complete. Mark the tenon piece width on the mortise piece, allowing for the horn, and square across one edge. From the top mark, come in the haunch width, which should be no greater than one-third the width of the tenon piece, and again square across the edge.

1. Transfer this haunch mark and the lowest mortise mark to the outer edge, to give the limits of the mortise. Set the mortise gauge and mark the thickness of the mortise, continuing 6mm (¼in) around the end of the horn to allow for the depth of the haunch. Cross-hatch the waste to distinguish it from the mortise.

2. Chop out the through mortise (*see* page 105). Extend the mortise on the outside edge to take the wedges.

3. To make the entry for the haunch saw down to the 6mm (¼in) gauge mark.

4. Then chisel out the waste. Mark up and saw the tenon.

5. Mark the depth of the haunch.

6. Then mark the width of the tenon against the through mortise on the mortise piece.

7. Cut two wedges from the waste on the tenon. Cut off the remaining waste to form the haunch.

8. Check the corners of the tenon for fit. If there is a gap at the shoulders check that the haunch is not too deep. If it is, deepen the haunch recess on the mortise piece rather than shortening the haunch. Glue and tap the mortise and tenon together. Glue and tap in the wedges alternately from the outside edge of the mortise piece. Then saw them off flush.

9. Saw off the horn.

A LONG AND SHORT SHOULDER MORTISE AND TENON JOINT

Edge

Side

Edge

THE FINISHED JOINT

View from face side

End

Tenon piece

Thickness

Width

Rebate

Long shoulder

Haunch

Short shoulder

Tenon

Cheek

Thickness

Depth

Width

Through mortise

Rebate

THE JOINT PULLED APART

Gauged line

Mortise piece

Squared line

THE WOOD MARKED UP

A long and short shoulder mortise and tenon joint

A rebated frame has tenon shoulders of different lengths. The width of the rebate can be variable whereas the depth is made one- or two-thirds the thickness of both mortise and tenon pieces, to coincide with the line of the tenon. Gauge the rebate on both pieces. From these marks set out the joint as for haunched mortise and tenons, ensuring that one shoulder bridges the gap made by the rebate (*see* page opposite). Chop out the through mortise. Then cut the tenon shoulders. Mark the width of the haunch against the through mortise and then cut it. Then cut the rebate (*see* pages 50, 58–9, 63 and 65). Cut the recess for the haunch on the mortise piece. This joint can also be wedged from the outside (*see* page 105) to strengthen it.

A MORTISE AND TENON JOINT WITH A MITRED FRONT

Edge

Side

Edge

THE FINISHED JOINT

Tenon piece   Length   Square shoulder

Cheek

Thickness

Tenon

Mitre shoulder

Width

Thickness

THE JOINT PULLED APART

Open mortise

Width

Mitre

Depth

Gauged line

Mortise piece

Squared line

THE WOOD MARKED UP

Making a mortise and tenon with a mitred front

Mark up the tenon and the open mortise (*see* page 107).
1. Mark the mitres on both pieces with a marking knife.
2. Then cut the mitre on the tenon piece, sawing slightly on the waste side of the marked line.
3. Ccut the tenon on the mitre side, holding the tenon piece at 45° in the vice so the saw cut is vertical.
4. Remove from the vice and pare the mitre on the marked line, using a chisel. Saw on the waste side of the tenon down to the square shoulder; then saw off the waste (*see* page 105). On the mortise piece, start by cutting the mitre just over a third of the way through the wood, finishing the cut accurately with the chisel.
5. To form the mortise, first bore out the base, drilling halfway in from each edge. Then saw down to the hole on the gauged lines.
6. Remove the waste and trim the base with the chisel.

Making a mortise and tenon with a mitred front

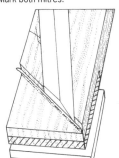
1. Mark both mitres.

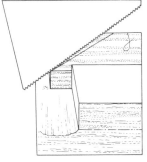
2. Saw close to the line.

3. Saw the tenon.

4. Chisel the tenon mitre.

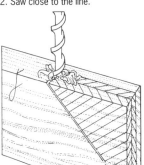
5. Bore out the mortise base.

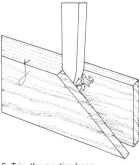
6. Trim the mortise base.

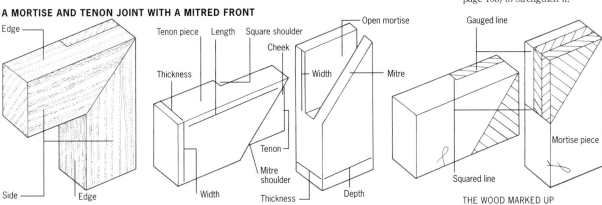

A PROJECTED AND WEDGED MORTISE AND TENON JOINT

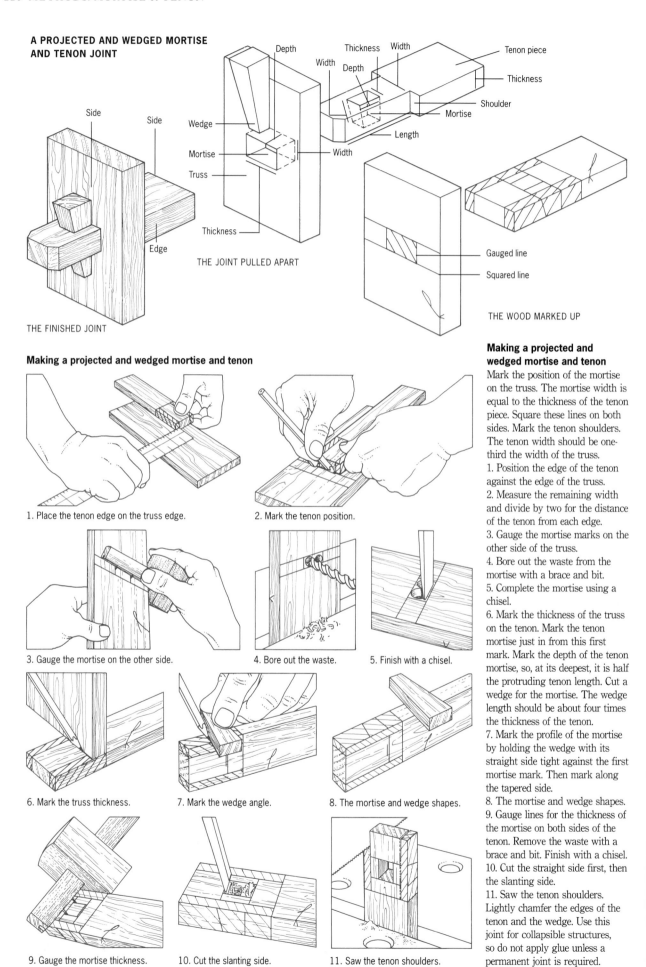

THE FINISHED JOINT

THE JOINT PULLED APART

Side
Side
Edge
Wedge
Mortise
Truss
Thickness
Depth
Width
Depth
Thickness
Width
Depth
Shoulder
Mortise
Length
Width
Tenon piece
Thickness

Gauged line
Squared line

THE WOOD MARKED UP

Making a projected and wedged mortise and tenon

1. Place the tenon edge on the truss edge.

2. Mark the tenon position.

3. Gauge the mortise on the other side.

4. Bore out the waste.

5. Finish with a chisel.

6. Mark the truss thickness.

7. Mark the wedge angle.

8. The mortise and wedge shapes.

9. Gauge the mortise thickness.

10. Cut the slanting side.

11. Saw the tenon shoulders.

Making a projected and wedged mortise and tenon

Mark the position of the mortise on the truss. The mortise width is equal to the thickness of the tenon piece. Square these lines on both sides. Mark the tenon shoulders. The tenon width should be one-third the width of the truss.

1. Position the edge of the tenon against the edge of the truss.

2. Measure the remaining width and divide by two for the distance of the tenon from each edge.

3. Gauge the mortise marks on the other side of the truss.

4. Bore out the waste from the mortise with a brace and bit.

5. Complete the mortise using a chisel.

6. Mark the thickness of the truss on the tenon. Mark the tenon mortise just in from this first mark. Mark the depth of the tenon mortise, so, at its deepest, it is half the protruding tenon length. Cut a wedge for the mortise. The wedge length should be about four times the thickness of the tenon.

7. Mark the profile of the mortise by holding the wedge with its straight side tight against the first mortise mark. Then mark along the tapered side.

8. The mortise and wedge shapes.

9. Gauge lines for the thickness of the mortise on both sides of the tenon. Remove the waste with a brace and bit. Finish with a chisel.

10. Cut the straight side first, then the slanting side.

11. Saw the tenon shoulders. Lightly chamfer the edges of the tenon and the wedge. Use this joint for collapsible structures, so do not apply glue unless a permanent joint is required.

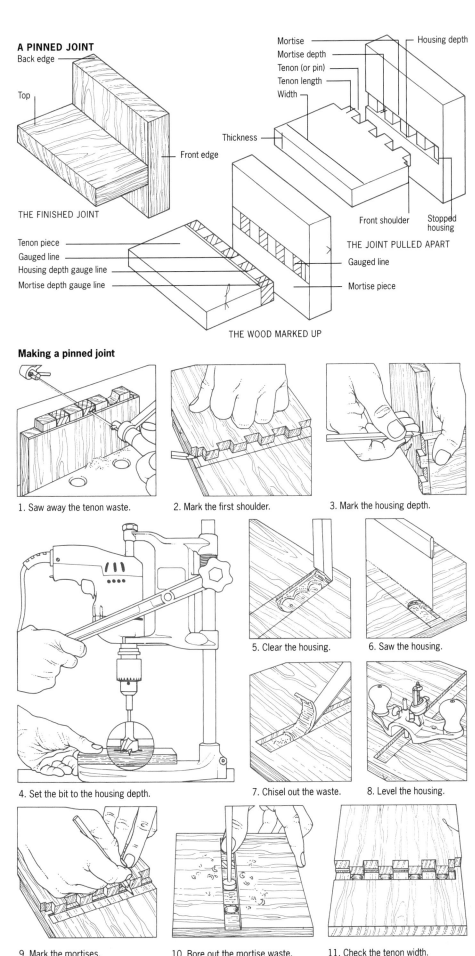

A PINNED JOINT

Back edge

Top

Front edge

THE FINISHED JOINT

Tenon piece

Gauged line

Housing depth gauge line

Mortise depth gauge line

THE WOOD MARKED UP

Mortise

Mortise depth

Tenon (or pin)

Tenon length

Width

Thickness

Housing depth

Front shoulder

Stopped housing

THE JOINT PULLED APART

Gauged line

Mortise piece

Making a pinned joint

1. Saw away the tenon waste.

2. Mark the first shoulder.

3. Mark the housing depth.

4. Set the bit to the housing depth.

5. Clear the housing.

6. Saw the housing.

7. Chisel out the waste.

8. Level the housing.

9. Mark the mortises.

10. Bore out the mortise waste.

11. Check the tenon width.

Making a pinned joint

Mark the thickness of the tenon piece on the mortise piece in pencil. Then mark just inside the line with a marking knife to ensure a tight fit. Set the cutting gauge to the mortise depth and gauge around the tenon piece, except on the back edge. Gauge around 3mm (⅛in) inside the first line except on the front edge. This gives the housing depth. The front edge of the mortise piece takes the form of a stopped housing. Gauge the front shoulder line on the top, end and bottom of the tenon piece 10mm (⅜in) from the edge, as far as the housing gauge mark. Mark the front of the first tenon a further 10mm (⅜in) in from the front edge to guard against splitting. Gauge this line on the top, end and bottom to the mortise depth gauged line. Divide the remaining width of the tenon piece into equal spaces for the tenons. Gauge the width for each tenon on the top, end and bottom of the tenon piece, between the mortise gauge marks. Saw off the front shoulder. Then saw down the sides of the tenons on the waste side of the lines.

1. Remove most of the waste with a coping saw. Finish with a chisel.
2. Place the tenon piece on the mortise piece and mark the position of the front shoulder.
3. Mark the depth of the housing on the edge of the mortise piece.
4. Set a Forstner bit to drill to this depth. Bore a series of overlapping holes at the end of the housing to form clearance for the saw when cutting the sides of the housing.
5. Remove the waste at the stopped end of the housing with a chisel.
6. Saw down the housing sides.
7. Chisel out the waste.
8. Level out the housing to 3mm (⅛in) with a router.
9. From the tenons, mark the positions of the mortises in the housing, making sure the face edges are coincident. Set the Forstner bit against the front edge of the mortise piece to drill to the depth of the tenons.
10. Bore out most of the waste for the mortises with the Forstner bit.
11. Before chopping out the mortises, check the width of the individual tenons against them. Chisel out the waste, and try the joint. If it is too tight, plane the bottom of the tenons; do not attempt to widen the housing. This joint has a large gluing area, making it particularly strong.

A KNUCKLE JOINT

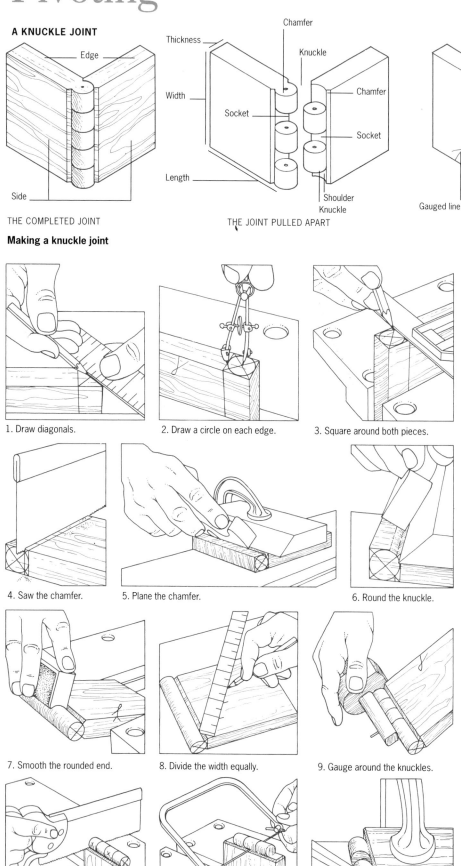

Edge

Side

THE COMPLETED JOINT

Chamfer

Thickness

Knuckle

Width

Socket

Chamfer

Socket

Length

Shoulder
Knuckle

THE JOINT PULLED APART

Gauged line

Squared chamfer line

THE WOOD MARKED UP

Making a knuckle joint

1. Draw diagonals.

2. Draw a circle on each edge.

3. Square around both pieces.

4. Saw the chamfer.

5. Plane the chamfer.

6. Round the knuckle.

7. Smooth the rounded end.

8. Divide the width equally.

9. Gauge around the knuckles.

10. Saw between the knuckles.

11. Remove the waste.

12. Shape the curve.

Making a knuckle joint

The pieces must be of equal thickness. Set the cutting gauge to the thickness of the wood; gauge round the sides and edges of both pieces.

1. Draw diagonals on the edges.
2. Set a compass to half the wood thickness and draw a circle on each edge.
3. Position a try square where the diagonals bisect the circumference of the circle near the gauged line and square around the sides and edges of both pieces to mark the chamfer lines.
4. With a dovetail saw, cut along each chamfer line to the circle. Before forming the chamfers, make a 45° backing piece; clamp it behind the chamfer line.
5. Plane the chamfer flush with the backing piece.
6. Partly round the knuckles from the chamfers using the shoulder plane. Round the end of the wood to the circle mark using first a smoothing plane and then the shoulder plane. With a gouge make a concave-shaped sanding block to fit the curve.
7. Using the block and a coarse and then a fine abrasive paper, smooth the rounded end of the work-piece.
8. Divide the width of the work-piece equally by the total number of pins in the knuckle (in this case, five).
9. Set the gauge for each mark and gauge around the knuckles from the face edge on each piece. Hatch in the waste areas.
10. Saw between the knuckles on the waste side of each gauged line allowing for a filed finish. Saw off the shoulders.
11. Remove the waste between the knuckles with a coping saw. Chisel the sockets clean.
12. Chisel the curve on the shoulders with a rocking motion and an in-cannel gouge.

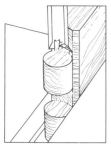

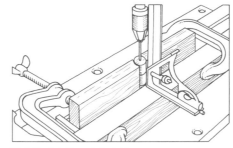

13. Pare the shoulders.

14. File the knuckles.

15. Drill a hole through the joints.

13. Pare vertically with an in-cannel gouge to the knuckle.
14. For a smooth movement, file the knuckle surfaces lightly and test the joint for friction. Complete the rounding of the sockets with a narrow chisel. Clamp the joint.
15. Bore a hole through the centre of the joint, working from both sides. To keep the drill vertical, position a try square alongside the bit or use a drill stand. Insert a steel pivoting rod through the hole and cut it flush.

A rule joint

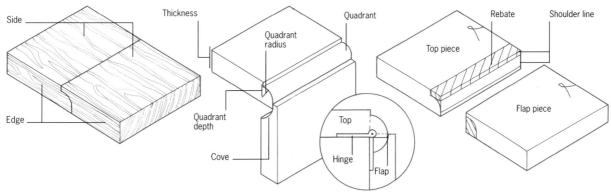

THE JOINT WITH FLAP UP

THE JOINT WITH FLAP DOWN

SECTION THROUGH JOINT

THE WOOD MARKED UP

Making a rule joint

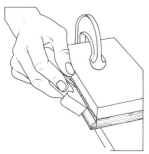

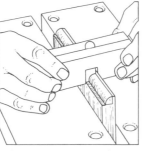

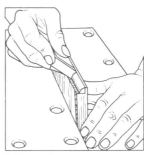

1. Plane to the quadrant mark.

2. Shape with a scratch stock.

3. Smooth the quadrant.

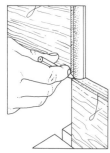

4. Mark the cove.

5. Form the cove.

6. Shape with the scratch stock.

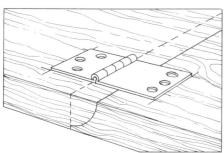

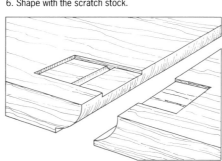

7. Mark around each hinge.

8. Chisel the knuckle recess.

Making a rule joint

Glue waste to the edges. Finger gauge a line 3mm (⅛in) down from the face side of the top along the end and both edges. Repeat on the underside. Set a plough plane to this distance – the radius of the quadrant – and cut rebates on the face of the top and underside of the flap. Square the shoulder line down one edge of the top; where it intersects the bottom shoulder line is the circle centre. Draw the quadrant with a compass.
1. Clamp a square backing piece flush with the shoulder and plane to the quadrant mark.
2. Shape the quadrant finally with a scratch stock made to fit.
3. Smooth the quadrant using a shaped sanding block.
4. Mark the cove from the quadrant. Chamfer the cove edge of the flap against a 45° backing piece.
5. Roughly form the cove profile with an out-cannel gouge.
6. Check the profiles of the edges together, then finish with the cove cutter in the scratch stock. Smooth. Chisel and plane off the waste wood. Square the rebate line around to the underside of the top.
7. Align the hinges, knuckles up and centred on the line. Mark around each hinge.
8. Chop out flap recesses with a scooping action. Mark and chisel the knuckle recess.

Dovetail

A CARPENTERS' THROUGH DOVETAIL JOINT

Edge

Side   End   End   Side

THE FINISHED JOINT

Socket piece

Tail piece

Socket   Pin   Tail   Shoulder

THE JOINT PULLED APART

Half thickness of socket piece

6mm (¼in)

Gauged line   Gauged line

THE WOOD MARKED UP

Dovetail proportions

6

1

SOFTWOODS

8

1

HARDWOODS

USING A DOVETAIL TEMPLATE

Dovetail proportions

The optimum slope for a dovetail is 1 in 6 for softwoods and 1 in 8 for hardwoods. Softwood cells compress more easily and so require a steeper slope. Too steep a slope produces a sharp dovetail, leaving weak, short grain at the corners. Too shallow a slope would be ineffective as the joint could be pulled apart. For repeated marking, make a dovetail template from hardwood or aluminium.

Making a carpenters' through dovetail

1. Set the gauge to the wood thickness.

2. Set out the tails.

3. Mark the tail slopes.

4. Saw the tails

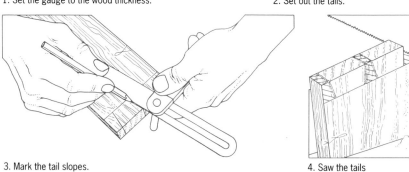

5. Cut the shoulders carefully.

6. Remove most of the waste.

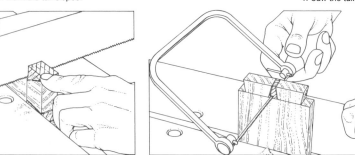

Making a carpenters' through dovetail

1. Set the cutting gauge to the wood thickness. Gauge the thickness of the socket piece all around the tail piece and the thickness of the tail piece on both sides of the socket piece. On each end of the tail piece mark in from the edge a distance equal to half the thickness of the socket piece. Measure the distance between the lines marked on the end as there should be a 6mm (¼in) gap for a pin between each tail. Subtract 6mm (¼in) for each pin.
2. Divide the remainder by the required number of tails to give the width of the tails.
3. Mark the tail slopes using a dovetail template or sliding bevel. Secure the wood in the vice at a slant so the saw cuts are vertical.
4. Saw on the waste side of the lines. Then change the angle of the tail piece and make the cuts on the other side of the tails. If the saw wanders from the marked line, continue in a straight line. (The sockets will be cut to fit the tails.)
5. Saw off the shoulders on the waste side of the line, keeping a finger against the waste to prevent it from suddenly falling away and causing the saw to slip.
6. Remove most of the waste between the tails quickly and neatly with a coping saw.

8. Chalk the end of the socket piece.

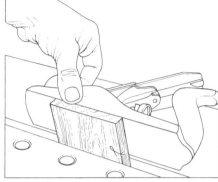

9. Line up the plane with the socket piece.

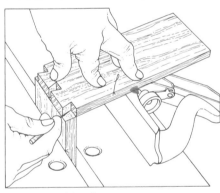

10. Mark around the tails.

7. Chisel out the remainder of the waste. Using as wide a chisel as possible, chop halfway through the tail piece, first from one side then from the other. Chop near the line first, chisel upright, bevel outwards. Then chop precisely on the line. When only a few tails are being made, a quick and simple method is to hold the wood by sitting on it. Mark the sockets directly from the tails. Use the following method whenever possible as it is simple, quick and accurate.

8. Rub chalk all over the end of the socket piece so that any scribed marks will show up clearly.

9. Lay a plane on its side close to the vice and secure the socket piece in the vice with the end level with the top of the plane. Tighten the vice and push the plane away. Rest the tail piece on the plane and the end of the socket piece, keeping the edges flush and the shoulders in line with the inside surface of the socket piece.

10. Mark round the tails with a scriber.

11. Square the marked lines down to the cutting gauge mark. Place the socket piece back in the vice, projecting it only slightly to minimize vibration.

12. Make vertical saw cuts just inside the scribed lines. Remove most of the waste with a coping saw.

13. Finish by chopping out the sockets with a chisel held at an angle, following the slope of the tail. Chisel halfway from each side.

14. Remove the inside sharp corners of the tails with the chisel to give the sockets a lead-in. Dovetail joints fit correctly only once, so try the joint by tapping only partly into position. Remove, smooth the inside surfaces and glue both pieces.

15. Then, using a piece of waste wood to spread the pressure, hammer the joint home.

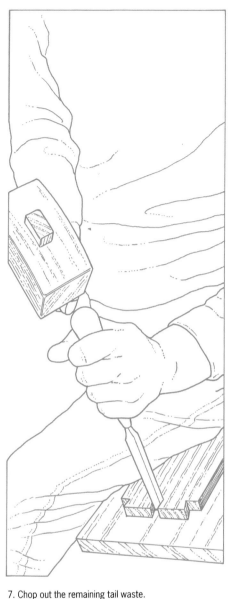

7. Chop out the remaining tail waste.

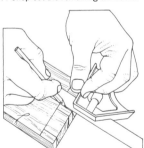

11. Square the lines down.

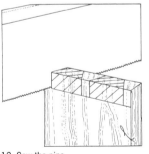

12. Saw the pins.

13. Chop out the sockets.

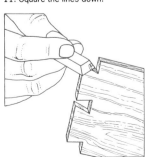

14. Remove the sharp corners.

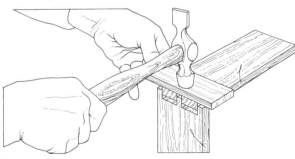

15. Tap the joint home.

A CABINETMAKERS' DOVETAIL JOINT

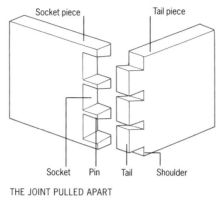

Socket piece   Tail piece

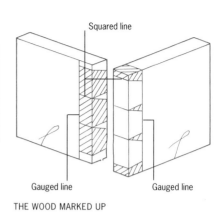

Squared line

Edge

Side   End   End   Side

THE FINISHED JOINT

Socket   Pin   Tail   Shoulder

THE JOINT PULLED APART

Gauged line   Gauged line

THE WOOD MARKED UP

Making a cabinetmakers' dovetail

1. Square the tail marks.

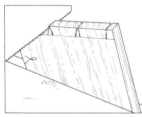

2. Make the vertical saw cuts.

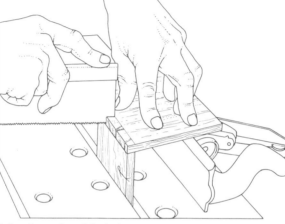

3. Draw the saw through the kerfs.

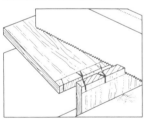

4. Saw the socket piece.

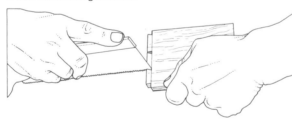

5. Clean out the waste with the saw tip.

Experienced cabinetmakers' method

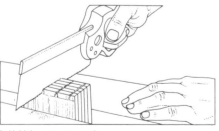

1. Hold the saw at an angle.

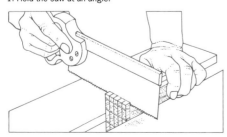

2. Saw off the shoulders.

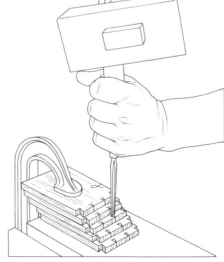

3. Chop out the tails.

Making a cabinetmakers' dovetail

Set the cutting gauge to the thickness of the tail piece and gauge round the socket piece. Set it to the thickness of the socket piece and gauge round the tail piece. Chalk all over the tail piece end grain; then mark and square across 6mm (¼in) from each end. Divide the distance between by the number of tails required.

1. Square across and mark in the tail slopes.

2. Cut the tails. Chalk the end of the socket piece and set it upright in the vice. Rest the tail piece on the plane and the edge of the socket piece.

3. Draw a dovetail saw through each of the kerfs. Square the marks down the face side.

4. Align the tail piece with the socket piece, and saw just to the side of the marked line. Remove the waste with a coping saw and finish the sockets with a chisel. Chop out the tails with a 3mm (⅛in) bevel-edged chisel.

5. Clean out the waste using the chisel and the dovetail saw's tip.

Experienced cabinetmakers' method

Mark up the tails on all the relevant pieces. Put all the tail pieces together upright in the vice.

1. Make all the saw cuts for one side of the tails first, holding the saw at the angle of the tail slope. Then make all the cuts for the other side of the tails. Chalk and mark the socket pieces, pairing them with individual tail pieces.

2. Clamp the tail pieces back in the vice and saw off the shoulders. Stagger the tail pieces one on top of the other, and clamp. Chop the tails halfway through on each piece. Turn the wood over.

3. Stagger and clamp the pieces. Complete the tails. Stagger and clamp the socket pieces similarly and chop out the pins and sockets.

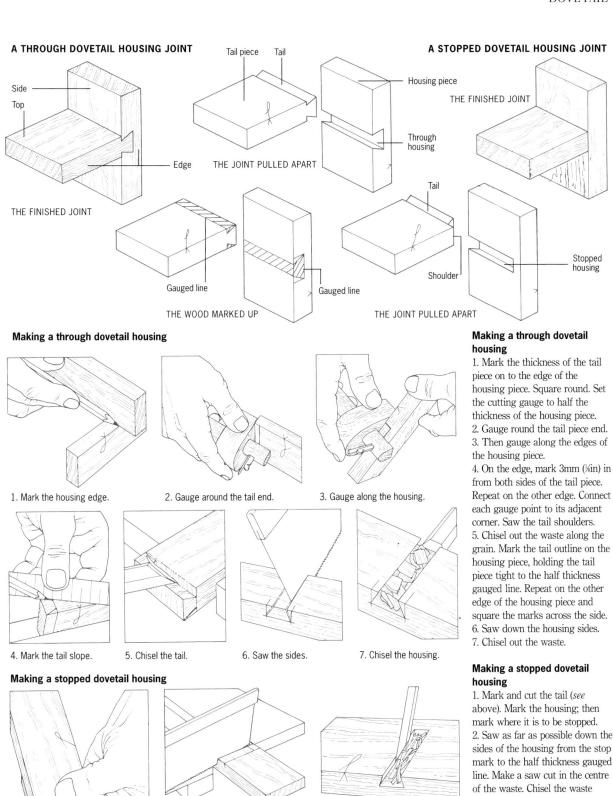

A THROUGH DOVETAIL HOUSING JOINT

Side
Top
THE FINISHED JOINT
Edge

Tail piece   Tail
THE JOINT PULLED APART

Housing piece
Through housing

A STOPPED DOVETAIL HOUSING JOINT

THE FINISHED JOINT

Gauged line
THE WOOD MARKED UP
Gauged line

Tail
Shoulder
THE JOINT PULLED APART

Stopped housing

Making a through dovetail housing

1. Mark the housing edge.
2. Gauge around the tail end.
3. Gauge along the housing.

4. Mark the tail slope.
5. Chisel the tail.
6. Saw the sides.
7. Chisel the housing.

Making a stopped dovetail housing

1. Mark the stopped housing.
2. Saw down the housing sides.
3. Chisel out the housing.

4. Mark the tail length.
5. Saw off the waste.

Making a through dovetail housing

1. Mark the thickness of the tail piece on to the edge of the housing piece. Square round. Set the cutting gauge to half the thickness of the housing piece.
2. Gauge round the tail piece end.
3. Then gauge along the edges of the housing piece.
4. On the edge, mark 3mm (⅛in) in from both sides of the tail piece. Repeat on the other edge. Connect each gauge point to its adjacent corner. Saw the tail shoulders.
5. Chisel out the waste along the grain. Mark the tail outline on the housing piece, holding the tail piece tight to the half thickness gauged line. Repeat on the other edge of the housing piece and square the marks across the side.
6. Saw down the housing sides.
7. Chisel out the waste.

Making a stopped dovetail housing

1. Mark and cut the tail (*see* above). Mark the housing; then mark where it is to be stopped.
2. Saw as far as possible down the sides of the housing from the stop mark to the half thickness gauged line. Make a saw cut in the centre of the waste. Chisel the waste horizontally, going no deeper than the saw cuts. (Or bore a series of overlapping holes along the housing, using a Forstner bit set to the half thickness gauged line.)
3. Chisel the waste from the houseing, starting vertically in the middle: work towards the sides.
4. Mark the housing length on to the tail.
5. Saw off the waste at the tail shoulder. Saw it off across the grain first.

A THROUGH DOVETAIL JOINT WITH MITRE

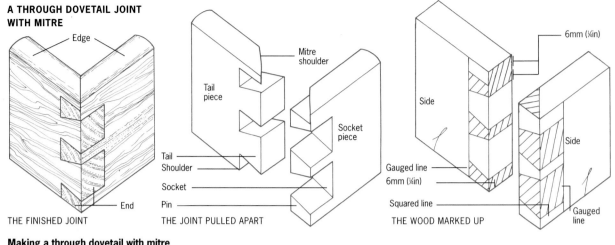

Edge

Mitre shoulder

Tail piece

Socket piece

Side

6mm (¼in)

Side

Tail Shoulder

Socket

Pin

Gauged line 6mm (¼in)

Squared line

End

Gauged line

THE FINISHED JOINT

THE JOINT PULLED APART

THE WOOD MARKED UP

Making a through dovetail with mitre

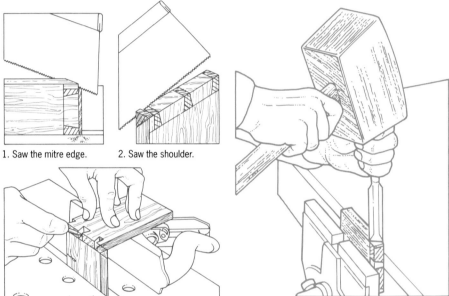

1. Saw the mitre edge.

2. Saw the shoulder.

3. Mark sockets from the tail piece.

4. Finish the mitre with a chisel.

Making a through dovetail with mitre

Both pieces must be the same thickness. Set the gauge to this thickness and mark the sides and bottom edge of the tail piece. Gauge both sides of the socket piece. Mark the mitre on the face edge of both pieces with a marking knife. Mark 6mm (¼in) from the face edge of the tail piece for the mitre shoulder and then another 6mm (¼in). Mark 6mm (¼in) in from the bottom edge. Set out the tails between these marks.
1. Saw the mitre edge on the tail piece near the mitre. Finish with a chisel.
2. Then saw down to the mitre shoulder. Finish with a chisel. Saw and remove the waste between the tails.
3. Mark the sockets from the tail piece. Saw the mitre.
4. Finish with a chisel. Round the mitre edge with a plane and a fine abrasive.

A THROUGH DOVETAIL JOINT WITH REBATE

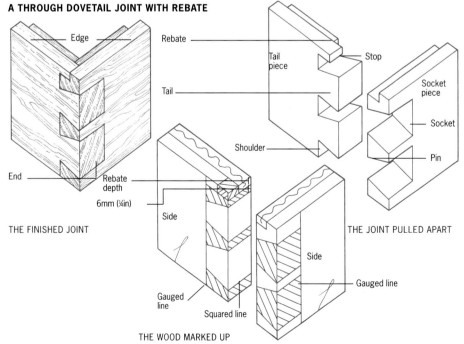

Edge

Rebate

Tail piece

Stop

Tail

Socket piece

Socket

Shoulder

Pin

End

Rebate depth

6mm (¼in)

Side

Side

THE FINISHED JOINT

Gauged line

Squared line

Gauged line

THE JOINT PULLED APART

THE WOOD MARKED UP

Making a through dovetail joint with rebate

Leave a projection on the shoulder of the tail piece to act as a stop for the rebate on the socket piece. Cut the rebates first. Mark in the depth of the rebate on the edge of the tail piece. Mark 6mm (¼in) in from the rebate for the first tail. Mark 6mm (¼in) in from the bottom edge for the last tail. Set out the tails between these marks and make saw cuts between the tails. Remove the waste between the tails. Chalk the end grain of the socket piece. Mark and chop out the sockets (*see* pages 114–15). Cut the rebate shoulder and the shoulder on the bottom edge of the tail piece.

A DECORATIVE THROUGH DOVETAIL JOINT

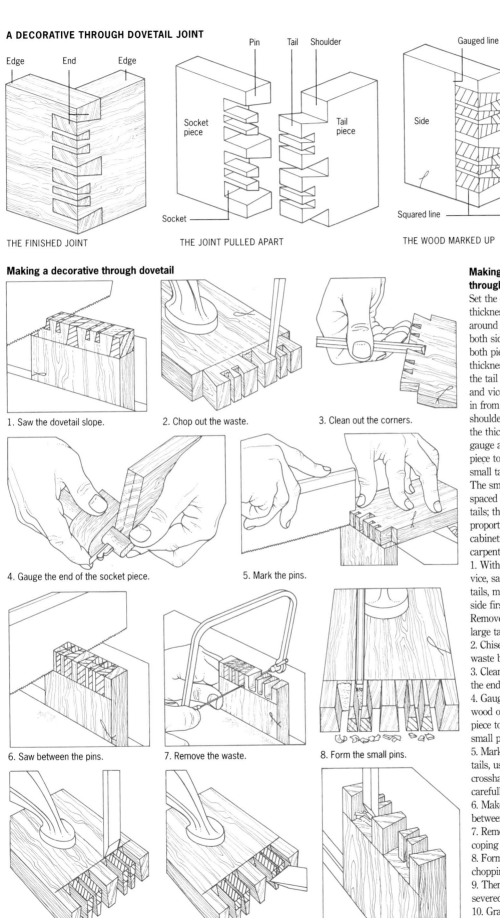

Edge   End   Edge

THE FINISHED JOINT

Pin   Tail   Shoulder

Socket piece

Socket

Tail piece

THE JOINT PULLED APART

Gauged line   Gauged line

Side   Side

Squared line

THE WOOD MARKED UP

Making a decorative through dovetail

1. Saw the dovetail slope.

2. Chop out the waste.

3. Clean out the corners.

4. Gauge the end of the socket piece.

5. Mark the pins.

6. Saw between the pins.

7. Remove the waste.

8. Form the small pins.

9. Chisel to the cut fibres.

10. Work down to gauged line.

11. Chop two pins at once.

Making a decorative through dovetail

Set the cutting gauge to the thickness of the wood and mark around the tail piece and along both sides of the socket piece. (If both pieces are not of the same thickness, set out the thickness of the tail piece on the socket piece and vice versa.) Mark 6mm (¼in) in from each edge for the shoulders. Set the gauge to half the thickness of the wood and gauge across the sides of the tail piece to give the length of the small tails. Set out the tails. The small tails need not be spaced equally within the large tails; they should be finely proportioned – more like cabinetmakers' dovetails than carpenters' dovetails.

1. With the wood upright in the vice, saw down the slopes of the tails, making all the cuts on one side first. Saw off the shoulders. Remove the waste between the large tails with a coping saw.

2. Chisel out any remaining waste between the tails.

3. Clean out the corners. Chalk the end of the socket piece.

4. Gauge half the thickness of the wood on the end of the socket piece to mark the depth of the small pins.

5. Mark the pins from the tails, using a saw. Hatch and crosshatch the waste areas carefully.

6. Make vertical saw-cuts between the pins.

7. Remove the waste with a coping saw.

8. Form the small pins by chopping across the grain.

9. Then chisel as far as the severed fibres.

10. Gradually work down to the half thickness gauged line.

11. Using a wide chisel, chop out two pins at once for a cleaner line.

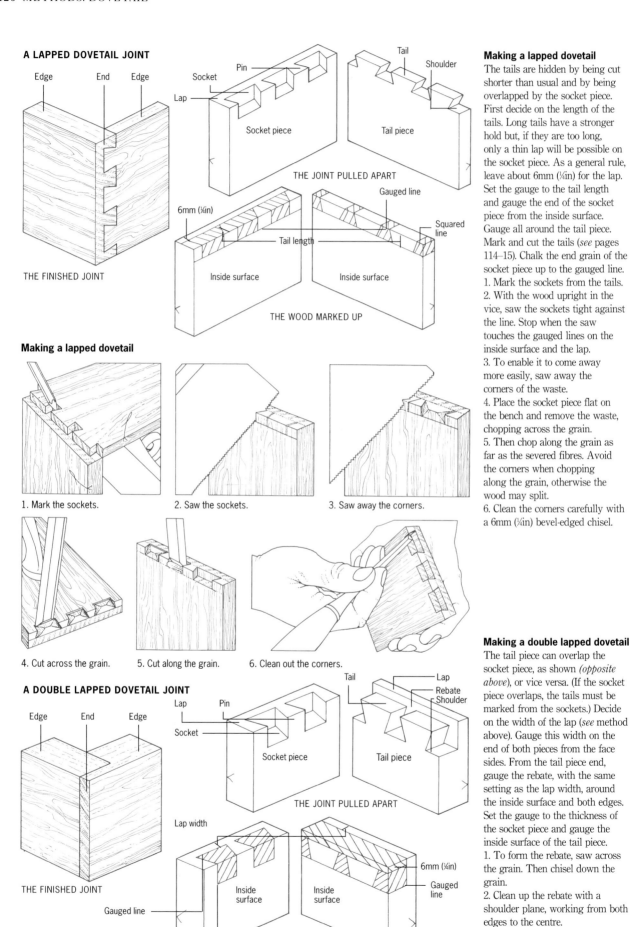

A LAPPED DOVETAIL JOINT

Edge   End   Edge

THE FINISHED JOINT

Socket
Lap
Pin

Socket piece

THE JOINT PULLED APART

Tail
Shoulder

Tail piece

6mm (¼in)

Gauged line

Tail length

Squared line

Inside surface   Inside surface

THE WOOD MARKED UP

Making a lapped dovetail

1. Mark the sockets.   2. Saw the sockets.   3. Saw away the corners.

4. Cut across the grain.   5. Cut along the grain.   6. Clean out the corners.

A DOUBLE LAPPED DOVETAIL JOINT

Edge   End   Edge

THE FINISHED JOINT

Gauged line

Squared line

Lap   Pin
Socket

Socket piece

Tail   Lap
Rebate
Shoulder

Tail piece

THE JOINT PULLED APART

Lap width

6mm (¼in)
Gauged line

Inside surface   Inside surface

THE WOOD MARKED UP

Making a lapped dovetail

The tails are hidden by being cut shorter than usual and by being overlapped by the socket piece. First decide on the length of the tails. Long tails have a stronger hold but, if they are too long, only a thin lap will be possible on the socket piece. As a general rule, leave about 6mm (¼in) for the lap. Set the gauge to the tail length and gauge the end of the socket piece from the inside surface. Gauge all around the tail piece. Mark and cut the tails (*see* pages 114–15). Chalk the end grain of the socket piece up to the gauged line.

1. Mark the sockets from the tails.
2. With the wood upright in the vice, saw the sockets tight against the line. Stop when the saw touches the gauged lines on the inside surface and the lap.
3. To enable it to come away more easily, saw away the corners of the waste.
4. Place the socket piece flat on the bench and remove the waste, chopping across the grain.
5. Then chop along the grain as far as the severed fibres. Avoid the corners when chopping along the grain, otherwise the wood may split.
6. Clean the corners carefully with a 6mm (¼in) bevel-edged chisel.

Making a double lapped dovetail

The tail piece can overlap the socket piece, as shown *(opposite above)*, or vice versa. (If the socket piece overlaps, the tails must be marked from the sockets.) Decide on the width of the lap (*see* method above). Gauge this width on the end of both pieces from the face sides. From the tail piece end, gauge the rebate, with the same setting as the lap width, around the inside surface and both edges. Set the gauge to the thickness of the socket piece and gauge the inside surface of the tail piece.

1. To form the rebate, saw across the grain. Then chisel down the grain.
2. Clean up the rebate with a shoulder plane, working from both edges to the centre.
3. Mark 6mm (¼in) in from each edge of the tail piece and set out the tails between these marks.

Making a double lapped dovetail

1. Saw the rebate for the lap.

2. Clean up the lap.

3. Set out the tails.

A SECRET MITRE DOVETAIL JOINT

Edge

THE FINISHED JOINT

Mitre

Mitre shoulder

Socket

Socket piece

Tail

Mitre shoulder

Mitre

Pin

THE JOINT PULLED APART

End

Inside surface

Inside surface

6mm (¼in)

End

Gauged line

Squared line

THE WOOD MARKED UP

Gauged line

Making a secret mitre dovetail

1. Mark the mitre on the edges.

2. Mark the pins with the template.

3. Saw the mitre edge.

4. Form the mitre lap.

5. Mark the tails from the pins.

6. Saw the mitre.

7. Chop out the waste.

Remove the waste at the shoulders and between the tails in the same way as chopping out the sockets in the lapped dovetail joint. Chalk the end grain of the socket piece and mark the sockets from the tails. Saw and chisel away the waste, cutting the corners away first to ease the chiselling process.

Making a secret mitre dovetail

Both pieces must be the same thickness. Set the cutting gauge to the thickness of the wood and gauge the inside surfaces of both pieces from the end. To mark the rebates, set the gauge to 6mm (¼in) and, on both pieces, gauge the end from the face side and the inside surface from the end.

1. Mark the mitre on the edges of both pieces, using a knife or chisel. Square the rebate line down to the mitre line on both edges. Cut both rebates (see method above). For this joint it is necessary to form the pins and sockets before the tails. Chalk the end of the socket piece. Mark lines 6mm (¼in) in from the edge of the rebate on the socket piece, parallel to the edge. Then mark in a further 6mm (¼in).

2. Mark the pins using a cardboard template the same width as the widest part of the tails and with the required slope on each side. For marking in a rebate, a cardboard template is more convenient than a wooden one, which would be awkward and the sliding bevel could not be adjusted close enough. Square the marks down the inside surface.

3. Saw the mitre edges on each side. Then saw down to the mitre shoulders. Chop out the sockets in the same way as in the lapped dovetail joint. Place a backing piece, cut and planed to 45°, behind the socket piece and align it with the top of the mitre shoulder. Secure it in position so it supports the plane.

4. Form the mitre lap with a shoulder plane. (The backing piece is needed as the mitre area is so small.

5. Mark the tails from the pins on the inside surface of the tail piece. Square the lines into the rebate.

6. Saw the mitre.

7. Then chop out the waste between the tails and the waste between the mitre shoulders and the tails. Plane the mitre lap.

A BEVELLED DOVETAIL JOINT

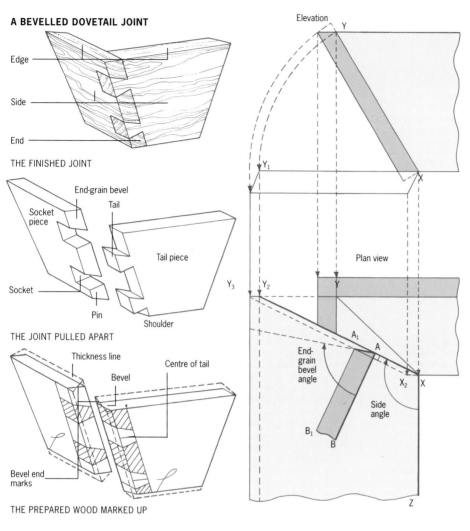

Edge

Side

End

THE FINISHED JOINT

Socket piece

End-grain bevel

Tail

Tail piece

Socket

Pin

Shoulder

THE JOINT PULLED APART

Thickness line

Centre of tail

Bevel

Bevel end marks

THE PREPARED WOOD MARKED UP

Elevation

Y

Y_1

X

Plan view

Y_3 Y_2 Y

End-grain bevel angle

A_1 A

X_2 X

Side angle

B_1

B

Z

Making a rod for a bevelled dovetail

Before this joint can be made, the true shape of the end must be obtained from a rod, or full-size drawing, because the sides as seen in elevation and in plan are sloping and are therefore foreshortened. Draw the elevation showing the slope and the thickness of the wood. Directly underneath, draw the plan view. If the side elevation is pivoted to lie flat, the true shape is seen when looking straight down on it. On paper in the elevation, pivot Y around X to Y_1. Project Y_1 vertically to Y_2, that is, until the line is level with Y in the plan view. Join X in the plan to Y_2. The angle between XY_2 and XZ is the angle of the sides. To work out the end-grain bevel angle, draw the outside edge of the side on the plan (Y_3X_2). From any point on line XY_2, draw a line AB at right angles . Draw a line A_1B_1 parallel to AB, the thickness of the wood away, reaching to line Y_3X_2. Join A to A_1. The angle between AB and AA_1 represents the end-grain bevel angle.

Preparing the pieces for jointing

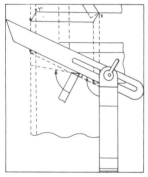

1. Set the side angle.

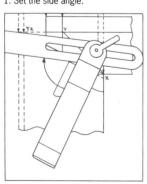

3. Set the end-grain bevel.

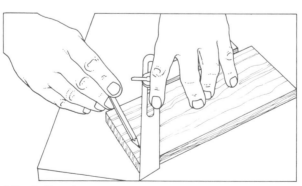

2. Transfer the angle.

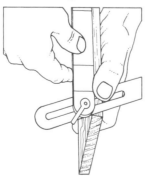

4. Mark this on the edges.

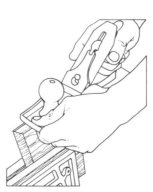

5. Plane the end grain.

Preparing the pieces for jointing

Both pieces of wood must be the same thickness.
1. Set the side angle using a sliding bevel against the rod.
2. Transfer the angle to both pieces of wood. Saw and plane the ends. Check the angles with the sliding bevel.
3. Set the sliding bevel to the end-grain bevel angle against the rod.
4. Mark this angle on the top and bottom edges of each piece. Connect up the lines along the inner and outer sides of each piece.
5. Plane the end grain to these lines. Check with the sliding bevel.

Cutting the tails and sockets

1. Mark out the thickness of the wood.

2. Saw the tail slopes.

3. Chop out the waste.

4. Mark the socket lines parallel with the edges.

A MACHINE DOVETAIL JOINT

Side

Groove

Front

A

B

Back

C

D

Side

PARTS OF A DRAWER OR BOX

Stop screws

Stop screws

B

A

C

D

B

C

D

A

ORDER OF CUTTING THE JOINTS

Making a machine dovetail

1. Insert the guide collar.

Clamping bar

A

B

Stop screws

Clamping bar

2. Clamp the pieces in the jig.

3. Clamp the template on top.

4. Cut the joint.

5. Let the bit cut each tail.

6. The completed cut.

Cutting the tails and sockets

1. Mark the thickness of the wood on both sides of each piece. Set out the centres of the tails parallel to the top edge. Then set out each tail relative to its centre line. Place the wood in the vice so one set of tail slopes is vertical.

2. Cut these. Change the angle and complete the cuts. Connect the two thickness lines across the edges. With the thickness lines vertical, saw off the shoulders. Saw out the waste between the tails.

3. Chop out the remaining waste, working to the centre from each side. Chalk and mark the socket piece from the tails (see page 115).

4. Mark the socket lines on the side parallel with the edges. With socket lines vertical, saw away most of the waste. Chop out the sockets. Plane a bevel on the top and bottom edges so they are horizontal when the joint is put together. The angle is the same as the end-grain bevel.

Making a machine dovetail

Through or lapped dovetail joints can be cut with the power router fitted with a dovetail bit guided by a jig and template. Both sides of the joint are cut at the same time. The sides are offset against stops so that, as the router follows the template fingers, it cuts the recess between tails in the vertical piece at the same time as it cuts a socket in the horizontal piece. For a four-sided box or drawer, mark the pieces and make the cuts in the order shown. Always cut a joint in waste pieces first to determine the depth of cut. If the drawer sides are grooved to take the bottom, cut the groove first.

1. Insert the template guide collar into the router sole plate. This will ride against the template. Cut and plane the pieces to size.

2. Clamp them with face sides against the jig and the ends flush and abutting against the stop screws on the jig; this will automatically give the required amount of offset. Use the stop screws on the left or the right according to which of the four corners are being jointed.

3. Clamp the template on top.

4. To cut the joint, run the router fully round the contour of the template fingers.

5. The guide collar runs against the template, while below it the bit makes the tail cut.

6. When the cut is done, unclamp the pieces and cut the next joint.

Housing

A THROUGH HOUSING JOINT

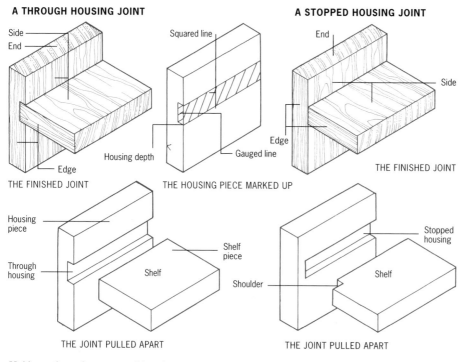

Side
End
Squared line
Housing depth
Gauged line
THE FINISHED JOINT
THE HOUSING PIECE MARKED UP

A STOPPED HOUSING JOINT

End
Side
Edge
THE FINISHED JOINT

Housing piece
Through housing
Shelf piece
Shelf
THE JOINT PULLED APART

Stopped housing
Shoulder
Shelf
THE JOINT PULLED APART

Making a through or stopped housing

1. Mark the shelf thickness.

2. Gauge the housing depth.

3. Chisel on the lines.

4. Chisel horizontally.

5. Level with a hand router.

6. Chisel the stopped end square.

A BAREFACED HOUSING JOINT

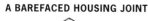

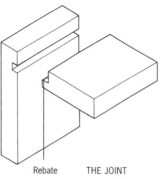

THE FINISHED JOINT

Rebate
THE JOINT PULLED APART

Housing width
Thickness
Housing depth
THE WOOD MARKED UP

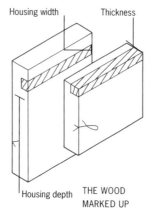

Making a through or stopped housing

1. Mark the thickness of the shelf piece on the side of the housing piece with a marking knife or a chisel. Square the lines across the face side and down both edges.
2. Set the marking gauge to one-third of the thickness of the housing piece and gauge the housing depth between the squared lines on both edges. With a bevel-edged chisel and mallet cut across the grain inside the squared lines.
3. Then chisel on the lines.
4. To provide shoulders for the hand router to run against, chisel horizontally to a depth of approximately 3mm (⅛in). Work into the centre from both edges.
5. Level the housing with a router. Test the joint for fit; if it is too tight, plane a shaving off the bottom of the shelf piece. (For other methods *see* pages 50, 58–9, 63, 65, 111 and 117.) In a stopped housing joint a shoulder must be cut in the face edge of the shelf piece. Mark the thickness of the shelf on the housing piece in pencil. Square the lines down the rear edges, and gauge the housing depth between these marks. With the gauge at this setting, gauge around the face side, underside and face edge of the shelf. Decide how far in from the edge the housing will be stopped and cut a shoulder at this point on the shelf piece. Re-mark the thickness of the shelf on the housing with a marking knife or chisel. Mark the stopped end of the housing. Clear the stopped end by drilling a few overlapping holes with a Forstner bit. Chisel shoulders for the saw to run against.
6. Chisel the stopped end square. Cut the housing in the same way as the through housing joint.

A barefaced housing joint

Pencil the thickness of the top on the housing piece. Square the marks down the edges. Mark the housing width to one-third of this measurement. Square the lines down the edges. Gauge the housing depth from the inside surface. Cut the housing. Gauge the housing width on the end of the top and gauge the depth on the edges. Saw across the grain down to the gauged marks. Gradually chisel down to the sawn line. Finish the rebate with a shoulder plane.

Dowel

A DOWEL JOINT

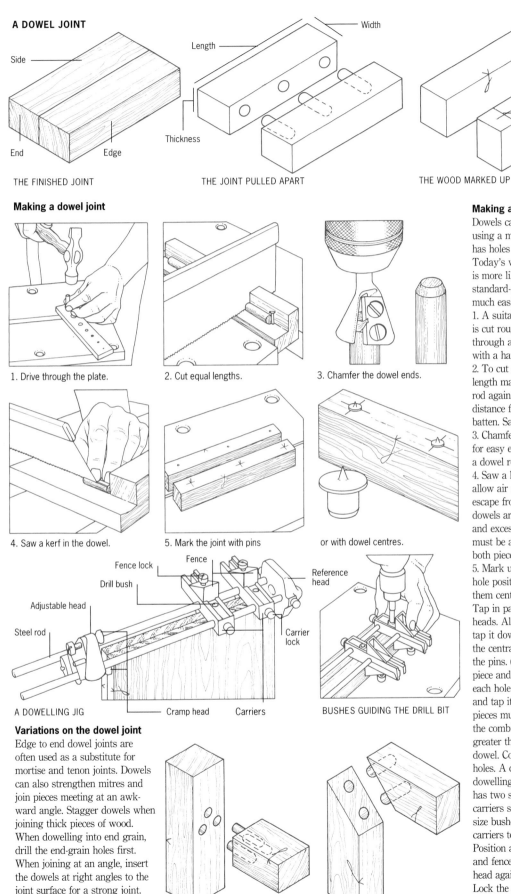

Side

End · Edge

Length

Width

Thickness

THE FINISHED JOINT

THE JOINT PULLED APART

Squared line

Gauged line

THE WOOD MARKED UP

Making a dowel joint

1. Drive through the plate.

2. Cut equal lengths.

3. Chamfer the dowel ends.

4. Saw a kerf in the dowel.

5. Mark the joint with pins

or with dowel centres.

Fence lock

Fence

Drill bush

Adjustable head

Steel rod

Reference head

Carrier lock

A DOWELLING JIG

Cramp head

Carriers

BUSHES GUIDING THE DRILL BIT

Variations on the dowel joint

Edge to end dowel joints are often used as a substitute for mortise and tenon joints. Dowels can also strengthen mitres and join pieces meeting at an awkward angle. Stagger dowels when joining thick pieces of wood. When dowelling into end grain, drill the end-grain holes first. When joining at an angle, insert the dowels at right angles to the joint surface for a strong joint. Clamp the wood at an angle so that the holes are drilled vertically wherever possible.

EDGE TO END JOINT

DOWELLED MITRE JOINT

Making a dowel joint

Dowels can be made and sized using a metal dowel plate which has holes of varying sizes. Today's woodworker, however, is more likely to use proprietary, standard-sized dowels that are much easier and more reliable.

1. A suitable hardwood, eg, beech, is cut roughly to size and driven through an appropriate hole plate with a hammer.

2. To cut all dowels to the same length make a jig. Butt the dowel rod against a nail the required distance from a kerf in the back batten. Saw through the kerf.

3. Chamfer both ends of the dowel for easy entry into the hole or use a dowel rounder.

4. Saw a kerf along the dowel to allow air and surplus glue to escape from the hole. Modern dowels are fluted to allow air and excess glue out. Dowel holes must be accurately aligned in both pieces.

5. Mark up one piece, squaring the hole positions across and gauging them centrally along the wood. Tap in panel pins and cut off their heads. Align the second piece and tap it down. Remove it, revealing the central impressions. Remove the pins. (Or, drill holes in the first piece and insert a dowel centre in each hole. Align the second piece and tap it down.) All holes in both pieces must be the same depth, the combined depth being slightly greater than the length of the dowel. Countersink all dowel holes. A dowelling jig makes dowelling easier. The type shown has two steel rods on which two carriers slide. Select the correct size bushes and insert in the carriers to guide the drill bit. Position and tighten the carriers and fences, with the reference head against one end of the work. Lock the adjustable head against the other end. Drill the holes in one piece. Invert the jig and drill the second piece.

Edge, tongue & groove

A RUBBED GLUE JOINT   **A TONGUED AND GROOVED JOINT**   **A SLOT-SCREWED JOINT**

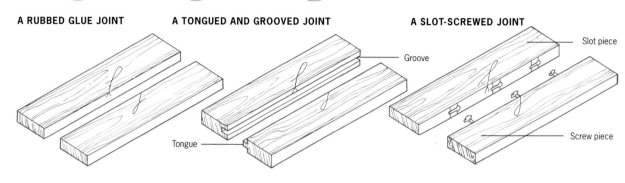

Groove

Tongue

Slot piece

Screw piece

Making a rubbed glue joint

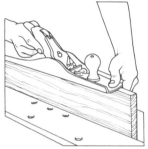

1. Plane the first edge.

2. Check the mating edge.

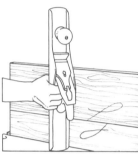

3. Check the alignment.

4. Glue both edges.

5. Rub the edges together.

6. Check the joint.

Making a tongued and grooved joint

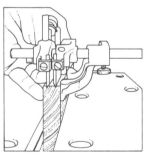

1. Make a cut at one end.

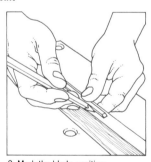

2. Mark the blade position.

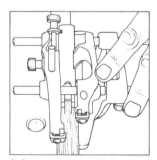

3. Centre the tonguing blade.

Making a slot-screwed joint

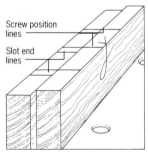

Screw position lines

Slot end lines

1. Square slot lines across.

2. Gauge along the edges.

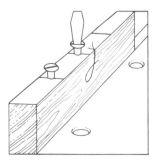

3. Insert the screws.

Making a rubbed glue joint

1. Hold one piece in the vice and plane the edge with the longest bench plane available. Try to plane a hollow in the centre of the piece. The length of the plane will make this difficult, but the attempt will help to stop the ends being rounded over. Finish planing by taking one continuous shaving. Check for perfect squareness.
2. Plane the mating edge similarly, checking it continually by moving it against the first edge to feel for points of friction at the ends.
3. Check the alignment of the sides with the plane edge.
4. Hold the edges of both pieces in contact, and glue them.
5. Rub the edges together to remove any air. Clamp the joint with three sash clamps for even pressure.
6. Apply light pressure at first; then tighten, checking the evenness of the joint as the pieces are tapped down flush.

Making a tongued and grooved joint

Cut the whole joint with a plough plane or use a router.
1. To centre the groove, make a cut at one end with the rebating blade. Then reverse the plane and make a second cut. When the cuts coincide, cut the groove.
2. Lay the rebating blade centrally on the edge of the tongue piece and mark its position.
3. Guided by the marks, centre the tonguing blade and cut the tongue.

Making a slot-screwed joint

Select the face sides and mark. Mark screw positions 44mm (1¾in) from each end and at intervals of 150mm (6in). Place the pieces in the vice with the screw piece offset by 13mm (½in). Square screw position lines across both pieces.
1. Square slot lines across the slot piece 13mm (½in) to the left of the screw position marks.
2. Gauge half the wood thickness along the marked edges.

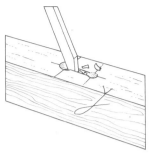

4. Bore holes at the slot ends.

5. Chisel the slots.

6. Tap the ends flush.

3. Insert the screws, leaving the heads projecting by 13mm (½in). Bore holes for the screw-heads in the slot piece on the screw position marks, 13mm (½in) deep.
4. Drill holes to take the shanks at the end of the slot lines, 13mm (½in) deep.
5. With a narrow chisel, cut slots 13mm (½in) deep.
6. Fit the larger holes in the slot piece over the screws and tap the ends flush.

A MITRE JOINT WITH LOOSE TONGUE

A KEYED MITRE JOINT

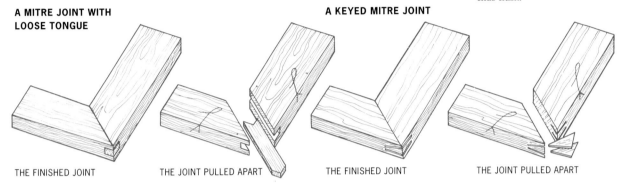

THE FINISHED JOINT   THE JOINT PULLED APART   THE FINISHED JOINT   THE JOINT PULLED APART

Making a mitre joint with loose tongue

1. Mark the tongue width.

2. Measure across the mitre.

3. Gauge around the mitre.

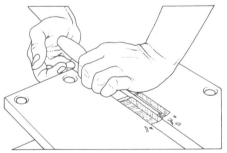

4. Chisel the groove.

5. Mark the waste on the tongue.

Making a keyed mitre joint

1. Saw two kerfs.

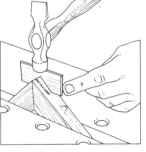

2. Tap the key into the kerfs.

3. Saw the keys off flush.

Making a mitre joint with loose tongue

Cut the mitre in a mitre box. Cut a strip of wood for the tongue about one-third of the thickness of the mitred pieces and 16mm (⅝in) wide. Put the mitre pieces together.
1. Lay the tonguing strip centrally on top and mark its width. Square the marked line parallel to the mitre and down both edges. Place the tongue on edge on a mitre end, flush with one side.
2. Measure across what remains of the mitre. Divide by two.
3. Set the marking gauge to this measurement and gauge around the mitre to the squared lines. Saw down the mitre to the squared lines.
4. Chisel the groove in the end of the mitre.
5. Fit the joint together with the tonguing strip in place and mark the waste on the tongue. Remove the tongue; saw it to size. Glue the joint and tongue together.

Making a keyed mitre joint

Cut and glue the mitre pieces; clamp and leave to dry. Position the mitre in the vice so the saw cuts level with the work surface.
1. Cut two kerfs, angling each inwards. Cut the key strips from 2mm (³⁄₃₂in) three-ply or veneer, depending on the size of the kerf.
2. Glue the key strips and kerfs and tap the keys into the kerfs. Allow to dry.
3. Saw the keys off and plane them flush with the joint.

Working manufactured boards

The most common manufactured boards are plywoods (three-ply, multi-ply), blockboard and laminboard, MDF (medium-density fibreboard), chipboard and hardboard. They make maximum use of wood material that might otherwise be wasted, and so they are usually more economical than solid wood. The natural figure in plywoods is generally plain due to the rotary slicing process; chipboard, MDF and hardboard have no figure.

The chief advantage of working with manufactured boards lies in the fact that they do not distort as a result of shrinkage or natural warping. Carcass construction is therefore made considerably simpler because allowance does not have to be made for dimensional change. Distortion in blockboard and laminboard is minimal as the plies sandwiching the solid wood strips restrain the tendency of the growth rings to straighten themselves. Any distortion that might occur in three-ply or multi-ply, where each veneer is laid at right angles to the next, is balanced out by its construction. Chipboard, MDF and hardboard have no natural grain direction across which they can shrink.

Manufactured boards, however, will warp if they are incorrectly stored. Damp boards usually warp and may even disintegrate. They should be stacked vertically against a dry wall resting fully on their edges with the top corners supported and protected from damage. Manufactured boards can only be used outside when specially treated. Tempered hardboard is impregnated with oil, and marine multi-ply is resin bonded, making it water resistant.

In addition to their stability, manufactured boards are particularly useful because they are supplied in large sheets. This makes them particularly suitable for wide, flat components. MDF, three-ply or five-ply are commonly used for panelling, for carcass tops, shelving and doors. For shelving, the solid core strips must run from end to end for greatest support. For doors, the strips should run vertically as screws do not hold in end grain. Chipboard is used mainly in cheap carcass construction, built-in fittings and as a substrate for veneer or plastic laminates.

Cutting

Manufactured boards, unless laminated, may be cut with a panel or a tenon saw in the same way as solid wood. A tenon saw with its fine teeth held almost horizontally is preferable for thin boards. Never use a rip saw. The resin adhesive in marine three-ply and chipboard quickly blunts saw teeth, so for these boards tungsten-carbide-tipped teeth are best. Make sure the saw blade always cuts into the face so any ragged edge that may result will be on the underside. To minimize this ragged edge, stick adhesive tape on the underside along the cutting line. When sawing, support both sides of the board close to the cutting line. To cut a large board, climb on to the workbench and kneel close to the cutting line. Have an assistant support a large overlap to prevent it from snapping off unevenly towards the end. Three-ply that is up to 3mm (⅛in) thick can be scored with a cutting gauge and snapped cleanly in two by holding it along the worktop edge against a stop and pressing on the overlapping piece. A laminated board can be sawn with a panel or tenon saw, but the leading edges on the teeth should be raked back more than usual. Always saw into the laminate and keep the teeth well clear of the laminate on the backward stroke to prevent it from chipping. To hold a laminated board firmly while sawing, clamp two battens close to the cutting line. Place blocks of the same thickness as the laminated board between the two battens at both ends. Then saw halfway across the board from both sides. This will leave a clean edge.

Cutting

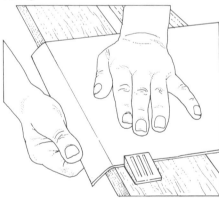

Hold thin ply against the worktop edge.

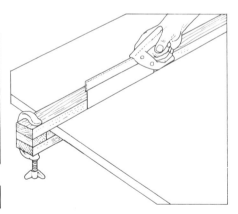

Saw halfway across a laminated board.

Smoothing

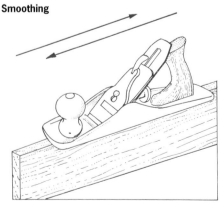

Plane the edges from the ends inwards.

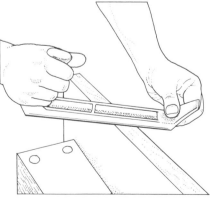

Smooth laminated board edges at an angle.

Smoothing

Wide surfaces of a manufactured board should not be planed, as they are pre-finished. Plane the edges from the ends in. If the plane runs off the end, chipping will occur. Cut resin-bonded boards to exact size to avoid planing as resin blunts the blades. Smooth chipboard edges with a Surform or rasp. Remove the woolly burr left on planed hardboard edges by glasspapering with a sanding block. Smooth the edges of laminated boards away from the laminate and at an angle with a Surform.

The edges of most manufactured boards reveal their construction and are both unsightly and easily damaged if they are not covered either with veneer or with solid wood. This procedure is known as lipping. MDF is the exception: its edges can be treated as for solid wood and can be smoothed and left exposed. It can be lipped if required and provides and excellent base for cabinet construction. Nails, screws and pins should be set somewhere between 100 and 150mm (4 and 6in) and should never be fixed closer than 13mm (½in) to the edges of any manufactured board material as the edges are liable to break. Use a twist drill for boring small holes and a Forstner bit for large holes. Special screws and nails are obtainable for use with some manufactured boards such as chipboard.

It is not always necessary to apply a surface finish as some manufactured boards are sold ready primed and sealed and many are either veneered and sealed or bonded with a plastic laminate. If not previously treated, plywood, MDF and blockboard may be finished in any way suitable for solid wood. Chipboard will require special treatment; all are porous and should be well sealed for finishing.

While plywood and hardboard are conducive to bending, MDF, blockboard and chipboard are rigid. The permissible curvature of plywood depends upon its overall thickness, the thickness and arrangements of its individual veneers and the species of wood used in its manufacture. Three-ply consisting of veneers of equal thickness will bend across the short grain of the outer layers. Synthetic resin bonded plywoods may be soaked in water, or steamed, to aid bending. Hardboard is most flexible when bent with the textured side to the outside of the curve.

LIPPING

VENEER LIPPING LAID SECOND

VENEER LIPPING LAID FIRST

SOLID WOOD LIPPING

FEATHERED LIPPING

GROOVED MULTI-PLY

GROOVED CHIPBOARD

GROOVED LAMINBOARD

LOOSE TONGUE LIPPING

TONGUED MULTI-PLY

PLAIN MDF

ROUNDED-OVER MDF

GROOVED MDF

Lipping
Where edges have split, re-glue them and clamp until dry before lipping. Hardboard is lipped only in combination with solid wood. If veneer lipping is laid after face veneer, the thin lipping edge will show on the face. If the lipping is done first, the face veneer will cover the lipping edge, but there is a risk of the face veneer lifting. To avoid both problems smooth the top edge of the face veneer to a 45° angle. All solid wood lipping that shows on the face side should be mitred. Lipping should be left proud of wide surfaces until the glue has dried. It can then be smoothed to any shape. Apply self-adhesive strip veneer lipping with a warm iron. Edges can also be lipped with solid wood. Feathered lipping does not show on the top surface. Lipping that is tongued and grooved provides the strongest join. Multi-ply, blockboard and chipboard may be grooved. Loose tongues can be used. It is always best to cut the tongue from solid wood if lipping blockboard or chipboard, though a tongue in multi-ply is quite strong. MDF may be finished without lipping. Its fine-textured, uniform structure allows its edges to be cut and smoothed by machine or by hand as with solid wood. It can be left square cut or profiled. When lipped with solid wood the MDF should be grooved and the tongue cut on the lipping.

Fixing

Three-ply, multi-ply and MDF can be fixed with screws or nails against a solid wood frame or another sheet of ply or MDF. Choose nail and screw sizes to ensure a firm grip in the underneath piece. Nails can be used to secure glue joints. Their heads must be left projecting above the surface so they can easily be withdrawn when the glue is dry. As well as fixing with nails, veneer pins, panel pins and oval brads can also be used. When using screws, drill a clearance hole, which can be countersunk. The most durable method of fixing these materials is with a combination of glue and nails or glue and screws. Nails and screws must not be fixed into three-ply and multi-ply edges as they will split the plies. Nails and screws should not be driven

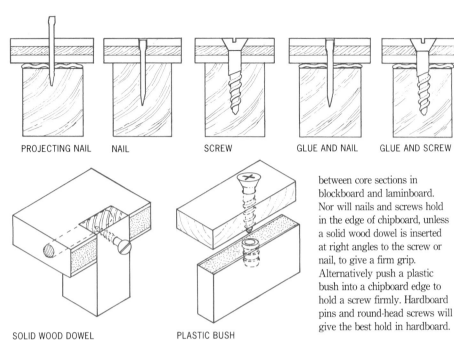

PROJECTING NAIL   NAIL   SCREW   GLUE AND NAIL   GLUE AND SCREW

SOLID WOOD DOWEL

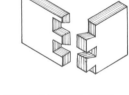

PLASTIC BUSH

between core sections in blockboard and laminboard. Nor will nails and screws hold in the edge of chipboard, unless a solid wood dowel is inserted at right angles to the screw or nail, to give a firm grip. Alternatively push a plastic bush into a chipboard edge to hold a screw firmly. Hardboard pins and round-head screws will give the best hold in hardboard.

Jointing multi-ply

A number of solid wood joints can also be cut in multi-ply. These include the barefaced housing joint and all other housing joints. Joints such as the through dovetail and decorative through dovetail can be cut, provided the tails and pins are coarse.

BAREFACED HOUSING JOINT   THROUGH DOVETAIL JOINT   DECORATIVE THROUGH DOVETAIL JOINT

Jointing boards other than multi-ply

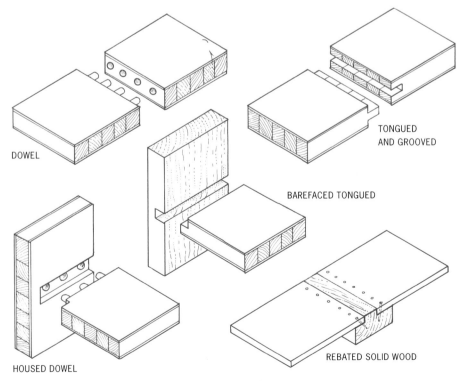

DOWEL

HOUSED DOWEL

BAREFACED TONGUED

TONGUED AND GROOVED

REBATED SOLID WOOD

Jointing boards other than multi-ply

In many respects MDF, blockboard and laminboard can be jointed in the same way as solid wood. Amongst the most suitable joints are dowel joints and housed dowel joints. A tongued and grooved joint can be cut across solid core strips – never along their length. MDF, blockboard and laminboard can be cut under similar conditions for a tongue but not a groove; a loose tongue can also be used. A barefaced tongued joint cut into solid wood is quite strong. Few of the traditional joints can be cut in chipboard as the fibres tend to crumble. Since hardboard is generally used for panelling in conjunction with a solid wood frame, hardboard rarely needs jointing. However, a strip of solid wood double rebated to take a sheet of hardboard on either side and secured with panel pins can make a strong joint for panelling.

Solid wood construction

Every piece of furniture can be classified into one or more of three types of unit – storage, supporting or seating. Each type of unit consists of components assembled into one of three basic constructions – frame, box or stool. From these basic constructions any kind of furniture unit can be made.

Common to all are the allowances for movement of the wood. When a solid board is fixed to another, splitting along their length may occur because wood shrinks across the grain. The development of frame and panel construction allowed for this movement in the wood as the panels are able to move independently of the frame. The direction of movement must be considered when boards have to be joined side edge to side edge, or end to end at right angles as for a corner joint. Wood moves across the grain and the growth rings tend to straighten as the wood dries, causing cupping. Join narrow boards side edge to side edge so that the movement of one board is counteracted by the next. Ideally, join boards with their growth rings at right angles to the wide surface.

Before assembling a carcass, have a preliminary unglued trial to ascertain the order of assembly and to check the fit. Wherever possible, break the carcass down into sub-carcasses each comprising several components, and assemble each unit separately. Assemble and roughly adjust all clamps; prepare any cross-bearers and clamping blocks. Collect the relevant tools: a hammer, a mallet and a striking block of waste wood, a soft pencil, measuring and testing tools, a damp rag for wiping off surplus glue and a quirk stick for cleaning glue out of corners. Mark joints and components with the soft pencil on the face side and number them with the order of assembly. Smooth all inside surfaces and inside all joints with a smoothing plane and abrasive paper. Glue and assemble the components into their parts. Any dowels or loose tongues can be glued into one side only; then check for length. Wipe off all surplus glue before it sets. Check for squareness and leave until the glue has set before assembling the units into a complete carcass. Remove heavy clamps as soon as possible.

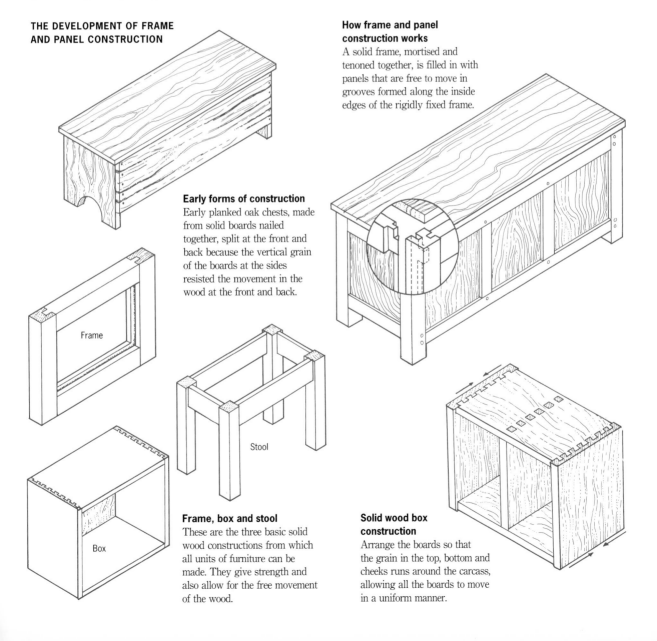

THE DEVELOPMENT OF FRAME AND PANEL CONSTRUCTION

How frame and panel construction works
A solid frame, mortised and tenoned together, is filled in with panels that are free to move in grooves formed along the inside edges of the rigidly fixed frame.

Early forms of construction
Early planked oak chests, made from solid boards nailed together, split at the front and back because the vertical grain of the boards at the sides resisted the movement in the wood at the front and back.

Frame

Stool

Box

Frame, box and stool
These are the three basic solid wood constructions from which all units of furniture can be made. They give strength and also allow for the free movement of the wood.

Solid wood box construction
Arrange the boards so that the grain in the top, bottom and cheeks runs around the carcass, allowing all the boards to move in a uniform manner.

Basic carcass construction

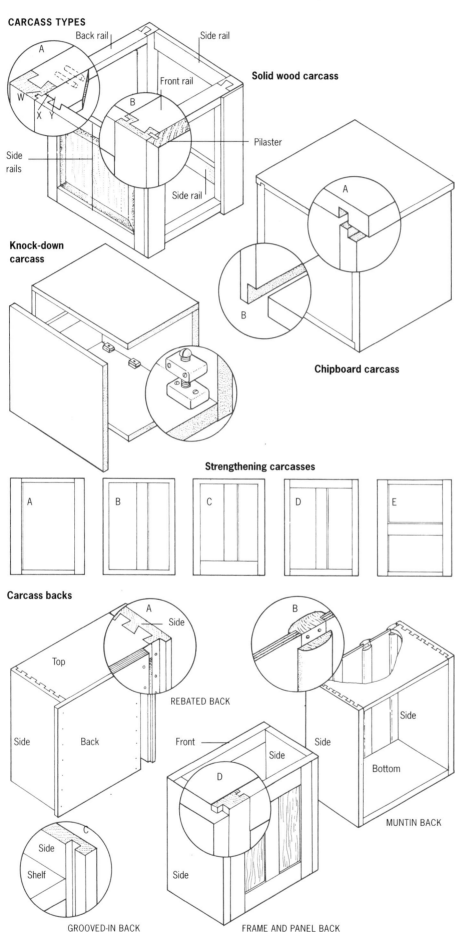

CARCASS TYPES

Back rail

Side rail

A

W

X Y

Side rails

Solid wood carcass

Front rail

B

Pilaster

Side rail

Knock-down carcass

A

B

Chipboard carcass

Strengthening carcasses

A   B   C   D   E

Carcass backs

A

Side

Top

REBATED BACK

Side   Back

B

Side

Side

Bottom

Front

Side

Side

MUNTIN BACK

C

Side

Shelf

D

Side

GROOVED-IN BACK

FRAME AND PANEL BACK

Solid wood carcasses
A. Rails are lap dovetailed to the corner posts, which are mortised to receive the tenons on the side rails. Posts and side rails are grooved to accept fielded panels. **B**. A triangular fillet, dowelled to the front or back rail and dovetailed to the side rail, is often added for strength. The short grain at x is weak and may split, so replace the acute angle at y with a right angle. w can be a tongue in a groove (as shown), or a mortise and tenon. Front pilasters, added for rigidity, may be tongued and grooved or attached with small glue blocks on the inside.

Chipboard carcasses
These can be simpler than solid wood as movement is negligible: tenons and dovetails are weak so corner joints can be **A** barefaced tongued and grooved, **B** rebated or mitred and glue blocked. For other joints *see* page 130. A lap joint can be reinforced by screwing and pelleting.

Knock-down carcasses
Most knock-down fittings, such as the block joint, have been designed for use with chipboard.

Strengthening carcasses
If a carcass is not rigid, doors and drawers can jam, and joints can fail. Methods of ensuring rigidity include fixed shelves and partitions, and **A** adding pilasters secured to the carcass front or back at the sides, **B** at the centre, **C** attached to a bottom rail, **D** in a T or **E** in an H form.

Carcass backs
A back does more than cover a gap: the carcass depends on it for rigidity and stability. **A**. The simplest form of back is a five-ply panel screwed into rebates in the sides and top. The carcass bottom is flush with or overlapped by the back. **B**. A muntin back consists of one or two grooved uprights, or muntins, tenoned or rebated and screwed into the top and bottom with fill-in panels, usually of three-ply. **C**. Hardboard can also be fitted in grooves worked in the sides. The carcass bottom and shelves must be flush with the groove to allow the back panel to slide in after assembly. **D**. A frame and panel back, suitable for a large carcass, can be screwed into a rebate, or tongued and grooved.

PLINTHS

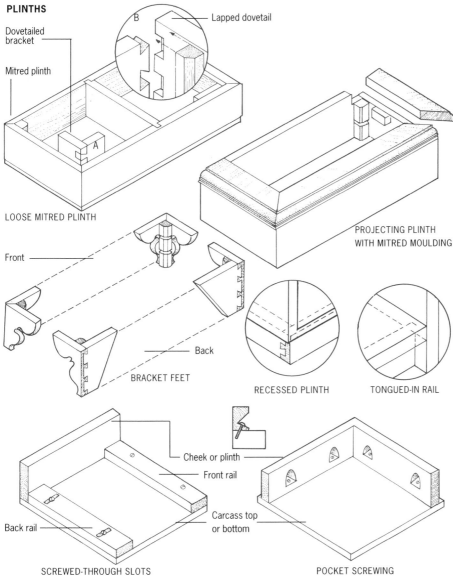

Dovetailed bracket

Mitred plinth

B — Lapped dovetail

A

LOOSE MITRED PLINTH

PROJECTING PLINTH WITH MITRED MOULDING

Front

Back

BRACKET FEET

RECESSED PLINTH

TONGUED-IN RAIL

Cheek or plinth

Front rail

Carcass top or bottom

Back rail

SCREWED-THROUGH SLOTS

POCKET SCREWING

Plinth construction

Complex secret dovetail joints may be used on plinths, but **A** it is more common to make a plain mitre joint at the front, reinforced by a glue block or dovetailed bracket. **B**. The back may be housed into the sides, tongued and grooved or lap dovetailed. A large plinth will require a cross-bearer, housed or slot dovetailed to front and back. A projecting plinth with moulding is constructed with mitred corners. The moulded board supports the carcass and is mitred at the front and glue-blocked in the corners beneath and along the sides. Bracket feet are used on antique and reproduction furniture. Front feet are mitred together and glue-blocked while the back feet are lap dovetailed. Recessed plinths, which do not require precise fitting, allow room to stand up against the furniture. A lapped dovetail at the front is typical. A variation used with cupboards and wardrobes is to bring the cheeks down to floor level and rest the bottom on an inset plinth rail tongued into the cheeks. Plinths and tops can be secured in the same way. Solid wood ones should be fixed by gluing and screwing to the front rails and screwing through slots at the back. Wooden buttons (*see* page 143) or metal shrinkage plates can be used. Plinths and tops of manufactured board can be glued and pocket screwed.

Fixing carcass tops

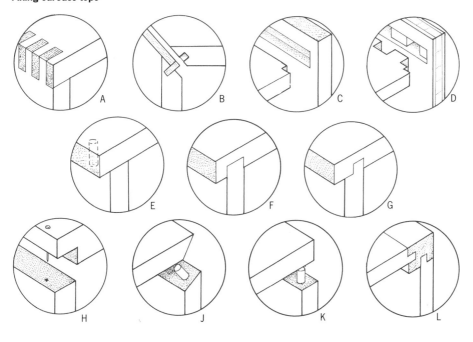

A

B

C

D

E

F

G

H

J

K

L

Fixing carcass tops

Where the top forms an integral part of the carcass and is not screwed on, dovetail or lapped dovetail are the most common joints. Use double lapped and secret mitre dovetails for hidden joints. **A**. A machine-made comb joint can also be worked. **B**. A mitre joint should be reinforced with a loose tongue. **C**. Tops that are set below the top ends of the carcass cheeks can be secured in a stopped housing. **D**. A pinned joint, because of the size of the gluing area, is stronger. With manufactured boards, oversailing tops can be fixed to the cheek ends by **E** dowels, **F** housings or **G** tongues. Flush tops can be **H** rebated, pinned and the holes filled, **J** mitred and dowelled, **K** butted and dowelled or **L** housed in a grooved corner block of solid wood.

Solid wood carcasses

Strong, well-fitting corner joints are necessary for strength and rigidity. In solid wood, **A** secret dovetails with a single lapped joint at the bottom and **B** a double lapped joint at the top are usual. Shelves increase strength and stop the cheeks bowing. All forms of housing joint are suitable, in any materials, although a through housing looks unsightly on the front edge. A stopped housing is neater and preserves the vertical line at the sides of the carcass. Adding stub tenons, making a pinned joint, increases the strength. **C.** A barefaced dovetail housing can be cut only in solid wood; it is strong as it resists any outward pull. The housing is tapered in its length and the shelf is inserted from the rear.

Manufactured board carcass with fixed shelves

Fixed shelves in manufactured boards may be **A** dowelled or **B** tongued to the cheeks. Other methods include knock-down fittings or screwing through the cheeks into the ends of shelves.

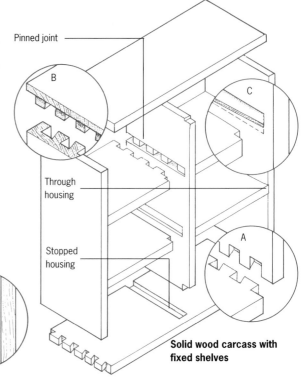

Pinned joint

Through housing

Stopped housing

Solid wood carcass with fixed shelves

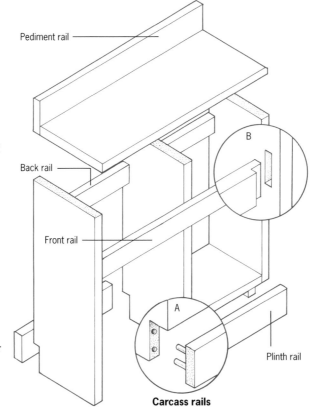

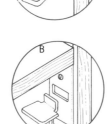

Manufactured board carcass with fixed shelves

Adjustable shelves

Adjustable shelves

These are best made from manufactured boards, which are less likely to warp. **A.** They may be supported by plastic studs tapped into holes in the cheeks; ideally the holes should be fitted with a metal or plastic bush. **B.** Metal bookcase fittings should be let flush into the cheeks. **C.** Magic wires provide concealed fittings (*see* page 159). When adjustable shelves are included it is advisable to have a back panel to ensure rigidity. Increase the strength by fixing one of the shelves permanently in position by the addition of a rail to the front or back, or by screwing through the back panel into the back edge of one or more shelves.

Carcass rails

In the construction of a carcass without a back, such as a bookshelf, that is likely to be subjected to heavy loading and have a tendency to racking, the addition of full-width rails will increase rigidity considerably. Most large knock-down cupboard or shelving units made of chipboard need rails to hold the side panels vertical. They may be pediment rails, front rails, back rails or plinth rails inset under the base. The rails may be lap dovetailed to the cheeks, **A** dowelled, **B** stud tenoned, tongued or secured with a knock-down fitting such as a block joint or a bolt and cross dowel. Rails can be used for fixing the carcass to a wall; this will increase the rigidity in the same way as the addition of a back. Rails may also be used for hanging the carcass.

Pediment rail

Back rail

Front rail

Plinth rail

Carcass rails

Hanging a carcass without a back

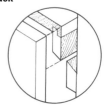

A bevelled rail tongued to the carcass or screwed to the carcass back can hook over a corresponding rail attached to the wall. Flushmount fittings and keyhole plates can also be used, as can cabinet hangers.

Basic frame for a chest of drawers with solids ends

A drawer needs planning at the start as the position of rails, runners, kickers and guides, and how to fix them, must be considered as should a central division. A basic chest of drawers with multi-ply or blockboard sides and bottom should have solid wood carcass rails and a drawer rail stub tenoned to the sides. Runners of solid wood are glued and screwed to the sides.

Basic frame for a chest of drawers in chipboard

A similar unit in chipboard should have solid wood runners screwed to the sides of the carcass and have dowelled rails.

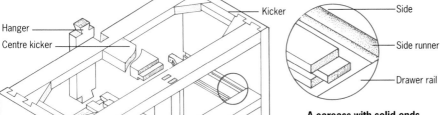

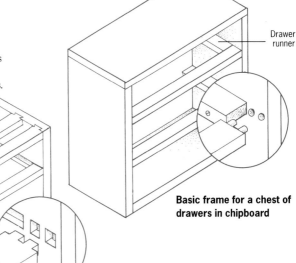

Basic frame for a chest of drawers in chipboard

Basic frame for a chest of drawers with solid ends

A CARCASS WITH A BACK AND DRAWERS

Drawer runner

RAILS, RUNNERS, KICKERS AND GUIDES

Fixing rails

Fix rails with a lapped dovetail. **A**. Use double tails for solid wood if the rail is wide enough. **B**. Make the single tail in block-board extra wide so it will hold in the varying grains of the core.

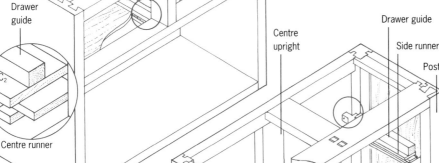

Hanger
Centre kicker
Drawer guide
C$_2$
Centre runner

Kicker
Side
Side runner
Drawer rail

A carcass with solid ends

Centre upright
Drawer guide
Side runner
Post

Drawer rail

Frame and panel carcass

The drawer rails are tenoned into the front posts and are cut around them at the back so that the rail ends touch the side panels. Their back edges are grooved to take the front ends of the side runners, which are stub tenoned. The side runners are set into grooves cut in the back posts and screwed into position. Guides on the side runners fill the space between the posts and the panels.

Frame and panel carcass

A carcass with solid ends

In a solid carcass, a drawer rail is grooved along its back edge, enabling a dustboard to be fixed and providing a means of securing the drawer runners, which are stub tenoned at the front. If no dustboard is required, a groove is cut locally to provide a mortise for the stub tenon. Side runners are grooved and fitted into stopped housings in the sides. No glue is used. At the back the wood is cut away at an angle and secured with a screw. If a centre upright is fitted at the back, it is often possible to cut a groove across it to accommodate the back end of the centre runner. If this is not possible, a hanger must be dovetailed to the top back rail and into the centre runner. Centre runners are stub tenoned to the front rail. Both edges of the centre runner may be grooved for a dustboard. The drawer guide is screwed to the top of the drawer runner. A solid top dovetailed to the sides acts as a kicker to prevent the drawer from tipping forwards when opened. In a carcass with solid ends, short kickers can be tongued into grooves in the rails or fillets. Secure them with two screws into the carcass sides, fixing the back screw in a slot to allow for movement in the wood. A centre kicker is stud tenoned into the front and back carcass rails.

Carcass rail

Drawers

The corners of drawers are always dovetailed into solid wood in quality work. The sides of the drawer are lap dovetailed to the front and through dovetailed to the back. This is a very strong form of construction as the dovetails resist the tendency of the front and back to pull away from the sides while the drawer is being pulled and pushed. One feature of the best hand-made drawers is that the corners of the lapped dovetails almost meet, giving a neat appearance because of the narrow pins. For large drawers, the front should be approximately 22mm (⅞in) thick. Medium-size drawers have fronts about 19mm (¾in) thick, and small drawers about 16mm (⅝in) thick. The sides and back should be kept as thin as possible, from 6–10mm (¼in–⅜in) thick.

Drawer grooves and slips

Groove the inside front to take the drawer bottom. The lowest front pin must be positioned low enough for the groove to be contained in the socket, otherwise the groove will show on the pin. If the sides are thick enough, they too are grooved level with the lowest dovetail. In the best-quality work the sides are too thin, so special grooved slips are glued in place to take the bottom. The simplest slip, commonly used with a three-ply bottom, has a quadrant moulding worked on its top edge. The drawer back must be arranged so that its bottom edge and lowest pin rest on the drawer bottom.

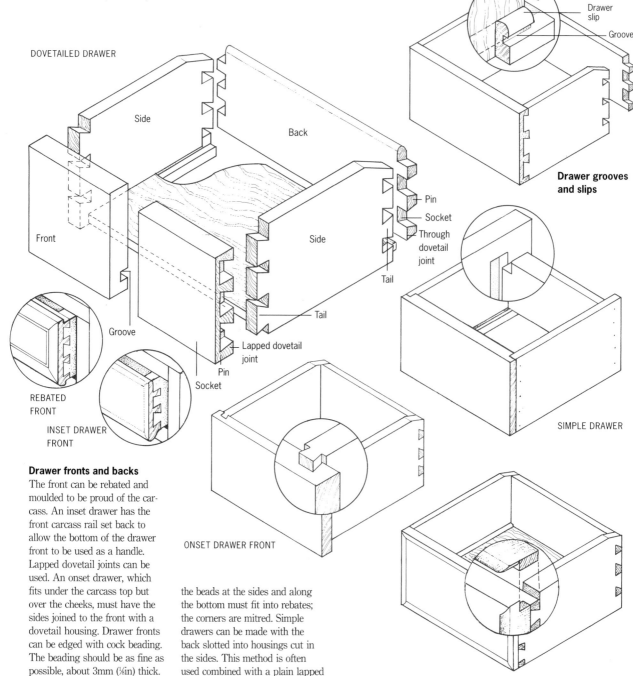

DOVETAILED DRAWER

Side

Back

Front

Groove

REBATED FRONT

INSET DRAWER FRONT

Pin

Socket

Lapped dovetail joint

Tail

Side

Tail

Pin

Socket

Through dovetail joint

Drawer slip

Groove

Drawer grooves and slips

SIMPLE DRAWER

ONSET DRAWER FRONT

COCK BEADING

Drawer fronts and backs

The front can be rebated and moulded to be proud of the carcass. An inset drawer has the front carcass rail set back to allow the bottom of the drawer front to be used as a handle. Lapped dovetail joints can be used. An onset drawer, which fits under the carcass top but over the cheeks, must have the sides joined to the front with a dovetail housing. Drawer fronts can be edged with cock beading. The beading should be as fine as possible, about 3mm (⅛in) thick. The top length of beading covers the top edge of the drawer, but the beads at the sides and along the bottom must fit into rebates; the corners are mitred. Simple drawers can be made with the back slotted into housings cut in the sides. This method is often used combined with a plain lapped dovetail joint between the sides and front.

Drawer bottoms

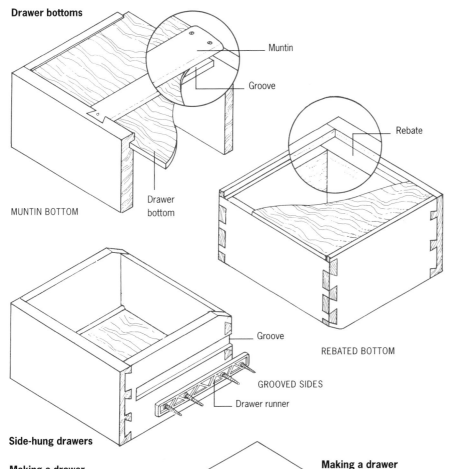

Muntin

Groove

MUNTIN BOTTOM

Drawer bottom

Rebate

REBATED BOTTOM

Groove

GROOVED SIDES

Drawer runner

Side-hung drawers

Making a drawer

Make each drawer to fit its own opening in the carcass. Cut the front and plane the edges to fit, in the correct order. Follow the same procedure for the back, which should have its top edge set down by 6mm (¼in) and its bottom edge resting on the drawer bottom. Fit the sides into the carcass and plane the ends square. Mark each side 'Left' and 'Right', and check they are equal in length. Gauge in grooves for the drawer bottom in the front and sides before marking out the dovetails. Mark mating ends A:A, B:B, C:C and D:D. Mark and cut the dovetails (*see* pages 114–5). Form the grooves; clean up the inside faces. To assemble the drawer, fix the front vertically in the vice, sockets outwards. Glue one side into the front. Remove from the vice. Glue the pins and sockets on the drawer back. Place the back in the vice and partially tap it into the glued side and front. Release from the vice. Place the U-frame, front upwards, on the bench and tap the joints fully home. Glue the tails on the second side. Turn the frame upside down and tap the side home. Wipe off surplus glue and check for squareness. When

Making a drawer

Drawer front

Drawer side

dry, fit the bottom in place but do not secure it yet. Fit the drawer into the carcass, locating tight spots carefully. These are revealed by a shiny surface on the wood when the drawer is pushed in and pulled out of the carcass. Remove them by taking fine shavings with a plane. Clean up the drawer, supporting it with the vice and a board secured with the bench holdfast. If the drawer is racked about, the joints could fail. Then secure the bottom, using a few drops of glue in the front groove and screws or pins to secure the back.

Drawer bottoms

Three-ply is generally used, but make small drawer bottoms from hardboard. If solid wood is used, the grain must run from side to side, or the bottom may be pulled out of the side grooves. Cut the bottom to project at the back and secure it with screws in slots; then if it shrinks it can be unscrewed, tapped forward and re-screwed in place. Fit a muntin down the centre of drawers over 600mm (24in) wide. Dovetail it into the drawer front or stub tenon it. Notch and screw it to the back. For a shallower drawer, a bottom can be rebated in and secured by gluing and pinning.

Side-hung drawers

Modern drawers are often side hung, so the drawer sides must be grooved to take the runners. These are attached to the carcass side. (No guides or kickers are needed.) The runners can be wooden fillets screwed to the sides, or special plastic strips that are secured by pressing projecting studs into holes bored in the sides of the carcass.

Drawer stops

Stops keep the drawer in position and prevent it from hitting the carcass back. Gauge the drawer front thickness on the rail. Glue two stops and place them slightly forward of the gauged line. Carefully slide the drawer into place. Remove it and the stops will be correctly positioned. Fix them with pins.

Drawer front

Drawer bottom

Drawer rail

Hardwood stop

Drawer stops

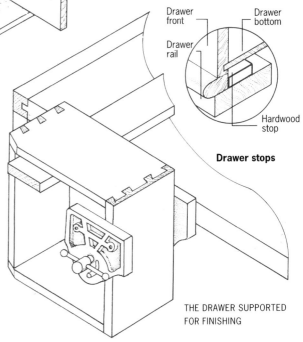

THE DRAWER SUPPORTED FOR FINISHING

Doors

A solid wood framework gives a frame and panel door its strength; it is made using mortise and tenon joints. Horns are left on the stile ends to prevent the wood from splitting during working. The exact construction of the frame depends on the method used to fit the panels. These are simply fill-in pieces and may be of solid wood or five-ply, fitted into grooves or rebates. Grooved-in panels are usually made of five-ply, while fielded and raised panels are normally made of solid wood. Flush panels may be of either material. All types of panels may be beaded into a rebated frame. To allow movement, solid wood panels must never be glued, and no glue should squeeze out of the joints during assembly. As it does not move as much as solid wood, five-ply may be glued to stiffen the structure. The panel area may be divided into smaller sections by muntins acting as vertical dividers. These are often used purely for visual effect, but they help to stiffen the panel area. Muntins are stub tenoned and glued in place.

Panel and frame construction

A grooved-in panel made from a manufactured board that is to have a brushed or sprayed surface finish should be assembled in its frame before finishing. If the finish is applied another way, or if the panel is of solid wood, the surface should be coated before assembly. Framed carcass backs need no finish. A haunched mortise and tenon is used for the frame. With a rebated frame, the panel can be fitted after assembly and application of a surface finish. A long and short shoulder joint is used. The panel is beaded in from the back. Moulding may be applied to the front edges of a plain frame to form a rebate. The panel is beaded in. In good moulded and rebated frames the moulding is worked in the solid. It is cut away locally at the mortise and mitred.

DOOR PARTS
1. Horn
2. Meeting stile
3. Hinging stile
4. Top rail
5. Middle rail
6. Bottom rail
7. Muntin
8. Top panels
9. Bottom panel

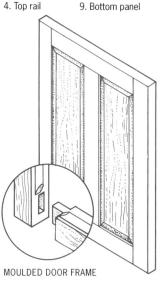

MOULDED DOOR FRAME

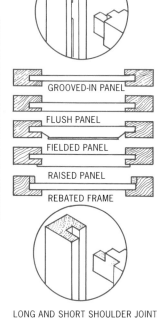

HAUNCHED MORTISE AND TENON

GROOVED-IN PANEL

FLUSH PANEL

FIELDED PANEL

RAISED PANEL

REBATED FRAME

APPLIED MOULDING

LONG AND SHORT SHOULDER JOINT

Making a frame and panel door

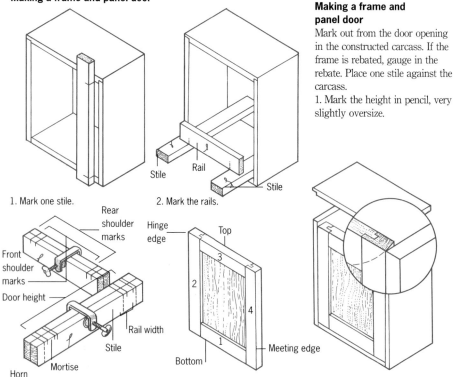

1. Mark one stile.

2. Mark the rails.

Stile   Rail   Stile

Rear shoulder marks
Front shoulder marks
Door height
Hinge edge
Top
Rail width
Stile
Horn   Mortise
Meeting edge
Bottom

3. Clamp the pieces together.

4. Plane the edges in order.

5. Bevel the meeting stile.

Making a frame and panel door

Mark out from the door opening in the constructed carcass. If the frame is rebated, gauge in the rebate. Place one stile against the carcass.

1. Mark the height in pencil, very slightly oversize.

2. Place the stiles in the carcass and mark the rails, adding a trimming allowance. This must also allow for the length of the tenons and long front shoulders.

3. Clamp the stiles and rails together to mark out the joints. Cut the joints, then the rebates. Glue and clamp the frame together.

4. Plane the edges of the frame in the correct order until it fits the door opening. Plane the bottom edge so that, combined with the hinging edge, the door fits the bottom right corner. To fit the top edge, rest the door on a piece of glasspaper placed on the carcass bottom, to give clearance for the surface finish. Plane the meeting edge, leaving it slightly oversize. Hinge to the carcass and complete the fitting on the meeting edge, giving the door a clearance fit.

5. Bevel the meeting edge slightly inwards.

Increasing use is being made of manufactured boards for flush doors. Multi-ply, laminboard and chipboard must have their edges covered to ease shaping and application of a surface finish and to conceal the core material. Wide edgings of solid wood are necessary to provide a secure grip for hinge and lock screws because manufactured boards do not give a secure grip on screws inserted into their end grain (*see* page 130). The edging can be butted and glued on, or tongued and glued into a groove for extra strength (*right*).

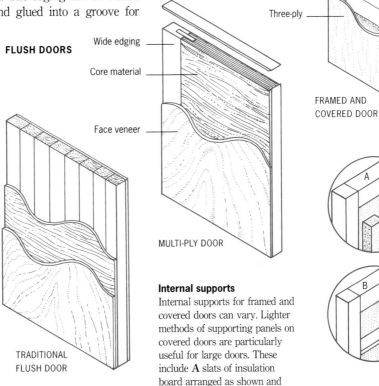

Tongue

Groove

Three-ply

Wide edging

Core material

Face veneer

FRAMED AND COVERED DOOR

MULTI-PLY DOOR

A

B

FLUSH DOORS

Flush door construction

A flush door is made with a core of straight-grained, seasoned wood formed of 50mm (2in) wide strips glued together. Smooth both sides, then face them with constructional veneer at right angles to the core's grain. Use veneers of the same thickness on both sides. Over the constructional veneers, lay decorative veneers with their grain parallel to the strips. Multi-ply and laminboard doors should have their grain at right angles to that of the face veneer. A framed and covered door has a solid wood frame covered with three-ply. The covering is supported by cross rails, drilled to allow the internal air pressure to equalize with that of the surrounding atmosphere, otherwise sinking or bulging may occur. Bore holes in the bottom rail, not in the top rail.

TRADITIONAL FLUSH DOOR

Internal supports

Internal supports for framed and covered doors can vary. Lighter methods of supporting panels on covered doors are particularly useful for large doors. These include **A** slats of insulation board arranged as shown and **B** cardboard honeycombing.

Door hinges

The butt hinge is most commonly used. The flaps can be recessed equally into the carcass and the door or the whole knuckle can be let into the door with one flap taper recessed. The other flap is recessed from the extreme edge of the carcass and tapered to the flap thickness in both lay-on and inset doors. Position a hinge its own length from the end of the stile. On a framed door line up the top end of the hinge with the inner edge of the rail.

Door hinges

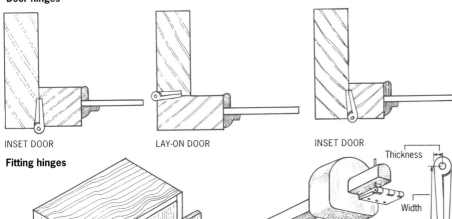

INSET DOOR

LAY-ON DOOR

INSET DOOR

Thickness

Width

2. Set the gauge.

Fitting hinges

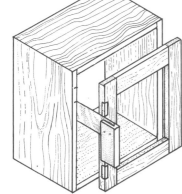

1. Square hinge position across.

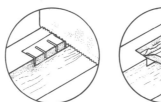

3. Saw the waste.

4. Chisel the recess.

Fitting hinges

1. To position a hinge, square pencilled position marks across the door frame and carcass.
2. Set a marking gauge to the hinge. Gauge its width and thickness from the knuckle to the edge on the door frame.
3. Make vertical saw-cuts in the waste and on the waste side of the gauged lines.
4. Chisel across the ends. Pare the recess flat. Form the recesses in the carcass and screw the door in position, centre screws first.

Sliding door construction

These are usually made of chipboard or laminboard edged all round with hardwood. Lightweight doors have a softwood frame faced with three-ply. The best way to make doors slide is to cut grooves in the carcass top and bottom or attach grooved hardwood, fibre or stainless steel guides to it. Doors may be tongued to slide in the grooves. Grooves must be slightly wider than the the door or tongue, for easy running. Allow extra depth in the top grooves for the doors to be inserted by pushing them up and then dropping them into the bottom groove. Fibre track reduces friction. Glue it into grooves worked in the carcass top and bottom. Let mating plastic gliders into a groove in the bottom of the door, which should fit close to the carcass bottom. At the bottom, fit the fibre track in

two lengths. Glue the first piece in place, slide in the doors, then glue in the remaining length.
A Large doors are usually top hung with two wheels per door, running in channels. **B** Buffer stops stop doors pinching fingers. **C** The door bottoms slide in nylon guides.

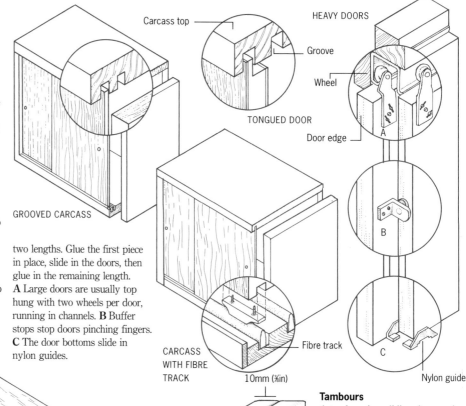

Carcass top

Groove

HEAVY DOORS

Wheel

Door edge

A

B

C

TONGUED DOOR

GROOVED CARCASS

CARCASS WITH FIBRE TRACK

Fibre track

Nylon guide

10mm (⅜in)

6mm (¼in)

Tambours

Feed-in groove

False interior

Locking rail

Finger grip

Fixed end-stop

Baseboard

Edging strip

Edging strip

Clamping block

SLAT ASSEMBLY

Various tambour slat profiles

Tambours

A tambour is a sliding door made of wooden slats glued to a canvas backing. Tambours can be pulled down to close, pushed up or into the sides. Surface finish the slats before assembling them face down on a board between edging strips and a fixed strip at one end, all slightly thinner than the slats. With a clamping block at the other end lightly clamp up the slats. Ensure absolute squareness. Then nail or screw the clamping block to the board and remove the clamps. Glue fine canvas over the slats, stretching it well. Leave sufficient canvas at one end for it to be attached to the locking rail. The tambour runs in grooves in the carcass sides. Widen the grooves around the curves so that the slats can negotiate the curves. Run out the side grooves at the carcass back, which must be detachable, so the tambour can be slid in after the carcass has been assembled and finished. Then fill in the feed-in grooves. The locking rail, which is thicker than the slats and is rebated at the ends, is then sprung into the grooves from the front after the tambour is in place. The canvas is then beaded into a rebate cut in the back of the rail (*see* inset). To prevent the contents of the carcass from interfering with the travel of the tambour, and for appearance, fit a false top, sides and back.

FALL FLAPS

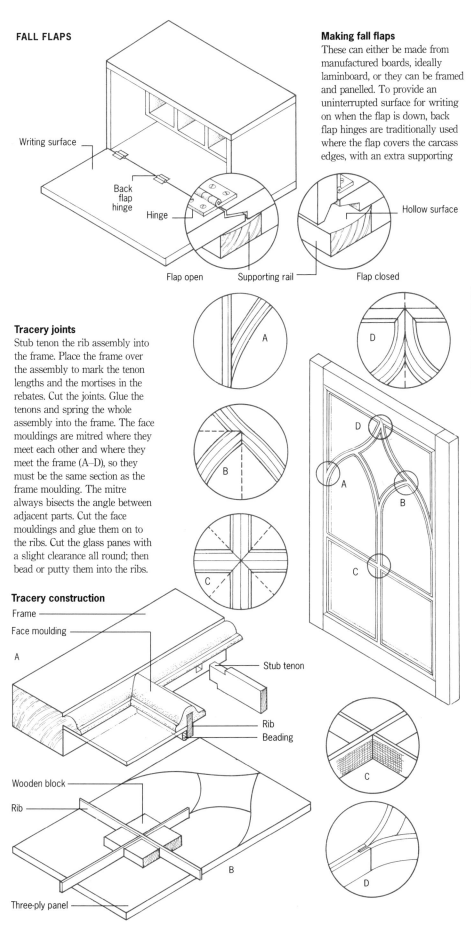

Writing surface

Back flap hinge

Hinge

Flap open

Supporting rail

Hollow surface

Flap closed

Making fall flaps

These can either be made from manufactured boards, ideally laminboard, or they can be framed and panelled. To provide an uninterrupted surface for writing on when the flap is down, back flap hinges are traditionally used where the flap covers the carcass edges, with an extra supporting rail fitted under the front edge of the carcass bottom. This rail is hollowed out so that it can accommodate the swing of the fall flap. Pivot hinges can be recessed into the side edges of the flap and the inside of the carcass. Stopped pivot hinges hold small flaps in the open position without additional support. All but the smallest flaps need more support than can be provided by the hinges alone. Lopers (horizontal arms that extend below the flap as it is lowered) can be built into the carcass beneath the flap, or a stay must be fitted to support it.

Tracery joints

Stub tenon the rib assembly into the frame. Place the frame over the assembly to mark the tenon lengths and the mortises in the rebates. Cut the joints. Glue the tenons and spring the whole assembly into the frame. The face mouldings are mitred where they meet each other and where they meet the frame (A–D), so they must be the same section as the frame moulding. The mitre always bisects the angle between adjacent parts. Cut the face mouldings and glue them on to the ribs. Cut the glass panes with a slight clearance all round; then bead or putty them into the ribs.

Tracery construction

Frame

Face moulding

A

Stub tenon

Rib

Beading

Wooden block

Rib

B

Three-ply panel

A

D

D

A

B

C

C

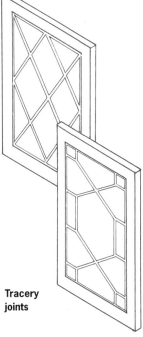

Tracery joints

Tracery construction

A. The tracery in barred doors comprises a face moulding with a separate stiffening rib grooved into the back to form rebates for the glass, which is beaded or puttied in. Lay out the ribs first on a three-ply panel that has been cut to fit the exact size of the door frame rebates. Set out the pattern, working to the centre of the moulding. **B.** Cut the ribs and hold them in place with wooden blocks pinned to the three-ply panel. Join the ribs together with cross halving joints or **C** simple butt joints reinforced with glued canvas. **D.** Two curved ribs meeting an upright can be spliced together and slotted into the end of the upright.

Tables

Straight legs

The mortise and tenon is the most common joint. **A**. Wide underframe rails should have haunched tenons as the haunch supports the upper third of the rail without it pulling free. **B**. Mitre tenons where they meet within the leg. Leave a small gap between the mitred faces to allow for the contraction of the leg and so that the shoulders can be pulled tight. **C**. To avoid the haunch showing on the top of the leg, use a tapered haunch resting in a correspondingly tapered mortise. **D**. A dowel joint between rail and leg is simpler but not so strong. Stagger the dowels. **E**., **F**. Reinforce leg and rail joints with blocks glued to the inside.

Round legs

To join rails to round legs, either **A** scribe the shoulder of the rail so that it fits the leg, where a dowel joint is easiest, or **B** plane a flat section on the leg and work a mortise and tenon joint.

Round legs

Canted legs

When a table has canted legs, **A** cut the tenon shoulder to slant at the same angle or **B** plane an area flat at the top of the leg to take a standard tenon. For a strong frame, first join the four rails together with through dovetails. Then saw and plane off the corners of the frame. Hold a leg in the vice. **C**. Place the frame corner on top and scribe its outline on the end of the leg. Saw and chisel out a recess in the leg to the frame depth. **D**. Slide the frame into the recess. Reinforce the joint with glue blocks and with a screw that is long enough to run through the leg and the joint and bite into the leg on the other side.

Cabriole legs

Tables with cabriole legs are constructed differently from other styles. Make the leg and rail frame with mortise and tenon joints. Glue the joints and allow them to dry. Then fit the ear pieces to each leg. **A**. These should be dowelled for the strongest fixing. **B**. They can also be glued, and have screws driven into counterbored holes and then be pelleted.

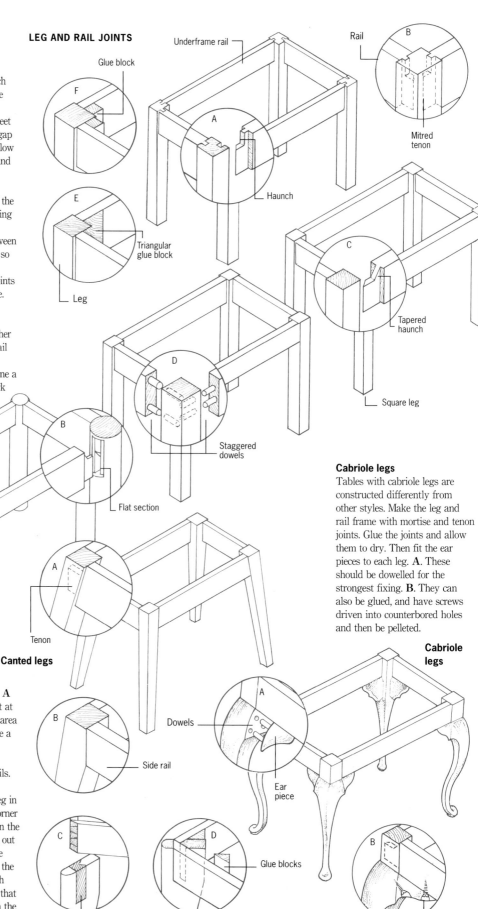

LEG AND RAIL JOINTS

Glue block

F

Underframe rail

A

Haunch

Rail

B

Mitred tenon

E

Triangular glue block

Leg

C

Tapered haunch

Square leg

D

Staggered dowels

A

B

Flat section

A

Tenon

Canted legs

B

Side rail

C

Recess

Dowels

A

Ear piece

D

Glue blocks

Cabriole legs

B

Pellet

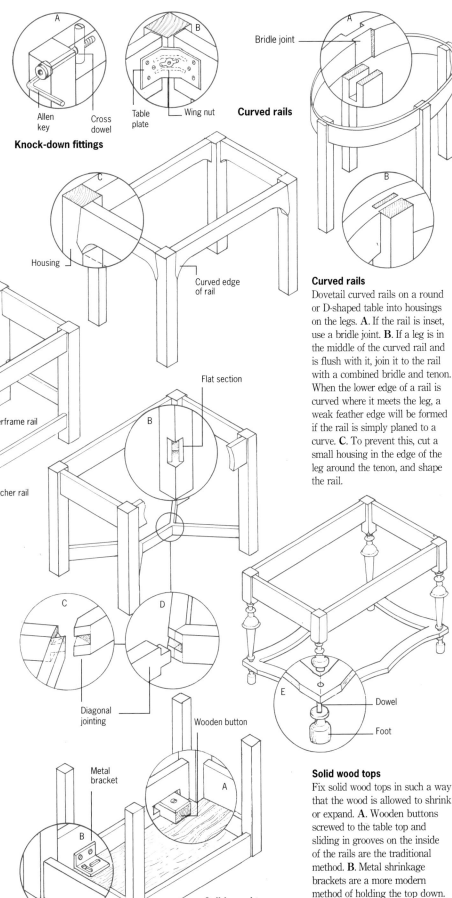

Knock-down fittings

These can be particularly useful on tables. **A**. Make firm secure fittings with a bolt and cross dowel. Insert the steel cross dowel in the rail at right angles to the threaded bolt, which passes through the leg and is screwed into threads in the dowel by an Allen key. **B**. The table plate is a straightforward fitting. Screw each side to a rail. Screw a threaded bolt into the corner of the leg and secure the table plate with a wing nut. Use two short locating dowels with knock-down fittings to prevent the components twisting. Do not glue the dowels if the table is to be dismantled.

Stretcher rails

Stretcher rails add strength and rigidity to the whole frame. They are usually thinner and narrower than the underframe rails and are joined to the leg in the same way, but without a haunch. **A**. If the rail is very thin, it can be fitted completely into the mortise; the tenon, however, should have a top shoulder to give it a definite length and to enable the top edge of the rail to be moulded. **B**. If stretchers run diagonally, work a flat section on each leg. **C**. Where diagonal stretchers join a central stretcher to form a Y, tenon them into the central stretcher, or **D** mortise them to receive the tenon on the central stretcher. Flat stretchers are sometimes required. Make up the stretcher frame with mortise and tenon joints or tongued mitres.
E. Secure turned feet with dowels passing through holes bored in the stretcher frame and into the bottom of the leg.

Curved rails

Dovetail curved rails on a round or D-shaped table into housings on the legs. **A**. If the rail is inset, use a bridle joint. **B**. If a leg is in the middle of the curved rail and is flush with it, join it to the rail with a combined bridle and tenon. When the lower edge of a rail is curved where it meets the leg, a weak feather edge will be formed if the rail is simply planed to a curve. **C**. To prevent this, cut a small housing in the edge of the leg around the tenon, and shape the rail.

Solid wood tops

Fix solid wood tops in such a way that the wood is allowed to shrink or expand. **A**. Wooden buttons screwed to the table top and sliding in grooves on the inside of the rails are the traditional method. **B**. Metal shrinkage brackets are a more modern method of holding the top down. These have slots on one face for the screws to slide along.

Knock-down fittings

Allen key · Cross dowel · Table plate · Wing nut

Curved rails

Bridle joint

Stretcher rails

Housing · Curved edge of rail

Underframe rail · Stretcher rail · Top shoulder

Flat section

Diagonal jointing

Metal bracket · Wooden button

Dowel · Foot

Solid wood tops

Chairs

The chair is the most used and abused piece of furniture in the average household. It has to withstand being rocked backwards and sideways as well as having to stand up to the torsional stresses imposed by the continual readjustment of the sitter's position. All chair joints must fit well and be strong. Make up front and back frames first and then join them to the side rails. Always make a full-size drawing of the projected chair to enable angles to be measured correctly. Any design more elaborate than a simple dining chair should be made up in softwood as a full-size working model to test the design and construction.

The modern dining chair can be quite simple to construct. Use mortise and double stub tenon joints to fix the front and back rails to their legs. Attach the side rails with dowels. Increase the strength and rigidity of the frame by gluing and screwing stout corner blocks in place. Screw a fillet to the back rail to support the three-ply base of the seat. Tenon any stretcher rails if they are used. Position them so as not to catch the back of the sitter's legs and so that they cannot conveniently be used as footrests. Make the chair back from a dowelled frame; pad and screw it to the back posts from the inside. Take the cover over to hide the frame.

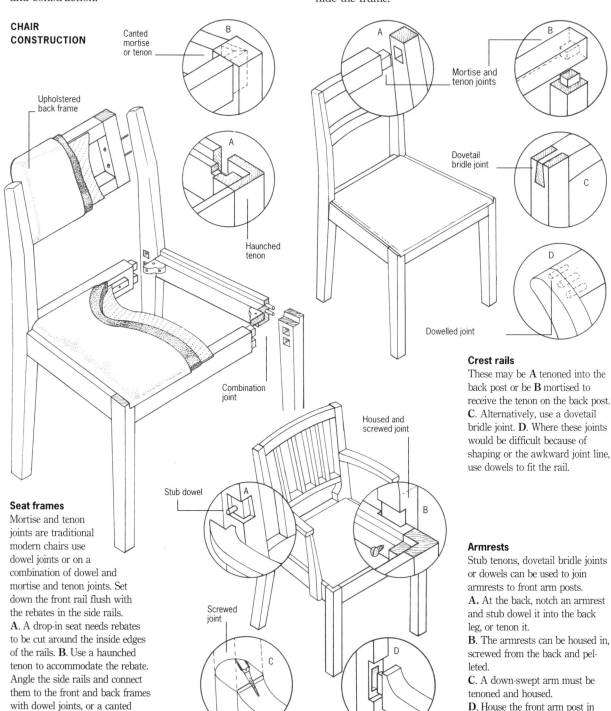

CHAIR CONSTRUCTION

Canted mortise or tenon

Upholstered back frame

Haunched tenon

Combination joint

Mortise and tenon joints

Dovetail bridle joint

Dowelled joint

Stub dowel

Screwed joint

Housed and screwed joint

Seat frames

Mortise and tenon joints are traditional modern chairs use dowel joints or on a combination of dowel and mortise and tenon joints. Set down the front rail flush with the rebates in the side rails.
A. A drop-in seat needs rebates to be cut around the inside edges of the rails. **B.** Use a haunched tenon to accommodate the rebate. Angle the side rails and connect them to the front and back frames with dowel joints, or a canted tenon or mortise. If the leg is flush with the rail, plane off the outer part of the leg after assembly.

Crest rails

These may be **A** tenoned into the back post or be **B** mortised to receive the tenon on the back post. **C.** Alternatively, use a dovetail bridle joint. **D.** Where these joints would be difficult because of shaping or the awkward joint line, use dowels to fit the rail.

Armrests

Stub tenons, dovetail bridle joints or dowels can be used to join armrests to front arm posts.
A. At the back, notch an armrest and stub dowel it into the back leg, or tenon it.
B. The armrests can be housed in, screwed from the back and pelleted.
C. A down-swept arm must be tenoned and housed.
D. House the front arm post in to the seat rail, and glue and screw it.

Beds

BEDFRAME CONSTRUCTION

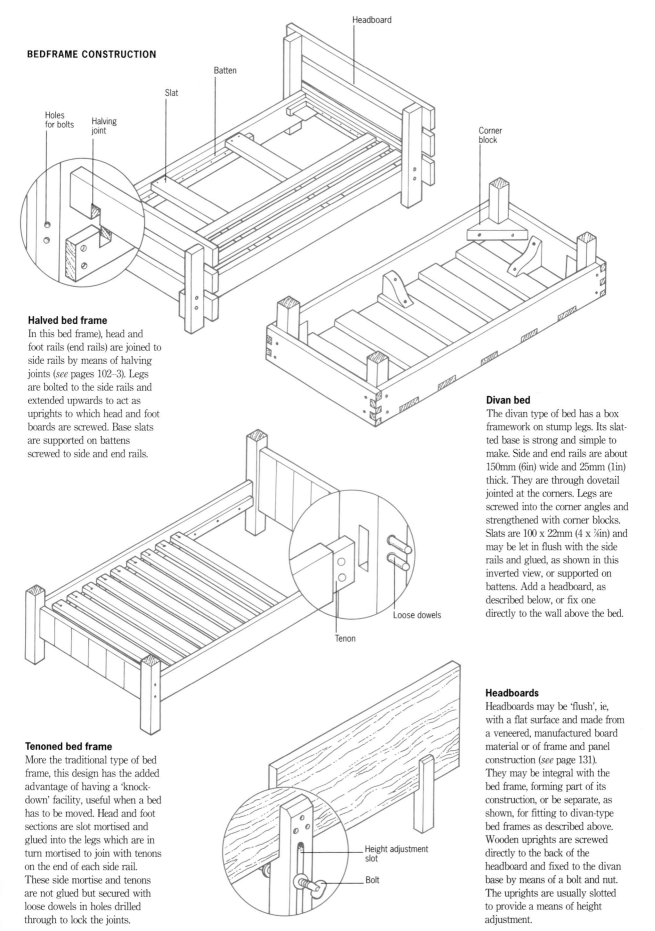

Headboard

Batten

Slat

Holes for bolts

Halving joint

Corner block

Loose dowels

Tenon

Height adjustment slot

Bolt

Halved bed frame
In this bed frame), head and foot rails (end rails) are joined to side rails by means of halving joints (*see* pages 102–3). Legs are bolted to the side rails and extended upwards to act as uprights to which head and foot boards are screwed. Base slats are supported on battens screwed to side and end rails.

Divan bed
The divan type of bed has a box framework on stump legs. Its slatted base is strong and simple to make. Side and end rails are about 150mm (6in) wide and 25mm (1in) thick. They are through dovetail jointed at the corners. Legs are screwed into the corner angles and strengthened with corner blocks. Slats are 100 x 22mm (4 x ⅞in) and may be let in flush with the side rails and glued, as shown in this inverted view, or supported on battens. Add a headboard, as described below, or fix one directly to the wall above the bed.

Headboards
Headboards may be 'flush', ie, with a flat surface and made from a veneered, manufactured board material or of frame and panel construction (*see* page 131). They may be integral with the bed frame, forming part of its construction, or be separate, as shown, for fitting to divan-type bed frames as described above. Wooden uprights are screwed directly to the back of the headboard and fixed to the divan base by means of a bolt and nut. The uprights are usually slotted to provide a means of height adjustment.

Tenoned bed frame
More the traditional type of bed frame, this design has the added advantage of having a 'knock-down' facility, useful when a bed has to be moved. Head and foot sections are slot mortised and glued into the legs which are in turn mortised to join with tenons on the end of each side rail. These side mortise and tenons are not glued but secured with loose dowels in holes drilled through to lock the joints.

Surface finishes

The purpose of applying a surface finish to wood is to protect it from oil, grease, liquids and other general pollution by sealing the pores. If it is transparent rather than opaque, the surface finish will enhance the natural beauty of the wood. To prevent wood from shrinking and the finished surface breaking down, any centrally heated room should contain a humidifier or an abundance of plants to maintain adequate levels of moisture in the air.

Choosing the best materials for a particular piece of work can cause confusion especially as they must be compatible. The eventual use of the piece is the prime consideration. Will it be subject to wear and tear or have liquids spilled on it? Does it need to be heat resistant? (The qualities of the main surface coatings are described on pages 150–51.) Will the piece look more attractive if it is coloured? If so, will a stain be satisfactory or would an opaque finish be more suitable? Is an open-grained surface preferable – or a close-grained woodfilled one?

Before applying any surface finish, it is essential that the wood is thoroughly prepared and its surface is absolutely clean. Any residual grease and dirt will repel the materials and thus give an uneven finish. Plane all protruding joints; punch nails and panel pins below the surface and remove any pencil marks, oil and grease stains, paint and bruises. Fill in any holes later.

Once the wood has been prepared, consult the chart (*right*) for the order in which the appropriate surface finishes should be applied.

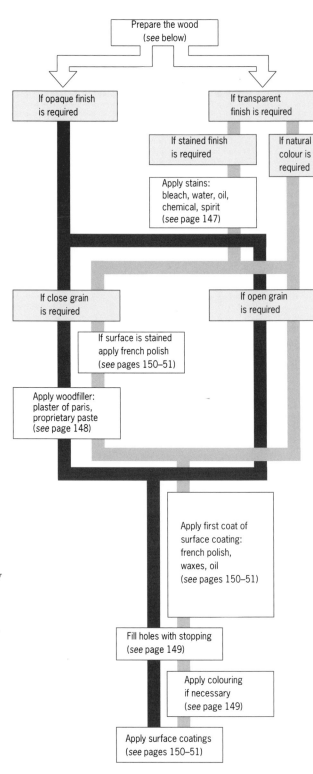

Preparing the wood

1. Press with a warm iron.

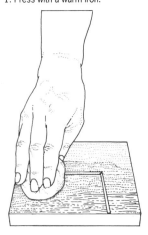

2. Thoroughly clean the wood.

Preparing the wood

Surface finishes tend to accentuate rather than conceal bruises and they are repelled by dirt so special care should be taken with the preparation of the piece of work. Any bruises in the wood must be removed before any finish is applied. Dampen the damaged area with a wet cloth. Heat an old iron file or an electric soldering iron so that the warmth from the iron can be felt 150mm (6in) from the face.
1. Place a wet cloth over the bruise and press with the iron, moving it about gently. The resultant steam causes the wood fibres to expand and rise, thus removing the bruise. Smooth the area with glasspaper.
2. To clean the wood, rub the surface vigorously with a cloth and clean water. The water will raise the grain. When the wood has dried completely, smooth it with a grade 6/0 or 7/0 garnet paper and dust off. The wood is then ready for its first surface finish.

Finishing surfaces

To ensure that the appropriate materials are applied in their correct order once the wood has been prepared, follow the arrows in the chart. Starting from the top of the page, follow the shaded boxes, which indicate the type of finish selected, and complete the actions mentioned in the unshaded boxes, in the order in which they appear.

On a transparent surface coating, a stain will often emphasize the figure of the wood as well as colour it. A stain is unnecessary if an opaque coating is to be applied.

There are four groups of stains: water, chemical, oil and spirit. Only stains in the same group are intermixable. Each group of stains is diluted by its base solvent.

Use plenty of the stain at the outset and allow a couple of hours for the wood to dry after staining. Any polishing carried out on wet wood will, at a later stage, cause a reaction that will spoil the final finish.

Water stains (direct dyes)

These are made by mixing dry pigments with water. The powders are intermixable and a wide range of shades can be achieved. The depth of the colour is determined by the amount of powder used: the more powder, the darker the stain. Pigment powders are comparatively cheap and large quantities can be made up from small amounts. Some powders take a while to dissolve, so leave the mixed stain for an hour before use so the final colour is certain.

Chemical stains

Some chemicals such as blue copperas and ammonia can be mixed with water and applied to wood as a stain. They react with the tannic acid present in the wood and change the wood colour. The problem is that the woodworker cannot see what colour these stains will make until they are applied to the wood. Some other chemical stains such as bichromate of potash and copper sulphate have a little colour content of their own while others, eg, ammonia and caustic soda, are colourless.

Oil stains

These are available in a variety of mixable colours. They are simple to use but are relatively expensive. Oil stains do not penetrate the wood fibres and will not raise the grain, so they tend to be stronger than other stains.

Spirit stains

Spirit stains are made by dissolving dry pigment powder in methylated spirit and then adding one part french polish as a binder to four parts methylated spirit. The rapid evaporation rate of the solvent in spirit stains does tend to make them difficult to use on large surfaces. They also have a tendency to fade.

Bleaches

There are three main bleaches that can be used on wood: sodium hypochlorite, oxalic acid and super bleach.

Sodium hypochlorite can be used for removing dark marks, without substantially altering the wood colour. Oxalic acid – a poisonous white crystalline powder that is saturated in water or methylated spirit – has similar uses. It should be neutralized with acetic acid and water. Super bleach is extremely powerful. Wear gloves and avoid splashing. It is available as a two-pack bleach. The first solution is an alkaline: apply liberally and allow to soak into the wood. This may temporarily darken the wood. The second solution is concentrated hydrogen peroxide. When it is applied to the wood after the first solution, the bleaching action takes place. If the reduction in colour is not sufficient, repeat the process. After use, wash the wood with clean water and allow it to dry completely.

The effect of stains and bleaches on various woods									
	Mahogany	Vandyke	Black	Blue copperas	Bichromate of potash	Ammonia	Sodium hypochlorite	Oxalic acid	Super bleach
Beech	reddish	brown	grey	greyish	light tan	brown	slightly lightens	slightly lightens	almost white
Mahogany	red	brown	subdues red; produces greyish tone	eliminates red; produces browny-grey	deep rich brown	deep brown with greyish tone	removes dark marks	slightly lightens	lightens considerably
Oak	red	deep brown	grey	grey-blue	greenish-brown	slightly greenish-deep-brown	removes dark marks	slightly lightens	almost white
Pine	reddish	brown	grey	greyish	pale yellow	greenish-brown	removes dark marks	slightly lightens	almost white
Teak	reddish	brown	grey	greyish	yellowish-brown	greenish-brown	removes dark marks	slightly lightens	lightens considerably
Walnut	reddish	brown	grey	greyish	pale yellow	greenish-brown	slightly lightens	slightly lightens	lightens considerably
Manufactured boards	reddish	brown	grey	greyish	deep brown	greenish-brown	removes dark marks	removes dark marks	almost white

Woodfillers

Woodfillers are used to fill the pores of wood to obtain a full-grained finish and for a high-gloss finish; they are rarely used on carved wood. They are based on chalk to which colouring, oils and solvents are added. Woodfillers are cheaper, quicker and more effective than french polish or any other surface coating that could be used as a filler.

Plaster of paris and proprietary oil-based fillers are readily available. The former is used when the work is to be french polished. Combined stain and woodfillers are available, but are generally unsatisfactory. Some surface coatings require specific woodfillers, so ask the suppliers. Always use a filler that is slightly darker than the wood.

Woodfillers can be applied to stained and unstained surfaces. Stained surfaces must be sealed with a thin coat of french polish before applying the woodfiller. If left unsealed, the stain might be lifted later on.

The art of woodfilling is to apply the filler quickly and evenly over the whole surface before the filler begins to dry. Clean all corners and recesses with a quirk stick and let the woodfiller dry for at least four hours before glasspapering, dusting and applying the surface coating.

Woodfilling with a proprietary paste

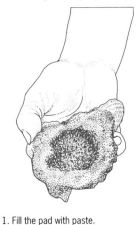
1. Fill the pad with paste.

2. Rub into the surface.

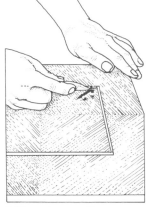
3. Clean out any mouldings.

Woodfilling with a proprietary paste

1. Fill a loose pad of hessian with paste. If too thick, dilute the paste with turps.
2. Rub paste into the wood surface with a circular motion. Work the paste well into any corners and mouldings. Keeping the pad loose, rub the paste across the grain. While the filler is still wet, wipe away the excess with hessian and then a soft, absorbent cloth.
3. With an appropriately shaped quirk stick clean corners, edges and recesses where any woodfiller remains. Leave to dry.

Woodfilling with plaster of paris

1. Mix the powders and plaster.

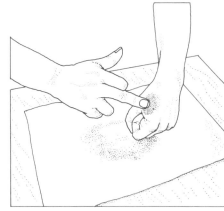
2. Test the colour.

Woodfilling with plaster of paris

Tip out some superfine white plaster on to a piece of newspaper and add the required pigment powders.
1. Mix together the powders and plaster by tipping them about in the newspaper.
2. To test the colour, put water on the back of your hand, dip a finger into the plaster mixture and rub it on your wet hand. The colour will appear much chalkier than desired, but this whiteness will be removed later. Soak a piece of hessian in cold water.
3. Squeeze it out gently and press it into the plaster mixture.
4. Rub the filler into the grain with a circular motion. When the entire surface has been filled, wipe it clean across the grain with clean hessian held loosely. Clean edges, corners, and recesses with a quirk stick. Leave to dry for about four hours. The water from the plaster will evaporate and leave a white residue. Remove this with linseed oil on a soft cloth, applied with a circular motion. Smooth the still-wet wood with 320-grit glasspaper, rubbing lightly along the grain. Wipe across the grain with clean dry hessian, pushing the excess filler into the grain pores. Rub up with a dry cloth.

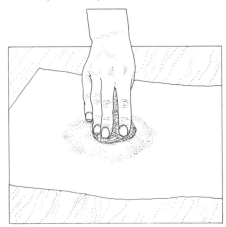
3. Press the pad into the mixture.

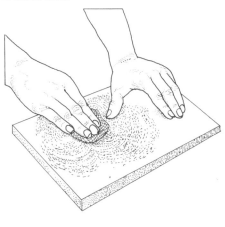
4. Rub into the grain.

Filling holes and cracks

This process is known as stopping. For an opaque finish, stopping is done after woodfiller has been applied (if a full-grained finish is desired) but before any surface coating is applied. For a transparent finish, stopping and colouring are done after the woodfiller and after one layer of surface coating has been applied. If woodfiller is not used the surface for a transparent finish must still be coated once before stopping and colouring.

Several materials are suitable for filling holes. Some, such as beaumontage and shellac, are known as 'hard stopping' and are melted in use, while others, such as beeswax and japan wax, are applied cold and are better suited to filling small holes. Shellac is immensely sticky and it is much cleaner to use beaumontage. Any of these stopping materials can be coloured by melting them down and mixing in dry pigment powders.

Colouring and staining

Colouring entails touching up a surface to one overall colour. It is best to make up spirit stains in strength and then mix them together. Bismarck brown and spirit black are the two main spirit stains that, combined in varying quantities, will give warmer or colder shades. To lighten dark spots in wood combine lemon chrome, orange chrome and titanium white. The colour should blend completely into the background and not show up as an obvious blob of colour.

Two thin coats of spirit stain are better than one thick one so bear this in mind when mixing up a colour. If more than three applications are required, seal the stain in with a layer of the selected surface coating before continuing with the colouring. Failure to do this could cause the stain already on to drag off later.

The professional way to apply french polish is with a rubber. A rubber is a piece of absorbent wadding covered in soft absorbent material. The wadding is carefully folded so that it is pear-shaped with a point at one end. Pound wadding is best as it stays soft and springy for a long time while medicated cotton wool and upholsterers' wadding tend to harden very quickly. Rubbers should be stored in an airtight container such as a lidded jar.

Stopping

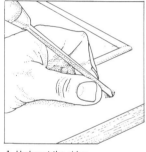

1. Undercut the sides.

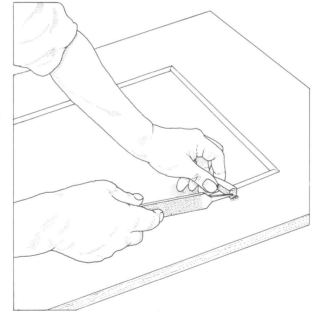

3. Chisel away the excess.   2. Melt the beaumontage stick.

Stopping

Proprietary wax sticks, made in a variety of colours, can be used; as an alternative make a beaumontage stick by melting beeswax and carnauba wax in 10:1 proportions in a double pot. Add pigment powder. Cool down the mixture and bind with a little french polish. Allow to solidify.
1. Enlarge the hole to be filled so the stopping remains lodged in place. Heat the tang of a file so that when held 150mm (6in) away from the face the warmth can be felt. Wipe off the soot.
2. Hold the beaumontage stick over the hole and melt it into the hole with the hot tang. Press it in well.
3. With a chisel, held bevel downwards, gently scrape away the excess beaumontage. Smooth the surface by glasspapering lightly with a sanding block. Then glasspaper further by hand.

Filling small holes

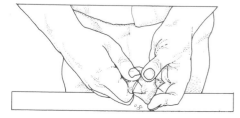

1. Remove shavings of coloured wax.

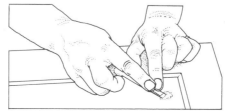

2. Press the shavings into the hole.

Filling small holes

Dip beeswax into the required pigment powders.
1. Remove shavings of the coloured wax, using a knife.
2. Press the shavings well into the hole with a chisel. Remove the excess wax with the chisel held vertically. Smooth the surface, first with the back and then with the front of a piece of glasspaper.

Surface coatings can be used both to protect a surface and to enhance the grain. Most protect against dirt and make cleaning easier. All protect against moisture to some extent. Some are heat resistant; others protect against insect or fungal attack. They all have good adhesive qualities provided the surface to which they are applied is absolutely clean. All work should be done in a well-lit room but not in direct sunlight. The room should be clean, and be at about a constant 18°C (65°F). The coatings discussed here are french polish, wax, semi-wax and oil.

French polish

French polish, although having little heat and moisture resistance, still remains popular among craftsmen. It is a sticky resinous mixture and so difficult to apply, but if applied correctly it gives one of the best finishes. The aim is to produce a high gloss with numerous thin coats of polish; this can then be matted down if required.

The basic ingredients of french polish are shellac – a substance exuded by the lac insect – and methylated spirit, which is used as a solvent. The main colours of polish are pale, button and garnet. French polish is also available tinted with dyes of black or red; black-dyed french polish is used to ebonize a surface over black stain. Sycamore, mahogany and birch are some of the best woods for ebonizing.

French polish should be worked in slowly using a rubber, gradually building up a film of polish, which is left to dry before the next coat is applied. Always lift the rubber promptly from the surface sides and ends to stop polish dripping over the edges. Rubbing and bodying up and down the grain is done to prevent the polish from streaking. It is easier to work on a number of surfaces in rotation so each surface has an opportunity to dry off before the next application of polish. Each coat of polish will partially dissolve the coat beneath so the layers will amalgamate. The quantity of polish worked into a surface determines the degree of gloss; for a full even gloss, apply many thin coats.

French polishing	
Beech	Use a pale polish on light or natural beech. Button polish may be used after staining.
Mahogany	Use button or garnet polish.
Oak	Use a pale polish on light oaks; button polish on stained oak.
Pine	Pale polish is normally used. Button polish is used on a stained piece.
Teak	Pale or button polish, depending on colour required.
Walnut	Pale polish is normally used. Button polish may be used for a cast.
Manufactured boards	Pale, button or garnet polish depending on colour required.

Wax and semi-wax polish

Wax gives an attractive shine and is easy to maintain, but it has only slight moisture resistance, little or no heat resistance and is easily marked. It also holds dust, which, unless the grain is sealed, will become embedded in the wood. Most proprietary waxes are based on soft paraffin wax and are unsuitable for application to unsealed wood. If using wax as a surface coating, carefully heat 0.45kg (1lb) of shredded beeswax with 280ml (½pt) turpentine and some carnauba wax. It is possible to colour beeswax with oil-soluble colours or dry pigment powders, and bleached beeswax is obtainable. Allow the mixture to cool. Apply the wax paste along the grain with a soft brush or cloth. Leave it to dry, and then burnish it with a soft dry cloth. On uneven surfaces, apply wax with a short-bristled brush made of bear hair or mixed hair and burnish with a dry soft-haired brush. Once the surface has been sealed with the beeswax mixture use further coats of proprietary wax to produce a finish with depth and warmth.

To apply a semi-wax polish, first seal the wood with a couple of coats of sealer, using a cloth or brush. When dry, smooth with a 7/0 garnet paper and wipe clean. Then add wax polish to 000 or 0000 steel wool and rub down the surface. Burnish with a soft dry cloth.

Oil

The advantages of oil polish are that it does not crack, blister, or show heat or water marks. It gives effective protection to wood exposed to the open air and to liquids. It is therefore suited to garden furniture, table and bar tops, counters and spirit cabinets.

The traditional oil to use as a polish is linseed oil; this will produce a fine finish that will be moderately heat and water resistant. Its application takes a great deal of time, however, as it is slow-drying and requires numerous coats applied sparingly over a period of months. Each application must be hardened by oxidization and at least twelve coats are necessary. The addition of small amounts of turpentine and terebene makes it easier for working and will speed up the drying process. Add 5 per cent turpentine and 5 per cent terebene and simmer the mixture in a double pan for fifteen minutes. Vigorously rub the mixture into the wood with a clean cloth. Allow at least one day for the oil to dry; then smooth it with fine glasspaper and dust clean. Apply numerous coats in this way, leaving at least one week between sessions. Remove any dust that has settled on the surface between sessions and use a clean cloth for every session.

Proprietary oils containing oxidizing agents are now available and are more widely used. Compared with linseed oil, these dry more quickly and require fewer applications. The include teak oil, tung oil and Danish oil which are suitable for all wood, especially teak, oak, mahogany, walnut and cedar, as they enhance the grain and colouring. Oil is extremely combustible so always soak an oil-filled cloth in water overnight and wash it before disposing of it.

French polishing

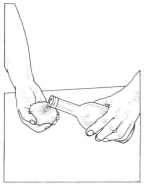
1. Charge the rubber with polish.

2. Rub the rubber along the grain.

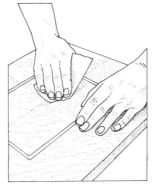
3. Smooth the surface.

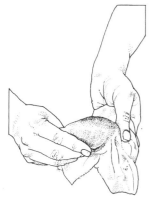
4. Fill the rubber with polish.

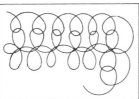
5. Work along the grain.

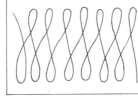
6. Work in figures of eight.

7. Work in circles.

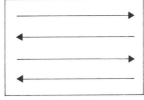
8. Work along the grain.

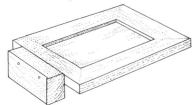
Using the rubber's nose in corners.

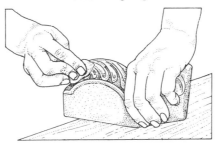
Using the rubber's nose in crevices.

Methods of holding work

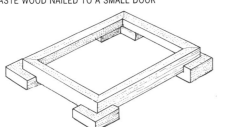
WASTE WOOD NAILED TO A SMALL DOOR

HEAVY DOOR LAID ON WEDGES

FRAME HELD WITH BENCH-STICKS

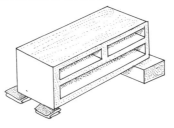
CARCASS PROPPED UP

French polishing

1. Remove the cloth and saturate the wadding with polish. Replace the cloth and squeeze until the polish oozes through.
2. Work the rubber along the grain with minimal downward pressure, overlapping each stroke. Too much downward pressure forces out the polish too rapidly, resulting in a sticky surface. Leave to dry for 10 minutes.
3. Rub 180-grit abrasive paper together to make it finer and smooth the surface. Dust with a soft cloth. Fill any holes and adjust the colour. Then body the surface with a rubber.
4. Charge with polish. Work the rubber in strict sequence.
5. First work along the grain, overlapping each stroke until the entire surface is covered.
6. Then work the rubber using a figure-of-eight movement.
7. Rub in a circular movement.
8. Finally work the rubber along the grain again. Leave the surface to dry off. Apply more coats, repeating this process until a high gloss has been achieved. Towards the end of the bodying process, lubricate the hardening rubber with a spot of linseed oil. Remove any excess oil with the dried-out rubber, using considerable pressure along the grain. Test the surface by breathing on it: if a mist forms, continue to rub until the oil has gone. With greater experience, methylated spirit can be used on the dried-out rubber, to give a perfectly smooth surface. Leave the surface to harden. Then smooth with fine abrasive paper.

Methods of holding work

Hold a small door by nailing a piece of waste wood at right angles to the unpolished bottom edge of the door. Lay a large or heavy door on four wooden wedges. The weight will keep it in position. Lay a table upside down to polish the legs and rails. Then stand it upright to polish the top. Polish a chair from the legs up. With a frame, first polish the inner and outer edges, then place the frame flat in home-made bench-sticks, nailed to the workbench, and polish the top. Prop up a carcass with a block of waste wood at one end and folded abrasive paper at the other so the grit is in contact with the carcass and the floor to prevent slipping. Hold a drawer from the inside.

FIXTURES & FITTINGS

As an extension to the earlier section on materials, the following pages describe those other items associated with, and often an integral part of, many constructions in wood. While many woodworking techniques and methods of assembly involve the use of interlocking joints fashioned in the wood itself, all of these – if intended to be permanent – are fixed with a glue of some kind. In some work, nails are used to fix wood to wood, sometimes in combination with glue, and screws too are used for the same purpose and for securing hardware such as hinges, locks and handles.

Until comparatively recent times there was only one glue in common use; now the range of adhesives has never been greater. And while nails – except panel pins and veneer pins – are not used to any extent in furnituremaking, they have their uses in other forms of woodwork. The use of screws in all aspects of working in wood seems to have increased in recent years and they are now available in a variety of material, finishes and special types. Quality brass hinges and other items of furniture hardware are also more readily available.

Screws, nails & adhesives

Screws are used to fasten wood to wood and for fitting hardware. They are sold by length and gauge (thickness): the higher the gauge number, the thicker the screw. They are usually made from brass, aluminium alloy or steel, which may be coated with chromium plating, zinc, black japan, cadmium or bronze. Screwdriver slots may be straight across or in the form of a cross.

When joining wood to wood the threaded part of the screw should penetrate the bottom piece. When joining two pieces of equal thickness, the screw length should be just less than the combined thickness. When joining very thick pieces, counterbore the top piece. Drill pilot holes when there is a danger of the wood splitting. Lubricate screws with grease or soap so they turn more easily, are protected against corrosion and can be withdrawn later. Always use brass screws in oak and sycamore, as steel is attacked by the acid in the wood and will corrode, staining the wood.

Both nails and screws are used in combination with glue when making permanent joints. Nails are made from steel, brass, aluminium alloy, iron and copper.

Screw parts

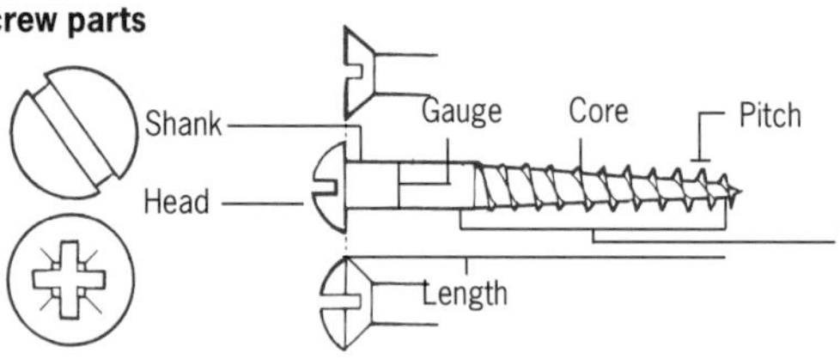

Countersunk, round- and raised-head screws have straight and cross slots. Length is that part sunk into the wood. Add 3 to the gauge number for the drill size in increments of 1/64in.

SCREWS

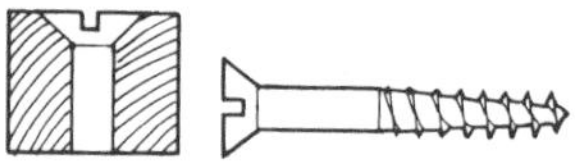

Countersunk screw
For general woodwork. The head is driven in flush with the surface of the wood.
Sizes: *see* chart below.

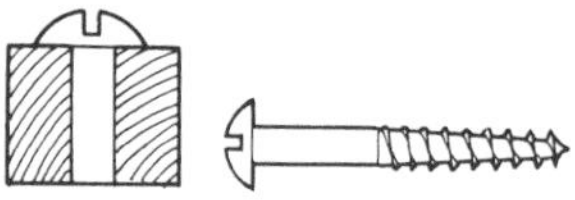

Round-head screw
For hardware fittings without countersunk holes to wood.
Sizes: *see* chart below.

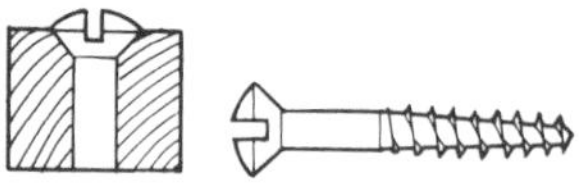

Raised-head screw
For decorative hardware such as door handle roses and plates.
Sizes: *see* chart below.

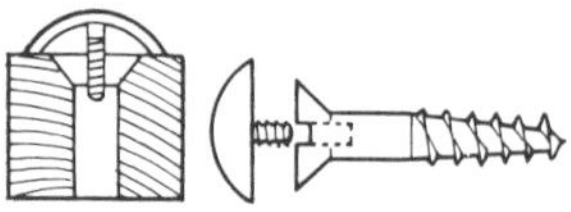

Dome-head screw
For mirrors and other fittings. It has a chrome-finished cap.
Sizes: 19–50mm (¾–2in).

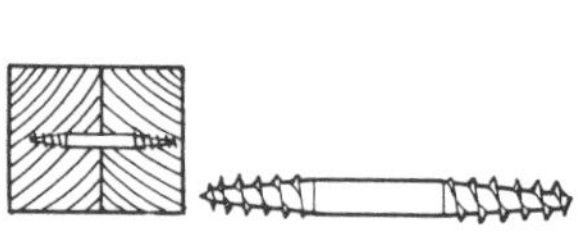

Dowel screw
For hidden joints. Screw the dowel into one piece of wood, then screw on the second piece.
Sizes: 19–88mm (¾–3½in).

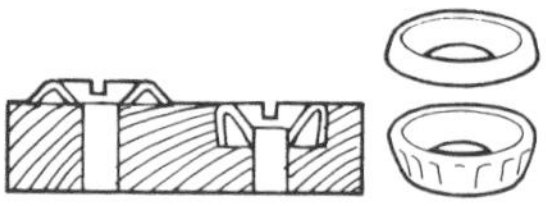

Screw cap and socket
For giving a neat finish. The cap is surface fitted, the socket let in flush.
Various sizes and shapes.

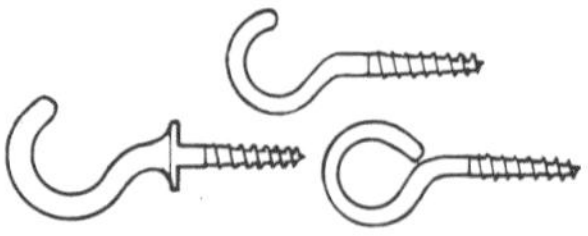

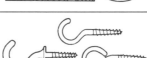

Screw hook and eye
For hanging items and for fastening doors. They are made from brass and coated steel.
Various sizes and shapes.

Screw lengths and gauges

Countersunk (Csk) · Round head (Rd) · Raised head (Rsd)
Straight head ⊘ · Cross head ⊕ · Straight and cross head ●

Gauge number	0		1	2		3		4			5			6			7		8			9	10			12		14		16	18	20
Length	Csk	Rd	Csk	Csk	Rd	Csk	Rd	Csk	Rd	Rsd	Csk	Rd	Rsd	Csk	Rd	Rsd	Csk	Rd	Csk	Rd	Rsd	Csk	Csk	Rd	Rsd	Csk	Rd	Csk	Rd	Csk	Csk	Csk
6 mm/¼ in	⊘	⊘	⊘	⊘	⊘			⊘	⊕																							
10 mm/⅜ in			⊘	⊘	⊘	●	●	●	●	⊘		⊕		●	●				⊘	⊕												
13 mm/½ in				⊘		●	●	●	●	●	●	●		●	●	●	⊘		●	●			⊘									
16 mm/⅝ in						⊘		●	●	⊘	●	●	●	●	●	●	●	⊘	●	●			⊘	●								
19 mm/¾ in						⊘		●	●	●	●	●	⊘	●	●	●	●	⊘	●	●	●	⊘	●	●		⊘	⊘					
22 mm/⅞ in								⊘						●	⊕		●		●	⊕												
25 mm/1 in						⊘		●	●	⊘	●		⊘	●	●	●	●	⊘	●	●	●	●	●	●	⊘	●	●	⊘				
28 mm/1⅛ in														●					●													
31 mm/1¼ in								⊘			⊘			●	●	●	●	⊘	●	●	●	●	●	●	⊘	●	⊘	⊘				
38 mm/1½ in								⊘						●	●	●	●		●	●	●	●	●	●	●	●	●	⊘	⊘	⊘		
44 mm/1¾ in														●			⊘		●	●	⊕	●	●	●	●	●	⊘	⊘		⊘		
50 mm/2 in														●	⊘		⊘		●	⊘	●	●	●	●	●	●	●	⊘	⊘	⊘	⊘	⊘
56 mm/2¼ in														⊘					●				●			●		●				
63 mm/2½ in														⊘					●	⊘		⊘	●	⊘		●	⊘	●		⊘		
69 mm/2¾ in																			⊘				⊘			⊘		⊘				
75 mm/3 in														⊘					●				●	⊘		●	⊘	●		⊘	⊘	⊘
81 mm/3¼ in																							⊘			⊘						
88 mm/3½ in																			⊘				⊘			⊘		⊘		⊘		
100 mm/4 in																			⊘				⊘			⊘		⊘		⊘	⊘	⊘
113 mm/4½ in																							⊘			⊘		⊘				⊘
125 mm/5 in																							⊘			⊘		⊘		⊘		
150 mm/6 in																										⊘		⊘		⊘		

Type	Description	Strength, durability	Moisture resistance	Gap filling	Assembly time	Setting time
Animal glue	Granules heated in water. Applied hot. Non-toxic. Reversible.	Good	None	No	Very short	12 hours
PVA (Polyvinyl acetate)	Ready to use liquid emulsion. Water soluble but not reversible when cured.	Very good	Poor (waterproof type is available)	Poor	Short	2 hours
UF Resin* (Urea formaldehyde)	Dry powder mixed with water. Or with separate hardener.	Very good	Very good	Yes	Medium	6 hours
Impact *	Latex based, contact adhesive. Ready-to-use.	Fair	Fair	No	Instant	2 mins
Epoxy *	Two-part. Resin added to hardener in equal amounts.	Very good	Good	Yes	Short	2 hours (normal type)

* These adhesives are flammable and toxic. Use in a well-ventilated space.

NAILS AND FASTENINGS

Round wire nail
For work where strength is more important than looks.
Sizes: 19–150mm (¾–6in).

Oval wire nail
For joinery. Its shape will minimize splitting.
Sizes: 13–150mm (½–6in).

Lost-head nail
For general use. The head is driven below the surface.
Sizes: 13–150mm (½–6in).

Panel pin
For cabinetwork and mouldings. It is also available with a twisted shank.
Sizes: 13–50mm (½–2in).

Veneer pin
For temporarily holding veneers in position on the ground before they are taped.
Sizes: 13–50mm (½–2in).

Hardboard pin
For hardboard. Its diamond-shaped head grips strongly.
Sizes: 19–38mm (¾–1½in).

Masonry pin
For fastening wood to masonry. It is made from hardened steel.
Sizes: 19–100mm (¾–4in).

Annular nail
For fastening manufactured boards especially three-ply. Its barbed surface aids grip.
Sizes: 19–75mm (¾–3in).

Twisted square-head nail
For general use. Its shank provides a screw-type grip.
Sizes: 19–100mm (¾–4in).

Corrugated fastener
For framed and batten joints.
Sizes: 6–22mm (¼–⅞in) deep; 22–31mm (⅞–1¼in) long.

Small brad
For carpentry. Used in place of round-head nails when extra holding power is required.
Sizes: 13–19mm (½–¾in).

Dowel nail
For fastening end to end and for hidden joints.
Sizes: 38–50mm (1½–2in).

Needle point
For fastening small mouldings. The head is cut off flush. It has a very fine gauge.
Sizes: 13–50mm (½–2in).

Chair nail
For upholstery. It is finished in copper, chrome and bronze.
Sizes: 3–13mm (⅛–½in) head.

Hinges

Mass production and self-assembly furniture have led to new types of hinge, often used with manufactured boards with limited screw-holding properties. However, the butt hinge and its variants remain among the most popular door hinges. The common butt hinge is the one that is used by most furnituremakers for hanging cabinet and cupboard doors. It should be recessed into the frame and the door stile so only the knuckle of the hinge is visible. On small to medium-sized doors, hinges are usually set at a distance equal to their own length from the end of the door stile; on a framed door hinges can be lined up with the inside of each horizontal rail. On a long door, hinges may be several centimetres from each end, with a central third hinge for heavy doors. The position of the centre of the knuckle determines the throw of the door and should be carefully set. Other butt hinges are shown, each with its own purpose. Surface-fitting hinges are easier to fit.

Recessing butt hinges

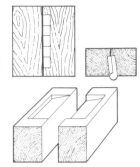

A simple method to recess a butt hinge is to let both flaps equally into the frame and carcass. Alternatively, the total thickness of the knuckle may be recessed into the door and one flap tapered into the carcass. If the swing of the door is restricted, move the hinge pivot point forward (*see also* page 139).

TYPES OF HINGE

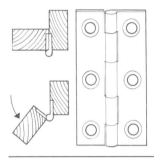

Common butt hinge
For all doors.
Fitting: Surface and recessed.
Sizes: Narrow, 25 x 16–75 x 35mm (1 x ⅝–3 x 1⅜in); broad, 38 x 22–100 x 60mm (1½ x⅞–4 x 2⅜in); strong, 38 x 25–100 x 75mm (1½ x 1–4 x 3in); extra broad, 25 x 25–75 x 63mm (1 x 1–3 x 2½in).

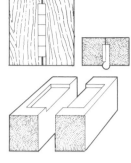

Piano hinge
For supporting long lengths such as chest flaps, piano lids and table flaps. It is available either as a drilled and countersunk flap or as an undrilled flap.
Fitting: Recessed.
Sizes: 1800 and 825mm (72 and 33in long (can be cut to length); 25 and 31mm (1 and 1¼in) wide.

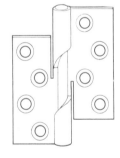

Rising butt
For room doors. As the door is opened, the hinge rises and the door is lifted clear of the carpet. The hinges are either left- or right-handed. The top of the door should have a taper bevelled to prevent it from jamming against the frame.
Fitting: Recessed.
Sizes: 75–100mm (3–4in).

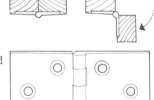

Back flap hinge
For table leaves and fall flaps on desks, bureaux and cabinets. Its wide flaps provide strong support.
Fitting: Surface and recessed.
Sizes: Light pattern, 25 x 41–75 x 125mm (1 x 1⅝–3 x 5in); heavy pattern, 31 x 75–75 x 150mm (1¼ x 3–3 x 6in).

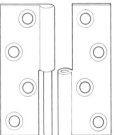
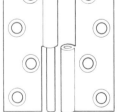

Lift-off hinge
For room and cabinet doors. This hinge, which can be left- or right-handed, is made in two parts so that one half can be removed yet still be attached to the door. The leaf with the pin must be fixed to the frame, countersunk side facing.
Fitting: Recessed.
Sizes: 38–150mm (1½–6in).

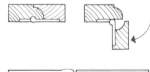

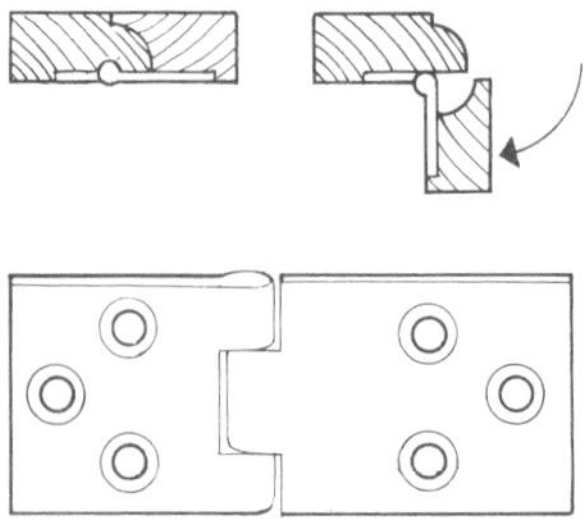

Rule joint hinge
For table extension flaps. The long flap is designed to clear the hollow in the cove of the rule joint. The knuckle is on the reverse to a normal butt hinge to permit a 90° drop. It has a bronzed finish.
Fitting: Recessed.
Sizes: 31 x 63–38 x 63mm (1¼ x 2½–1½ x 2½in).

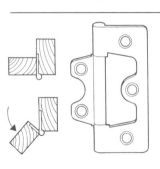

Flush hinge
For all types of door. This thin one-flap hinge has part cut away to act as a second flap. It is a weak hinge but has the advantage that it will support light doors without the need for recessing. It is made from coated steel.
Fitting: Surface.
Sizes: 38–75mm/1½–3in).

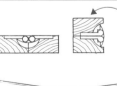

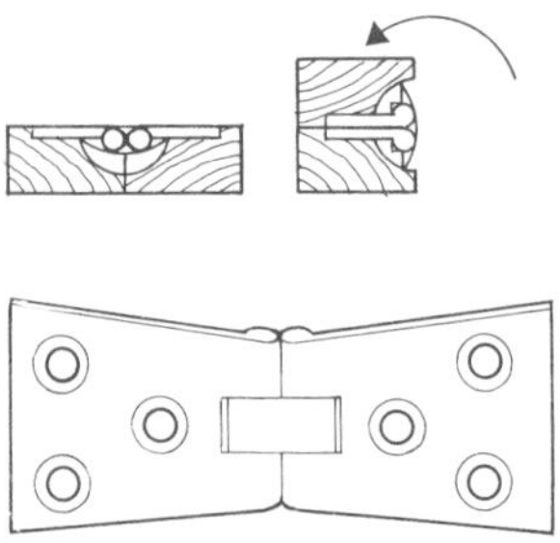

Counterflap hinge
For counters and tables with lift-up leaves. The hinge allows the flap to lie back flat along the counter. The most common type has a double pin connected by a smooth link let in flush with the hinge surface.
Fitting: Recessed, knuckle down.
Sizes: 31 x 75–38 x 113mm (1¼ x 3–1½ x 4½in).

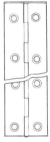

Stays, castors & handles

Stays are used to support the fall flaps of cabinets and bureaux, to restrict the swing of wardrobe doors and to support and hold lift-up flaps and box lids. Modern stays have plastic slides or stay housings, for a quiet action, and mechanisms that control the fall so that the flap is lowered smoothly. Most stays can be fitted on either side, but some stays are handed, that is, they can only be used on either the left- or the right-hand side of the carcass. The fitting of a stay is dependent on the carcass to which it will be attached, but as a rough guide a stay should be positioned at approximately 45° to a carcass or flap that is opened at 90°.

Castor wheels or balls are fitted to furniture to make it more manoeuvrable. Castor wheels are made from hard or soft rubber or plastics. The ball types are made from hardened plastics, solid brass and coated steel.

Glides have a greater bearing surface than ball or wheel castors, but create more friction. They are used to protect floor surfaces against scarring and are commonly made from nickel-plated steel and plastics. Height adjusters, or levellers, which are similar in design to glides, are fitted on to legged furniture to obtain even floor contact.

Handles, knobs and pulls for doors and drawers are available in a wide range of shapes and finishes to suit most types of furniture. The number and placing of handles on furniture is not critical as long as the door or drawer functions smoothly and efficiently. Handle styles should ideally be seen as an integral part of the furniture design from the beginning. Once these considerations have been taken into account, the final choice is a matter of personal taste.

STAYS

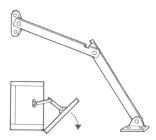

Cranked stay
For fall flaps or doors. The steel arm is hinged at the centre, enabling the stay to fold into the cupboard when the flap is closed. It is made right- and left-handed in nickel-plate and electro-brass finishes.
Size: 250mm (10in) long.

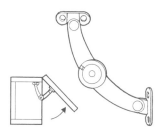

Cranked lift-up stay
For lift-up flaps on small storage units. The wide sturdy arm locks in the open position. To close, lift the flap slightly before lowering. Its friction mechanism prevents slamming. It is made left- and right-handed from nickel-plated steel.
Size: 125mm (5in).

CASTORS

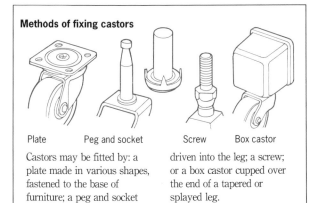

Methods of fixing castors

Plate   Peg and socket   Screw   Box castor

Castors may be fitted by: a plate made in various shapes, fastened to the base of furniture; a peg and socket driven into the leg; a screw; or a box castor cupped over the end of a tapered or splayed leg.

Ball castor
For all types of furniture. A heavy-duty ball-bearing castor capable of supporting loads up to 230kg (500lb).
Fitting: Plate, peg and socket, screw-in.
Size: 50mm (2in) diameter.

Wheel castor
For trolleys and beds. If the trolley is required to carry heavy loads, wheel castors should be used together with the ball castors.
Fitting: Plate, peg and socket, screw-in.
Size: 41mm (1⅝in) diameter.

HANDLES

Swan-necked handle
For high-quality furniture, such as chests of drawers. It is commonly available in solid brass and steel with various finishes and patterns.
Sizes: 88–113mm (3½–4½in).

Extruded aluminium pull handle
For doors and drawers, such as on built-in cupboards. It can be fitted vertically or horizontally.
Sizes: It is supplied in multiples of 75mm (3in), up to a maximum of 900mm (36in).

Knob
For cupboards, drawers and doors. Available in many shapes: round, oval, cylindrical and polygonal. It is made from wood, metal and plastics in numerous finishes.
Size: 50mm (2in).

Ring handle
For cupboards and drawers. The handle and its round- or square-shaped surround are made from solid brass and coated steel.
Size: 50 x 38mm (2 x 1½in).

Locks, bolts & catches

When fitting locks, bolts and catches for security, always fit the best quality available. Solid brass locks are better than those of folded or pressed brass or steel. Handed locks are also available. Viewed from the opening side, these are either left- or right-handed, according to the direction in which the bolt shoots when the key is turned.

Catches are required only to fasten doors or boxes and to hold them closed. Many are made from plastics or coated steel with plastic rollers for a smoother, quieter action on doors in constant use.

Unless specified below, the escutcheons for locks and striking plates for all the fittings are usually bought separately from the main fitting. They are available in a wide range of sizes and finishes.

Fitting locks

Surface   Recessed   Mortised

There are three basic ways in which cupboard locks and similar locks may be fitted. The straight cupboard lock is fitted to the door surface. The cut cupboard lock is recessed into the door. The mortise cupboard lock is mortised into the door thickness.

LOCKS

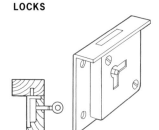

Drawer lock
For flush-fitting drawers.
Fitting: Recessed.
Some locks have two keyholes placed at right angles so that the lock can be used upright, in which case they are handed.
Sizes: 38 x 31–75 x 47mm (1½ x 1¼–3 x 1⅞in).

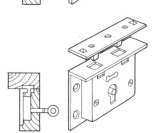

Box lock
For lift-up lids on boxes.
Fitting: Recessed.
The striking plate has two projecting tabs that fall with the lid and are engaged sideways by a bolt in the main part of the lock.
Sizes: 38–75mm (1½–3in).

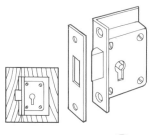

Spring lock
For drawers and cupboards.
Fitting: Recessed.
This spring-loaded lock can close without a key. It has a striking plate and is made left- and right-handed.
Sizes: 75 x 38–75 x 47mm (3 x 1½–3 x 1⅞in).

Escutcheon
For protecting the wood against scarring by the key.
Fitting: Pressing an open-based escutcheon into a hole (left); pressing a serrated escutcheon into a hole (centre); fixing a plate to the surface with escutcheon pins (right).
Sizes and finishes vary.

BOLTS

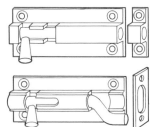

Barrel bolt
For cabinet doors.
Fitting: Surface.
Made from extruded brass with a steel shoot, the bolt is available either straight or necked for rebated doors.
Sizes: 50 x 25–150 x 25mm (2 x 1–6 x 1in).

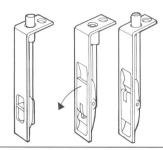

Flush bolt
For cupboard doors.
Fitting: Recessed.
The bolt can be operated by a knob or a concealed lever. It is made from brass or chromium-plated steel.
Sizes: 150 x 19–900 x 25mm (6 x ¾–36 x 1in).

CATCHES

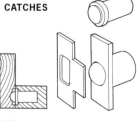

Single ball catch
For cabinet doors.
Fitting: Mortised.
It is made from brass and has a spring-loaded steel ball at the top. The edging gives a neat finish. It is supplied with striking plate.
Sizes: 3–16mm (⅛–⅝in) diameter.

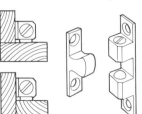

Double ball catch
For high-quality furniture.
Fitting: Surface.
Two spring-loaded steel balls adjusted by turning an integral screw to vary the pull of the door. It is made from brass, steel or plastics with a variety of finishes.
Size: 50mm (2in).

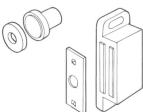

Magnetic catch
For cupboards and doors.
Fitting: Surface and recessed.
Made from hardened plastics and steel. Cylindrical recessed magnetic catches are used for lay-on doors.
Sizes: 44 x 16–60 x 16mm (1¾ x ⅝–2⅜ x ⅝in).

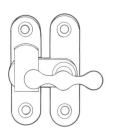

Showcase catch
For display cabinets and cupboards generally.
Fitting: Surface.
When fitting to a double door, fit a bolt to the inside of one of the doors. This catch is made from brass.
Sizes: 50–63mm (2–2½in).

Shelf fittings

One method of fixing a number of shelves into a carcass frame or cupboard is to use a series of housing joints (*see* page 124). With modern fittings and techniques there are now several alternatives, some of which make it possible for woodworkers to build a piece of furniture, such as a bookshelf, that was perhaps considered too complicated or time consuming to attempt hitherto.

Most shelf fittings currently available permit fully adjustable shelving arrangements which can be readily adapted for most storage purposes. All will support shelves made from solid wood or from manufactured board. Some are suitable for direct fixing to a supporting wall while others are specifically for use inside cabinets, bookcases and all types of built-in furniture.

Fittings for direct wall application range from simple, fixed, angle brackets, suitable for workshop and store room use, to various types which consist of lengths of metal channel mounted vertically on the supporting wall, into which specially shaped shelf bearers are inserted at any chosen position. Shelves are then attached on to the bearers. For adjustable shelves inside cupboards, etc, there is a choice of either small metal or plastic plugs of several kinds which are inserted into sockets in the upright sides of the cupboard, or spring wires that fit into each upright and into each end of the shelf. These last have the advantage of being completely concealed but they are not very strong. Strongest of all are the small metal brackets which fit into a slotted metal strip recessed and screwed into the cupboard or bookcase sides.

To avoid sagging under load, shelves should be sturdy, ie, between 19 and 25mm (¾ and 1in) thick, and with no more than 750mm (30in) between supports.

TYPES OF SHELF FITTING

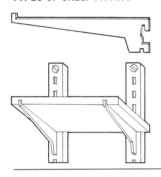

Heavy-duty shelving system

Comprises steel wall channels into which two-pronged brackets are inserted. The S-shaped bend between the prongs ensures that there is no lateral movement. Accessories include tilt brackets and book-ends. Each bracket can support 40kg (88lb).
Size: Channel 1000mm (40in); bracket 150 and 250mm (6 and 10in).

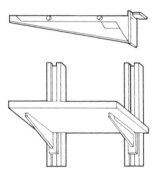

Lightweight shelving system

Comprises aluminium wall channels into which PVC locking strips are inserted to provide anchorage for the shelf brackets. Press fit each bracket in the horizontal position, then twist it until vertical. Shelf heights can be adjusted by tilting bracket up and sliding it. Each bracket supports about 15kg (33lb).
Size: Channel and brackets are cut to order.

Shelf bracket

For shelves in which the finish is secondary to strength, for example, in workshops and greenhouses. The bracket, which is made from zinc-plated or japanned steel, offers rigid support, the long vertical arm being capable of countering much leverage.
Size: 31 x 19mm (1¼ x ¾in).

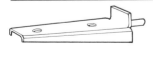

Cantilevered bracket

For moderate shelf support. The bracket is fitted by pushing the pin at the back into a pre-drilled hole in the wall and reinforcing it with a screw driven through the rear upturned part of the bracket. Screw the shelf to the zinc-coated steel bracket.
Size: 113mm (4½in).

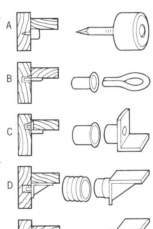

Stud shelf supports

For adjustable shelving in cabinets, bookcases and other fitted units. Fit the studs into holes about 150mm (6in) apart along the length of the carcass sides, according to requirements. Four studs – two at each end – will support most shelves. Some of the various types of stud shelf support available are: **A** a plastic stud with an integral nail; **B** a coated steel or brass eye and socket for lightweight shelves; **C** an angled, coated-steel stud and socket for supporting heavily laden shelves; **D** a plastic stud and bush; **E** a moulded plastic bracket stud; **F** and a two-piece shelf support. This last fitting comprises two plastic pegs. Fit the shelf between these two pegs so that the arms of the upper peg spread and grip the shelf. Once fitted, the shelf cannot be moved accidentally.

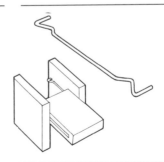

Magic wire

For fitting wooden shelves invisibly. Fit the ends of the wires into two holes positioned slightly closer than the length of the wire. Make stopped grooves in the ends of the shelf, which can then slide on to the wires. The shelf is given almost total support along its width.
Sizes: 138–219mm (5½–8¾in).

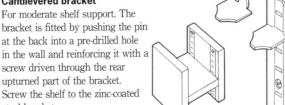

Bookcase strip

For bookcases or fitted units. Screw the strip along the length of the carcass sides and clip the studs into the horizontal slots. Both the strip and the studs are made in two finishes – zinc- or bronze-coated steel.
Size: 900mm (36in) length (can be cut shorter with a hacksaw); 19mm (¾in) width.

PROJECTS

Becoming a good woodworker requires both time and practice. The best way to learn how to do anything well is to do it. The materials need to be understood, the right tools must be chosen and their correct use in shaping and jointing wood must be mastered. Working methods, short-cuts, 'tricks of the trade', and ways of putting things right must all be learned. Such skills cannot be acquired without effort, nor can they be achieved by just reading a book.

The six projects that follow are intended to stimulate the creative interest inherent in all of us. Each project has been purposely designed to incorporate one or more of the joints described and illustrated in detail in the methods section of the book and to provide practice in their making.

The projects are the work of Andrew Crawford who designed them, made them and describes them especially for this book.

Essential tools

The following list comprises tools and materials that any keen woodworker should have to hand and these will be required to complete the projects. Extra items needed for specific projects are indicated where appropriate.

Abrasive papers: 180-grit garnet down to 1200, wet and dry if available
Brushes for glue, sealer and lacquer
Card or 1.5 mm plywood to make templates
Chisels: a selection: 6–38mm (¼–1½in)
Clear furniture wax
Coping saw
Clamps
Electric drill and various drills
Finish: sanding sealer, two-part lacquer, etc
Glue (PVA or similar)
Lubrasil paper (400-grit)
Mallet
Marking gauge
Masking tape
Pencil
Pins
Plane
Ruler
Sanding drum (for drill)
Scalpel/Craft knife
Screwdrivers
Screws
Scriber
Straight-edge
Tenon saw/Dovetail saw
0000 wire wool
45° fence

Measurements

The instructions for the six projects contain sets of both metric and Imperial measurements. Because these are not exact equivalents, nor intended as such, it is essential that you use either one set or the other, not both.

Desk box

The constructional strength of this elegant box comes from the keys cut into the mitred corners. I have made these and and decorative line around the lid from a sandwich of contrasting veneers. I recommend that you use a router to cut the keys and form the rebates.

CUTTING LIST

Maple
MAIN BOX
2   265 x 74 x 10mm (10½ x 3 x ⅜in)
2   195 x 74 x 10mm (7½ x 3 x ⅜in)

Birch plywood
LID
4mm 260 x 190mm (³⁄₁₆ x 10¼ x 7½in)

BASE
3mm 265 x 195mm (⅛ x 10½ x 7¾)

Figured maple veneer
2   270 x 200mm (10¾ x 8in)

Other materials
1m x 4mm (39 x ³⁄₁₆in) decorative line for the lid
4mm (³⁄₁₆in) veneer 'sandwich' or solid timber
      for mitre keys
2 hinges
2 'S'-hooks
2 A4 sheets of stiff card
Fabric (cotton moiré) 500 x 500mm
(18 x 18in)

EXTRA TOOLS NEEDED
Veneer press (or two smooth, rigid boards and four or five lengths of angle iron with two 75mm (3in) G-clamps for each piece of angle iron
Carpet underlay
Mitre saw or 45° shooting block and disc sander
Router

METHOD

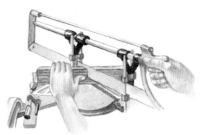

Cut the timber to shape
Prepare the timber to the dimensions in the cutting list. Cut the mitres using a mitre saw. Trim them using a plane on a 45° shooting block or disc sander to ensure that opposing pairs of pieces are identical in length.

Work the rebates in the underside to take the base and lid using a router, or a plough or rebate plane.

Plane the 2.5mm (³⁄₃₂in) chamfer around the top of the face edge of each piece.

If you are using a router, start to form the lid cut-off groove on the underside, cutting a 5mm (³⁄₁₆in) deep 3mm (⅛in) groove through half the thickness of the wood. Leave the router set up or keep a note of the exact setting.

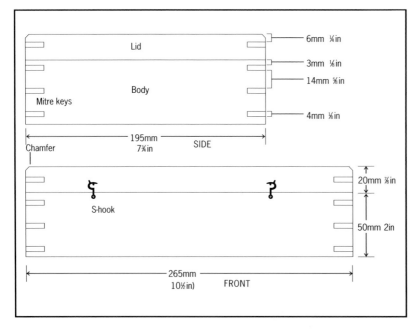

Lid

Body

Mitre keys

6mm ¼in

3mm ⅛in

14mm ⅝in

4mm ⅛in

Chamfer

195mm
7¾in

SIDE

S-hook

20mm ⅞in

50mm 2in

265mm
10½in)

FRONT

Assemble the body

Lay the timber in the correct order, outer side up. Put a piece of adhesive tape along the top and bottom of each side piece, making sure that it is long enough to be stuck firmly around each corner. Assemble in order, stretching the tape a little at each corner to make sure that the joints are really tight.

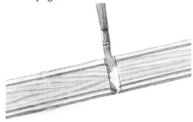

When you are satisfied with the fit, undo one corner, apply PVA to all the joints and then re-tape the corner. If you water the PVA down by 5 per cent, it will spread more easily and thinly, and will be less likely to form a layer separating the joints. It also slows drying time down a little. Wipe off any excess and set aside to dry for 2 hours.

Assemble the veneer

Tape one piece of veneer on to one of the boards with a piece of paper underneath (to stop the veneer sticking to the board). Tape only around the edge.

Apply an even coat of thinned PVA (10 per cent water) and place the ply on top. Apply another coat of glue to the ply, place the backing veneer on this (this prevents the lid bowing when dry), then another piece of paper and the carpet underlay.

Put the second board in place and either place in the veneer press or space the pieces of angle iron along the boards and apply the G-clamps. Set aside to dry for 2 hours.

Fit the lid and base

When the veneer is dry, remove it from the veneer press or clamped boards, measure, cut and plane it exactly to size and glue it in place with PVA. Cut and plane the base to size and glue it in place. Set aside to dry for 1 hour. Screw or pin the base to secure it.

Add the decorative line

I cut strips from a 4 mm (¾6in) glued-up sandwich that I also used for the mitre keys. You could also buy a ready-made line from veneer suppliers.

Separate the lid and box

If using a router, cut a 3mm (⅛in) wide groove 4.5mm (⁵⁄₃₂in) deep all round – almost deep enough to meet the first groove. Cut through the remaining 0.5 mm (½₂in) with a scalpel.

By hand, mark the correct position and carefully use a dovetail saw or other fine-toothed tenon saw to saw right through. Support the lid with small wedges where you have cut through at strategic points. Be very careful towards the end so that it does not break raggedly on the inside.

Clean up the inside edges. Glue some 180-grit garnet paper to the underside of one end of a piece of scrap about 75 x 300mm (3 x 12in). Work with a circular, grinding motion, ensuring that the opposite end of the scrap is touching the box surface to keep the edges level and square.

If using a router, cut an incomplete groove 2.5mm (³⁄₃₂in) in from the edge of the chamfer, just greater than veneer depth and just less than the width of your line, along each edge. Form the corners using a scalpel and a straight-edge. Open up the groove to its full width by trimming the inside edges with a scalpel and straight-edge. Alternatively, make up a small scraper the exact width of your line and run this along a firmly held straight-edge. Use the scraper to remove the waste down to the full depth. Or, mark the width of the line, then reinforce both sides of the channel using a scalpel and remove the waste with a narrow chisel. Form the corners carefully using a scalpel and straight-edge. Glue the line in and leave to dry for half an hour.

Form the mitre keys

Tape the box and lid together, mark out the cuts, and using either a router table and fence with a 'carriage', or sawing back to the marks, make the mitre key cut out for the keys. Cut the material for the keys into strips 18mm (¾in) wide, planing both edges absolutely square. Cut this into triangles 18 x 18 x 25mm (¾ x ¾ x 1in). Glue these in place, planed edge inwards, and set aside to dry for half an hour.

When the keys are dry, trim them back using a sharp, wide chisel, always working in from the corners.

Chamfer the hinge edge

Cut a fine chamfer along the back edge of both lid and box. The exact size of the chamfer will have a marked effect on how far the lid will open – just farther than 90° is ideal.

Fit the hinges

Mark out the width of the hinges on the back edges of the box and lid, cut down with a chisel and remove the waste to half the thickness of your hinges measured at the pins. Drill and screw the hinges into place on to the lid and then to the box, drilling for and fitting only one screw per hinge. Close the box to check that the lid and box line up. If they do not, mark for the next set of holes off centre in the direction in which you want the lid to move. This can take time to get right, but it is worth it. When you are satisfied, remove the hinges, thoroughly sand, apply finish to all of the exterior surfaces and set aside to dry for the time specified in the manufacturer's instructions.

Finish the outside

Smooth the box with 1200-grit wet-and-dry paper, then 0000 wire wool. Then wax it with a good quality clear furniture wax and buff.

Refit the hinges and drill and screw the 'S'-hooks in place.

Line the inside

Cut the card to fit the inside of the box (with a small allowance for the fabric). Cut the cotton moiré to size, allowing about 18mm (¾in) to wrap around to the back. Fix the fabric to the card using double-sided sticky tape. Check that all the pieces fit neatly and glue them in place in the following order using a latex adhesive: front and back first; then the sides; then the base. Repeat for the lid.

Modular wine rack

You can make as many modules as you need of this design – I have made three – each module holds four bottles. The top module has no vertical supports. Each module slots neatly and securely on top of another, but if you wish you could screw it together for added safety.

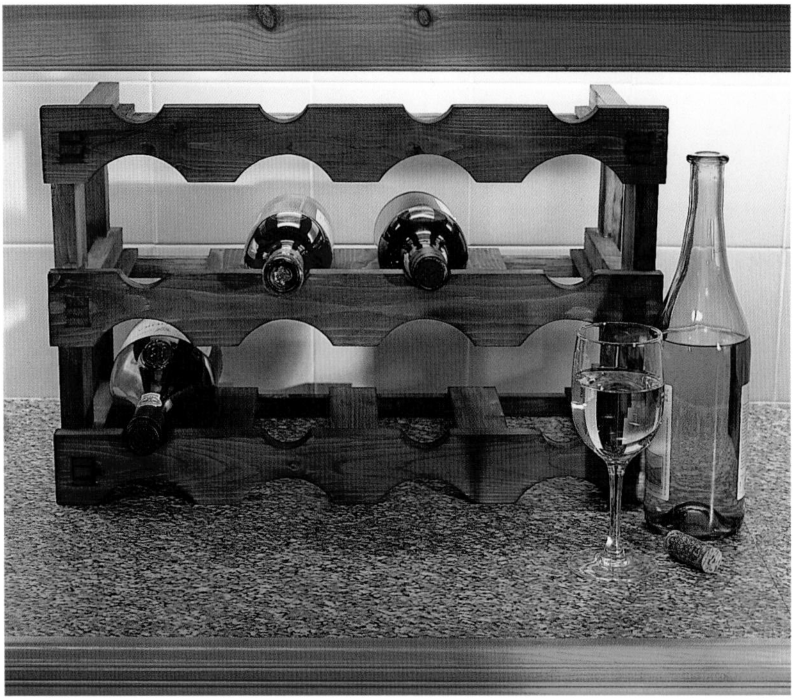

CUTTING LIST

Pine

FRONTS
3 500 x 60 x 18mm (20 x 2⅜ x ¾in)

SIDES
6 260 x 45 x 18mm (10 x 1¾ x ¾in)

SIDE SUPPORTS
Front
4 130 x 60 x 18mm (5⅛ x 2⅜ x ¾in)
Back
4 130 x 30 x 18mm (5⅛ x 1 3/16 x ¾in)

SLATS
9 242 x 45 x 6mm (9¼ x 1¾ x ¼in)
6 242 x 12 x 6mm (9¼ x ½ x ¼in)

SLAT SUPPORTS
Front
3 436 x 14 x 18mm (17¼ x⅝ x ¾ in)
Back
3 500 x 14 x 18mm (20 x ⅝ x ¾in)

Walnut

WEDGES
1 260 x 18 x 4mm (10 x ¾ x ⅛in)

Other materials

24 x no 2 (½in)screws
Thin ply 116 x 60mm (4½ x 2⅜in)

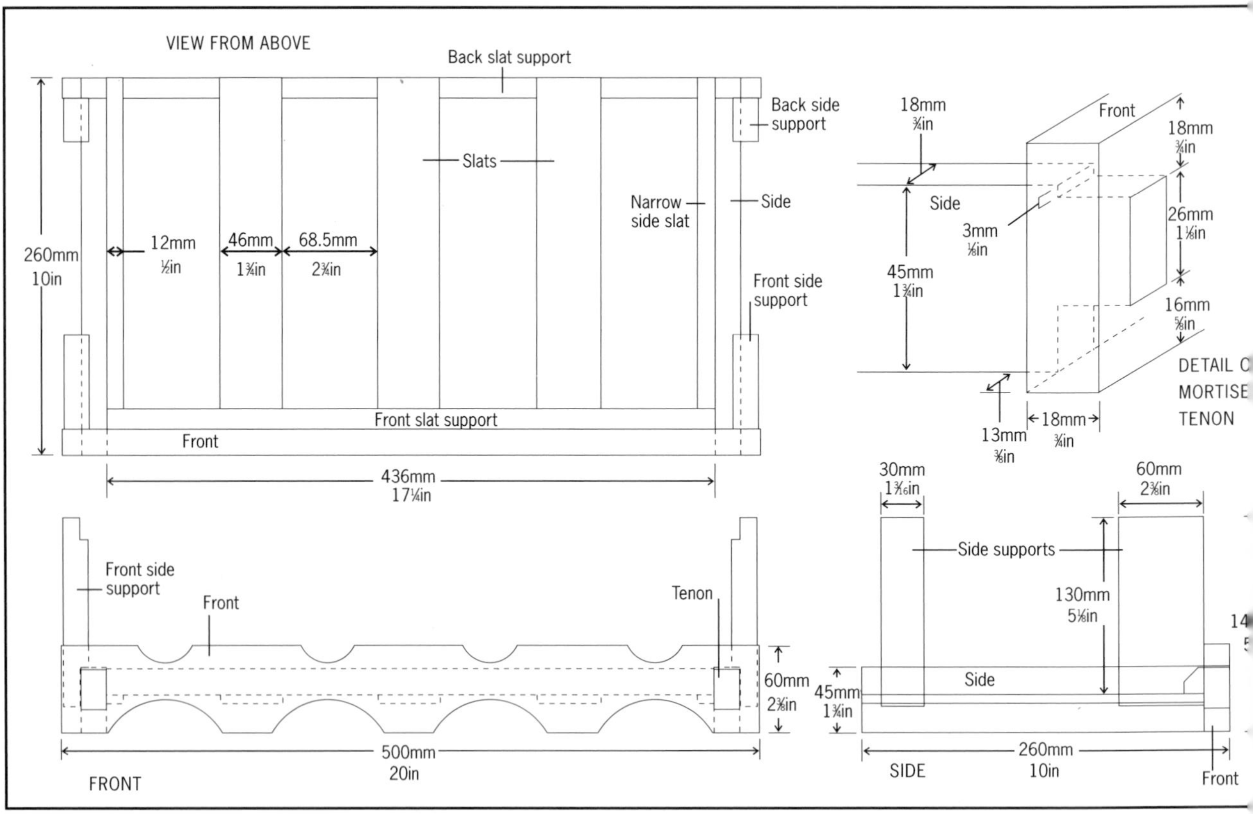
VIEW FROM ABOVE
Back slat support
Back side support
Slats
Narrow side slat
Side
260mm 10in
12mm ½in
46mm 1¾in
68.5mm 2¾in
Front side support
Front slat support
Front
436mm 17¼in
Front side support
Front
Tenon
60mm 2⅜in
500mm 20in
FRONT
18mm ¾in
Front
18mm ¾in
Side
3mm ⅛in
26mm 1⅛in
45mm 1¾in
16mm ⅝in
13mm ⅜in
18mm ¾in
DETAIL OF MORTISE TENON
30mm 1³⁄₁₆in
60mm 2⅜in
Side supports
130mm 5⅛in
45mm 1¾in
Side
260mm 10in
SIDE
Front

METHOD
Cut the timber to shape
Prepare your timber to the dimensions in the cutting list and make the template for the bottle curves from the plywood.

Make the tenons and shoulders
Tape the side pieces together in packs of three and mark the dimensions of the shoulders for the tenons (top: 3 x 18mm (⅛ x ¾in), underside: 16 x 18mm (⅝ x ¾in)). Hold them firmly in the vice and saw the shoulders using a tenon saw (*see* page 105) leaving tenons 26 x 18 x 18mm (1⅛ x ¾ x ¾in).

Repeat this process for the back slat supports on the underside of the sides (14 x 18mm (⅝ x ¾in)).

While the side pieces are still taped together, saw the slots in the tenons to take the wedges. There are two wedges per tenon, which you should space equally. Make the cuts slightly narrower than the walnut strip and to half the depth of the tenon (9mm (⅜in)). (*See* Wedging a through mortise and tenon, page 105.)

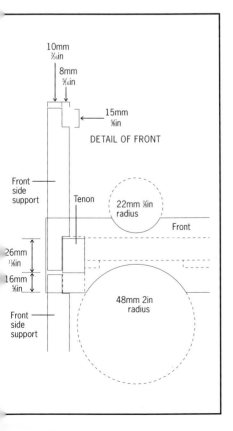

10mm
⅜in

8mm
⅜in

15mm
⅝in

DETAIL OF FRONT

Front side support

Tenon

22mm ⅞in radius

Front

26mm 1⅛in

16mm ⅝in

48mm 2in radius

Front side support

Cut the bottle curves in the front
Mark around the template on to one of the front pieces, starting 18mm (1in) from the end. Cut around just outside the lines with a coping saw. Smooth back exactly to the lines using a sanding drum mounted vertically or use 100- or 180-grit garnet paper on curved blocks. Use this as a template for all the other front pieces.

Mark and cut the mortises
Mark and cut the mortises 26 x 18mm (1⅛ x ¾in) (*see* page 105) on both faces of each of the front pieces using a marking gauge (18mm (¾in) from the top edge, 13mm (½in) from the side). Drill out most of the waste using a 16mm drill then chop the rest out with a chisel. Be careful not to break the grain away on the faces. Always work from the outside in, and not right through the mortises. Keep testing the fit.

Make the wedges for the tenons
Clamp the walnut strip to the bench with enough projecting to allow you to make a wedge 20mm (⅞in) long. Plane one face to a taper and cut the piece off at about 12mm (½in). Reposition the strip and continue until you have enough wedges.

Attach the front slat supports
Chamfer the inner top corners of the front slat supports and drill and screw these along the back faces of the fronts.

Join the front and sides
Apply glue to the mortises and tenons of one front and two side pieces and knock them together – use a piece of scrap to protect the wood. Apply a little glue to the wedge slots and hammer the wedges into place to tighten the tenons. Check carefully for squareness. Leave to dry for 1 hour.

Attach the back slat support
When the mortises and tenons are completely dry, screw the back slat support into place. NB The back supports stick out by about 14mm (⅝in) beyond each side piece – this is important as they lock against the side support to stop the top modules sliding forwards.

Tidy up the mortise and tenon joints
Carefully chisel off the waste from the ends of the tenons and wedges and sand completely flush. Repeat for all modules.

Attach the bottle support slats
Drill each end of the slats first to avoid splitting. Pin and glue the bottle support slats – including the narrow 12mm (½in) slats at each end – into place 68.5mm (2¾in) apart on top of the back support. Flip the module over and screw the front ends of the slats to the underneath of the front slat supports.

Attach the side supports
Carefully saw and chisel the rebates on the side supports (top:15 x 8mm (⅝ x ⁵⁄₁₆in); bottom: 26 x 8mm (1⅛ x ⁵⁄₁₆in)) and glue and screw them in place at the front and back of each side as indicated on the plan. Clamp and leave to dry for 1 hour.

Finishing
Sand the rack all over. It can be left untreated if you want, but I have given mine a coat of green aniline dye to add a bit of colour.

Breakfast tray

I have chosen cherry as it is a warm, neutral colour and not too heavy. It is also very fine grained which makes it ideal for dovetailing.

Dovetailing takes a bit longer than most other joints but it is still the most elegant solution to joining two pieces at right angles, both mechanically and visually.

CUTTING LIST

Cherry
MAIN FRAME
2   500 x 40 x 14mm (20 x 1⅝ x ⁹⁄₁₆in)
2   360 x 65 x 14mm (14 x 2⅝ x ⁹⁄₁₆in)

LIPPING
2   510 x 10 x 6mm (20½ x ½ x ¼in)
2   370 x 10 x 6mm (14½ x ½ x ¼in)

BASE
6mm (¼in) plywood
1   490 x 350mm (19½ x 13½in)

Other materials
Cork floor tiles or similar for interior
Screws
Sheet of stiff paper or card as a template
for the base

EXTRA TOOLS NEEDED
Bevel gauge

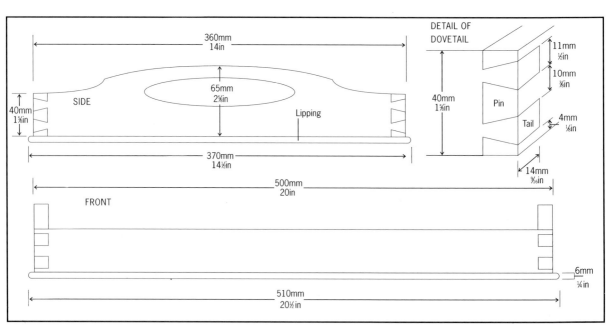

METHOD
Prepare the timber
Prepare your timber to the dimensions given in the cutting list and make a template for the shape of the handles from card or 1.5mm (¹⁄₁₆in) birch ply.

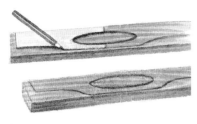

Mark and cut out the handles
Mark carefully around the prepared template for the handles on to each of the pieces for the ends (the shorter pieces) and cut the shapes for the handles out using a coping saw. (See page 42 for how to make interior cuts with a coping saw.)

Clean up the curves of the handles
Clean the curved shapes of the handles using either a vertically mounted sanding drum or of you are sanding it by hand 180-grit garnet paper around curved blocks. You may find that sandpaper wrapped around a piece of 1.5mm (¹⁄₁₆in) plywood is helpful – this will be firm but flexible enough to bend well around the various curves. Pay particular attention to the inside of the handle: the smoother it is the better the tray will feel.

Check the measurements
Make sure that the height at the end of the handle pieces is identical to that of the parallel sides and make any adjustments necessary by planing the straight edges.

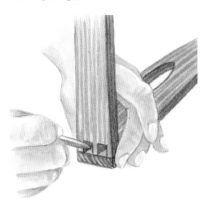

Mark up and make the dovetails
See pages 114–15 for how to mark and make the 'pins' and 'tails' of the dovetails following the dimensions shown on the plan. The dovetails should be at a slope of 1 in 6; the whole pins should be 10mm (¾in) at their narrowest; the half pins 4mm (¹⁄₈in) at their narrowest; and the tails 11mm (½in) at their widest. Make sure that you have the pieces of wood the correct way round: the narrow part of the pins and the wide part of the tails must be on the outside. First, mark and cut the pins on the long, unshaped sides, sawing with a coping saw just inside the marked lines.

Then mark and saw the tails on the handle sides, just inside the marked lines. Finally, chisel out the rest of the waste carefully, checking the fit with the other half of each joint until you have a neat push fit.

Fit the sides together
Do a dry run to check that all of the sides fit together properly and that the tray frame does not deviate from the square. Be careful when you are assembling and disassembling the dovetail joints, as a tug or twist in the wrong direction can split away the half pins at the edges of the long, unshaped sides.

When you are satisfied that all of the joints fit together neatly, apply glue and assemble them. You should not need to use clamps as the tapered shape of the pins and tails should pull the tray frame together, but do make sure that the tails – on the handle pieces – are pushed fully home into the gaps between the pins. As the fit should be quite tight, you may find that you need to apply a few strategic blows with a mallet – use a piece of scrap to avoid bruising the wood. Measure the diagonals to check for squareness and set aside to dry for 1 hour with a couple of weighted boards laid across to hold all four corners flat.

Sand the surface smooth
When the glue is dry, sand all of the joints completely flush on all of the outside faces and true up the top and bottom edges where the pieces meet. Give the whole frame a thorough sanding down to 320-grit.

Apply the lacquer
When you have a smooth, even surface, check that it is clean, dry and free of dust. Apply a coat of clear lacquer. Set the frame aside to dry between coats for the time specified in the manufacturer's instructions, apply another coat of lacquer, and, again, leave to dry according to the manufacturer's instructions.

Measure the base
Draw around the outside of the tray on to a piece of stiff paper or card as a template. Use this template to cut a piece of standard 6mm (¼in) plywood exactly 10mm (½in) smaller than your line drawing, taking into account any slight departures from the perfectly square that may have occurred despite your best efforts to avoid them!

Make the mitres in the lipping
Cut the mitres in the 10mm (½in) cherry lipping by sawing and then trimming them back to the exact length required using a disc sander and a 45° fence. If you don't have a disc sander, cut the mitres as accurately as you can. If the pieces of lipping become fractionally short, compensate for this by planing the inside edge. Do not overdo this or you will end up with a piece of narrower lipping down one side. Round over the outer edge of the lipping using a router or plane, or by sanding it, masking any minor differences at the corners. Alternatively, you could leave it square if you prefer.

Apply the lipping
Check that the lipping fits around the base without leaving any gaps at the corners. When you are completely satisfied, glue and tape each piece in place and leave it to dry. When the glue is completely dry, sand it smooth and level, apply two coats of laquer as before and set aside to dry according to the manufacturer's instructions.

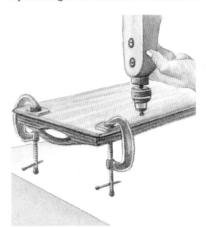

Fit the base to the sides
When both the sides and base are completely dry, use a marking gauge to mark a line 15mm (⅝in) in from the outer edge of the lipping all around the underside of the base – this should be about 5mm (¼in) inside of the inner edge of the lipping, ie, on the ply, not on the lipping. Clamp the base to the sides ensuring that the lipping projects the same distance beyond the sides all round. Drill equally spaced holes on the marked line and screw the base in place.

Add the finishing touch
To finish the tray, I have lined the interior of the base with some ready-sealed cork floor tiles which give a good-looking and practical, easy to clean surface, which is also heat-proof. These are stuck in place with contact adhesive.

Mirror frame

This mirror frame departs a little from the usual and the way in which I have joined the frame has given it has a slightly oriental feel. I have used ash here, but oak or straight-grained elm would do equally well. I have added some small ebony details at the corners of the finished mirror for added interest.

CUTTING LIST

Ash

2 700 x 50 x 14mm (28 x 2 x ⅝in)
2 550 x 50 x 14mm (22 x 2 x ⅝in)
1 260 x 50 x 14mm (10 x 2 x ⅝in)

3mm (⅛in) ply – or similar

2 510 x 25mm (20½ x 1in)
2 360 x 25mm (14½ x 1in)

Other materials

Scraps of ebony for decoration
2 mm (3/32in) mirror glass 480 x 330mm (19¼ x 13¼in)
3 mm (⅛in) hardboard 480 x 330 (19¼ x 13¼in)
Screws no 2 (½in)

METHOD

Prepare the timber

Prepare your timber to the dimensions given in the cutting list.

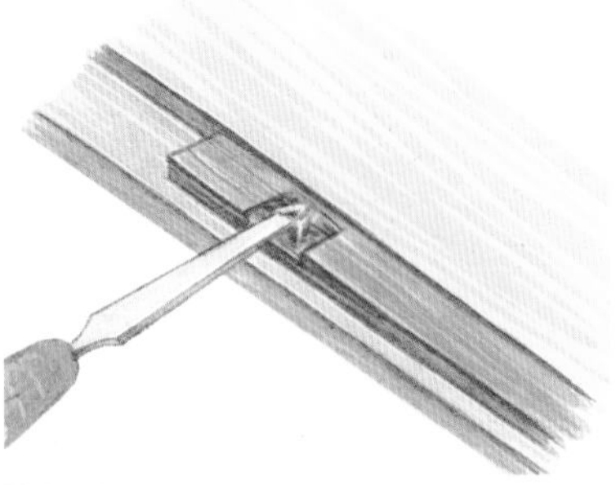

Make the cross-halving joints

Mark and cut the cross-halving joints 70mm (2¾in) from the ends, 50mm (2in) wide and 7mm (5/16in) deep, as shown on page 102, making sure that each piece of wood has one cut on the face and one on the back. Number all the joints.

Make the rebates

Mark the depth and width of the rebate using a marking gauge. It should be 10mm (⅜in) wide and 5mm (7/32in) deep along the inner edge of the back of each piece for the glass and hardboard. If your glass is thicker or thinner, adjust the depth of the rebate accordingly.

If you are using a router, set it up under a router table, as this is the best place for it for any small-scale work – and fit a 12mm (½in) or larger square cutter. Now take the rebate from the 'open' end, where the cutaway for the joint is at the back, to just short of the 'closed' end (this end must be finished by hand later).

If you are using a chisel, gradually remove the waste by chiselling using alternate vertical and horizontal cuts. To make it easier to remove the waste, you should make a saw cut across the grain roughly every 25mm (1in), but be careful not to saw over your marked lines.

You could also use a rebate plane with a 'bull-nose' facility.

Measure for the glass

When you have cut all four rebates, assemble the pieces in the correct order and measure across the back to make sure that the hardboard and glass will fit. These should sit snugly in place but not be too tight: allow 1mm (1/32in) all round. If necessary, trim a little more from the rebates.

Add the flares

Cut the fifth piece of ash into 16 equal pieces, 60 x 10 x 14mm (2⅜ x ⅜ x ⅝in), to form the flares. Glue these in place at the ends of the pieces in pairs, using PVA and ensuring that they are absolutely flush. Set aside to dry for 1 hour.

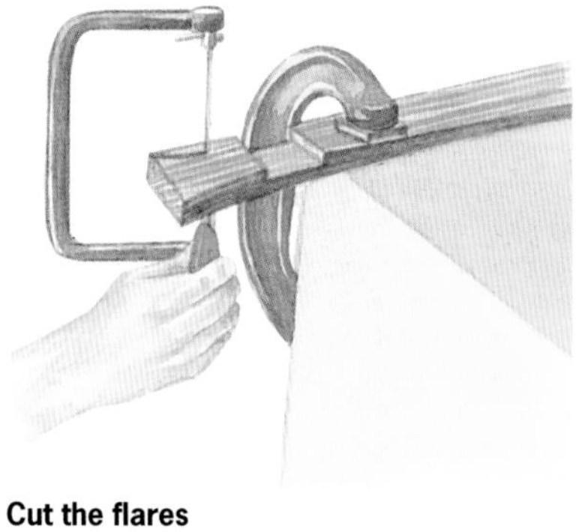

Cut the flares

Make a template for the flares out of card or 1.5mm (1/16in) birch ply cut to the exact shape of the flare (as shown on the plan *opposite above: right*) and draw around this on to each glued-on piece. Use either a bandsaw or coping saw to cut away the waste material. If you are using a coping saw, clamp the pieces firmly on to a bench and work the saw vertically. Whichever you use, you should cut fractionally outside the marked line.

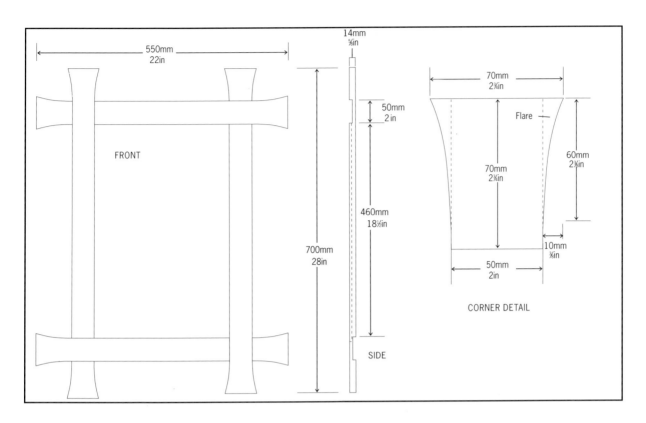

550mm
22in

FRONT

700mm
28in

14mm
⁹⁄₁₆in

50mm
2in

460mm
18½in

SIDE

70mm
2¾in

Flare

70mm
2¾in

60mm
2⅜in

10mm
⅜in

50mm
2in

CORNER DETAIL

Clean up the flares

Use a sanding drum mounted vertically to speed up cleaning. If you do not have one, use 180-grit garnet paper on a curved former for the basic cleaning and to remove the saw marks, then progress to 240. Be careful during the final shaping not to hollow the area where the flares join the main pieces as this would spoil the overall effect. Do not round off any sharp corners at this stage, leave that until after the frame has been glued up.

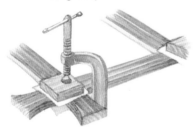

Assemble the frame

Do a dry run of assembling the whole frame first to make sure that the fit of the joints is not too tight and that the frame is properly squared up. When you are satisfied with the fit, glue the frame together using PVA. Clamp a single G-clamp at each joint and use a block of waste wood with paper at the top and bottom of each joint to help the corners glue up completely flush. (This will also stop the wood being bruised.) Set aside to dry for 1 hour.

When the PVA is completely dry, remove the G-clamps and clean up any adhesive that may have squeezed out from the between the joints and gently saw completely flush.

Tidy up the corners of the rebates

If you made the rebates for the mirror glass with a router, you will now need to finish the corners. Align a straight-edge with the body of each rebate and score along the incomplete part with a scriber or scalpel. Carefully chisel the waste away until it forms an exact corner with the completed rebate on the adjoining piece. Then repeat this process for the other three corners.

Sanding

Sand down the whole frame thoroughly with 320-grit garnet paper, softening any sharp corners. Again, take care not to hollow the areas where the flares join the main part of the frame.

Sealing

Apply a layer of sanding sealer or thinned two-part lacquer. Set aside to dry for for the length of time specified in the manufacturer's instructions. Sand the frame gently with 400-grit lubrasil paper and then rub all over with 0000 wire wool.

Add the decoration

I decorated my mirror with 10mm (½in) square blocks of ebony cut from scrap. Mark the exact position of the decoration on the frame, and remove the sealer or lacquer down to bare wood from where the glue will be applied. (This is essential, or the glue will not stick to the frame properly.) Apply the PVA and position the ebony blocks carefully. If necessary, use clamps and blocks of scrap to hold the ornamental scraps in position while they are drying. Set aside to dry for half an hour.

Fit the mirror glass and hardboard

To hold the mirror in place, I used pieces of 3mm (⅛in) birch ply, 25mm (1in) wide, 30mm (1¼in) longer than the mirror in each direction. Mark a line 15mm (⅝in) around the outside of the rebate, trim the strips to length so they fit just inside the line and mitre the corners for neatness. Drill through the ply for soem fine, 10mm (⅜in) countersunk woodscrews 8mm (⁵⁄₁₆in) from the outer edge, and 9mm (⅜in) into the frame 8mm (⁵⁄₁₆in) from the outer edge of the rebate. Put the mirror glass and hardboard in place, and screw the strips into position.

Hanging

Screw a flush picture hanging ring one-third of the way down each side, thread picture wire or strong cord through them and pull taught.

Finishing

Finally, mask the mirror glass and apply a good quality clear furniture polish and buff to a satisfying, warm, satin finish.

Spice rack

This walnut spice rack is designed so that the shelves are the right height to take small spice jars and herb pots. The drawer is optional – I have added air holes at the front so that it can be used to store garlic bulbs. The back is veneered, but you could use 4mm ($\frac{5}{32}$in) walnut instead.

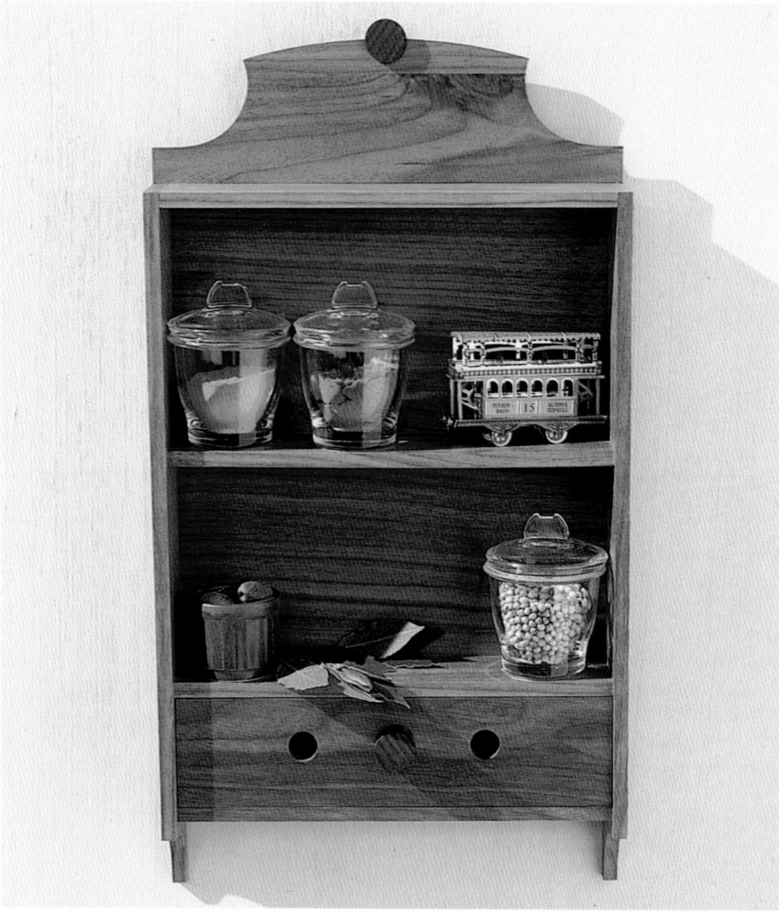

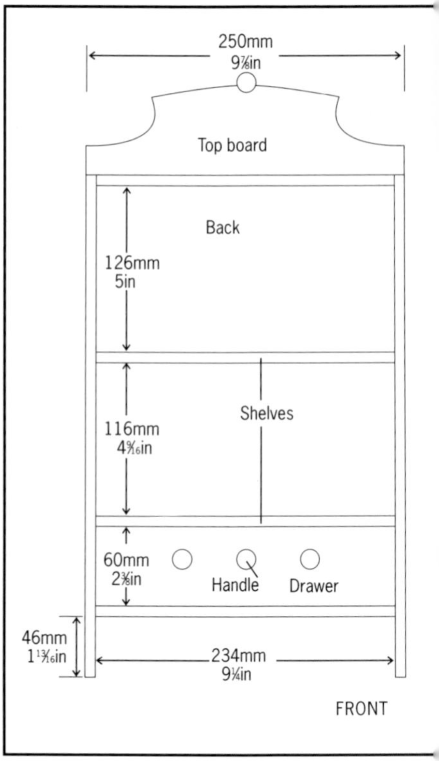

CUTTING LIST

Walnut

SIDES
2 383 x 66 x 8mm (15 x $2\frac{5}{8}$ x $\frac{5}{16}$in)

TOP
1 242 x 62 x 8mm ($9\frac{9}{16}$ x $2\frac{7}{16}$ x $\frac{5}{16}$in)

SHELVES
2 242 x 54 x 8mm ($9\frac{9}{16}$ x $2\frac{1}{8}$ x $\frac{5}{16}$in)

BOTTOM
1 242 x 58 x 8mm ($9\frac{9}{16}$ x $2\frac{5}{16}$ x $\frac{5}{16}$in)

TOP BOARD
1 250 x 75 x 8mm ($9\frac{7}{8}$ x 3 x $\frac{5}{16}$in)

DRAWER

Front
1 233 x 59 x 8mm ($9\frac{3}{16}$ x $2\frac{5}{16}$ x $\frac{5}{16}$in)

Back
1 233 x 59 x 4mm ($9\frac{3}{16}$ x $2\frac{5}{16}$ x $\frac{1}{8}$in

Sides
2 59 x 50 x 4mm ($2\frac{5}{16}$ x$1\frac{31}{32}$ x $\frac{1}{8}$in)

Base
1 231 x 48 x 4mm ($9\frac{1}{8}$ x $1\frac{7}{8}$ x $\frac{1}{8}$in)

3mm ($\frac{1}{8}$) plywood

BACK
325 x 246mm ($12\frac{13}{16}$ x $9\frac{3}{4}$in)

Walnut veneer

2 330 x 250mm ($12\frac{15}{16}$ x $9\frac{3}{4}$in)

Other materials

Pins
Screws

EXTRA TOOLS NEEDED

2 small sash clamps

METHOD

Prepare the timber

Prepare your timber to the dimensions given in the cutting list and mark and cut the curves at the bottom of the sides.

Veneer the back

See the Desk box (pages 162–3) for how to do this. When the veneer is dry, sand it thoroughly and apply two coats of the finish that you are using for the rest of the rack.

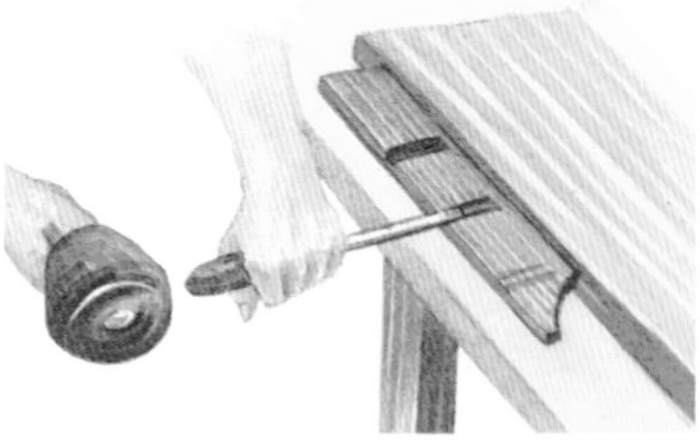

Cut the housings for the shelves

Mark the positions for the stopped shelf-housings. The barefaced housing (see page 101) for the top shelf is 4mm ($\frac{5}{32}$in) wide and the rest are 8mm ($\frac{5}{16}$in) wide. They are all 4mm ($\frac{5}{32}$in) deep and all stop 8mm ($\frac{5}{16}$in) short of the front edge. The top edges of the housings are at the following distances from the top of the side: top shelf 4mm ($\frac{5}{32}$in); second shelf 134mm ($5\frac{5}{16}$in); third shelf 258mm ($10\frac{3}{16}$in); bottom shelf 326mm ($12\frac{7}{8}$in).

If using a router, stop at least 8mm ($\frac{5}{16}$in) short of the front. Cut the front ends square by making firm cuts with a scalpel along a straight-edge and chiselling out the waste. If cutting the housings by hand, chisel or scalpel a clean cut along the marked lines and chisel out the waste.

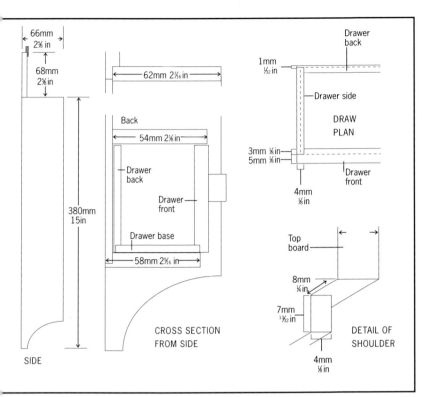

66mm
2⅝ in

68mm
2⅝ in

62mm 2⁷⁄₁₆ in

Back

54mm 2⅛ in

— Drawer
back

Drawer —
front

380mm
15in

Drawer base

58mm 2⁹⁄₁₆ in

CROSS SECTION
FROM SIDE

SIDE

1mm
¹⁄₃₂ in

— Drawer side

DRAW
PLAN

3mm ⅛ in
5mm ⅛ in

4mm
⅛ in

Drawer
back

Drawer
front

Top
board —

8mm
¼ in

7mm
¹³⁄₃₂ in

DETAIL OF
SHOULDER

4mm
⅛ in

Make the rebates to take the back
Cut a rebate 4 x 4mm (⁵⁄₃₂ x ⁵⁄₃₂in) along the inside back edges of the sides between the top and the housing for the bottom. Cut another rebate 4 x 4mm (⁵⁄₃₂ x ⁵⁄₃₂in) along the upper back edge of the bottom. The back will sit on this.

Shape the top
To allow the top to lay flush with the front of the sides, at the front of either end cut away a 4mm (⁵⁄₃₂in) deep shoulder 8 x 8mm (⁵⁄₁₆ x ⁵⁄₁₆in). Along the top edge of either end, cut a rebate 4 x 4 x 54mm (⁵⁄₁₆ x ⁵⁄₁₆ x 2⅛in) to form the barefaced housing joint with the tops of the sides.

Check the fit
Assemble the sides, shelves and top and bottom, planing the backs of the shelves if they protrude beyond the shoulder of the rebate for the back.

Apply the finish and sand
Disassemble the rack and give all the pieces a couple of coats of sanding sealer or a clear lacquer. Set aside to dry for 2 hours. Smooth all the surfaces, particularly those on the inside, with fine lubrasil paper and 0000 wire wool. Then wax and buff well.

Glue the rack together
Remove the wax and finish down to bare wood where glue is required. Apply PVA to the joints and fit the sides, shelves, bottom and top together.

Work on a level surface using two sash clamps to push the sides together. Use pieces of thick scrap to spread the pressure evenly. Measure the diagonals to check for squareness – correct minor discrepancies by skewing one of the sash clamps so that it acts slightly out of square. Set aside to dry for 1 hour.

Attach the back
Cut the back to size so that it overlaps the top by about 1mm (¹⁄₁₆in), smooth, wax, buff, and drill and pin into place, punching the pins in flush.

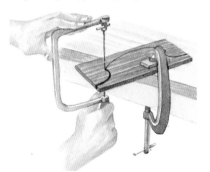

Cut the top board to shape
Draw the shape on to the timber and cut out with a coping saw. Mark and cut a rebate 7 x 4mm

(¼ x ⁵⁄₃₂in) along the front of the lower edge to overlap the top. Mark and cut shoulders 4mm (⁵⁄₃₂in) wide to fit over the sides. Finish as above.

Mark a shallow recess to take the circular decoration; cut carefully around the line with a scalpel or craft knife, chisel out the waste and glue the decoration in place.

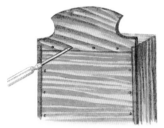

Attach the top board
Drill and countersink along the bottom back edge of the top board to take some fine brass countersunk woodscrews, 12mm (½in) long. Hold the board in position, mark through the holes, drill and screw in place.

The drawer
Cut rebates 3mm deep and 4mm wide (⁵⁄₃₂ x ⁵⁄₃₂in) for the sides along the inside ends of the front and back, and then 4mm deep and 3mm wide (⁵⁄₃₂ x ⁵⁄₃₂in) along the bottom inside edges of front, back and sides for the base. Drill the ventilation holes in the front, sand all the pieces thoroughly and apply finish, smoothing and waxing as before.

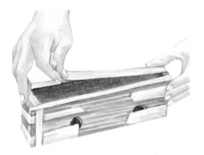

Check that all the pieces fit, and then glue up the drawer, using masking tape to hold the pieces together, and check for squareness.

Attach the drawer base
Cut the base to size, glue into place and set it aside to dry for 1 hour. Sand the bottom of the drawer completely flush.

Add the drawer pull
Fix the drawer pull using a piece of fine studding (threaded rod) or a small bolt with the head cut off, first screwed into the pull and then into the drawer. Alternatively, you could fit this from inside the front using a wood screw before assembly.

Hanging
If you intend to hang this unit, I suggest that you use a pair of flush picture hanging rings. Fix these in position by screwing through the top board into the back of the top shelf, using fine 15mm (⅝in) countersunk woodscrews and join them with some picture wire.

Child's playbox

The moving eyebrows and eyes on this playbox should make this a popular and useful addition to any child's bedroom, and the strong dowelled construction will ensure that it should stand up to heavy use. The aniline dyes that I used for the facial features are non-toxic.

CUTTING LIST

Beech
LEGS
   4   300 x 36 x 36mm (12 x 1½ x 1½in)
BATTENS
   3   300 x 14 x 14mm (12x ½ x ½in)
   2   200 x 14 x 14mm (8 x ½ x ½in)

12mm (½in) birch plywood
FRONT
   1   328 x 260mm (13 x 10¼in)
BACK
   1   328 x 190mm (13 x 7½in)
SIDES
   2   248 x 190mm (9½ x 7½in)
LID
   1   450 x 370mm (18 x 14½in)

4mm (⅛in) birch plywood
BASE
   1   352 x 272mm (14 x 10½in)

Other materials
black, blue and red aniline dyes
screws
waxed paper
36 dowels – 25 x 6mm (1 x ¼in)
pair of hinges 8mm (⅜in) deep
260mm (10½in) chain
Plus various bits for the facial features:
   3mm ply for the eyes, eyebrows and tongue
   Small block of birch for the nose

EXTRA TOOLS NEEDED
4 sash clamps
Drill stand or dowelling jig
Dowel centres for marking the dowel holes

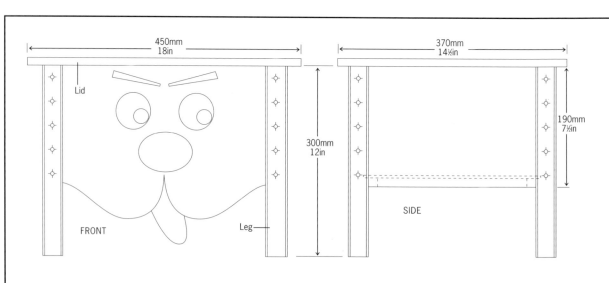

450mm
18in

Lid

300mm
12in

FRONT

Leg

370mm
14½in

190mm
7½in

SIDE

METHOD
Prepare the timber
Cut your timber and plywood to the dimensions specified in the cutting list. It is particularly important that the legs are exactly square.

Shape the front
Mark the outlines of the dog's face on the front. Cut the plywood to shape with a coping saw and sand the sawn edge smooth.

Drill the dowel holes
Mark a central line along each end of the pieces of ply. There are five dowels each for the front and back and four dowels each for the sides. Space the five dowels evenly down the front and back, and space the four dowels for the sides between them. No dowels are at the same height in one leg as this would weaken it.

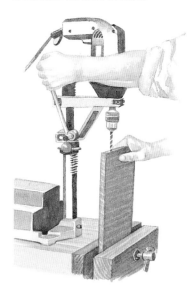

Drill to a depth of 13mm (⅝in), using a drill stand and a 6mm (¼in) drill. It is important that the ply is held absolutely square and vertical. You could also use sighting jigs and blocks and there are several dowelling jigs on the market that will cope with the

problems of squareness and lining up. Repeat this with all of the pieces. The best drills to use are 'lip and spur' bits. These have good sharp points that enable you to locate the holes exactly, and a sharp spur to cut a clean hole.

Shape the legs
Make 3mm (⅛in) chamfers along three corners of each of the legs (the fourth corner, the inside, will also have a chamfer, but this is done later).

Mark the dowel holes in the legs
Mark the centres of the holes on the legs as accurately as possible, using a set of 'dowel centres'. Number the pieces to be joined and simply push them together to give you your accurately marked centres. Drill to a depth of 13mm (⅝in), keeping the legs absolutely straight.

Make the final chamfer on the legs
Once you have a secure push fit for all pieces, assemble the box – without glue. On the inside, mark where the ply meets the legs. Take the box apart, and plane a wide chamfer on the fourth corner of the legs between the marked lines.

Attach the battens to support the base
Mark the position of the back and side battens along the bottom, inner edge of each piece. Measure their positions from the top and position the batten on the front, shaped piece accurately. Glue and screw all four battens using 22mm (⅞in) countersunk woodscrews.

Assemble the body
Glue the legs to the front and back. When these are dry, join the two sides. Cut the ply to size for the base. Drill and screw it in place, using 12mm (½in) countersunk woodscrews.

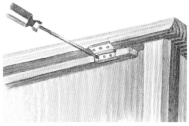

Fit the lid
Glue and screw the hinge batten at the top of the back. Round over the edges of the lid with a rounding-over cutter or by planing. Sand all surfaces. Attach the hinges to the underside of the back edge of the lid, mark their position on the hinge batten, carefully mark, saw and chisel out a recess to take the hinges to their full depth and screw the lid in place. Check for accurate fit.

Finishing
Remove the lid, apply a couple of coats of clear lacquer to the exterior surfaces and set everything aside to dry according to the manufacturer's instructions.

Apply the facial features
Make the eyes, eyebrows and tongue from plywood, colour them with aniline dyes and seal with a clear lacquer. The pupils should be off-centre.

Stick waxed paper on the back of the eyes and eyebrows and fix in place with one central screw each. Drill tight holes for the screws and do not screw them in too tightly, so they will be free to move and you can change the expression. Camouflage the screw heads with black paint.

Fix the tongue and nose on from behind with two screws each, re-attach the lid and fit the chain so that it holds the lid vertically when it is open.

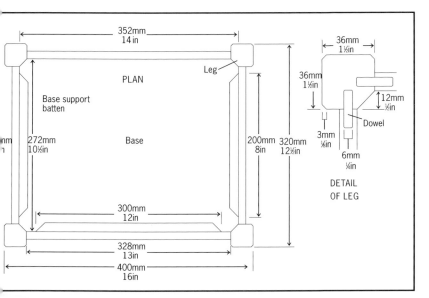

Glossary

Abrasive paper A general term for paper such as garnet paper and glasspaper. Sometimes referred to as sandpaper.
Adhesives Substances, such as glue, used to stick objects together.
Air-dried Timber seasoned in open air but protected from direct sun and rain.
Animal glue A glue made from gelatinous materials, eg, animal skin and bone after boiling.
Arbor A steel shaft or spindle integral with a tool or accessory for fixing into a CHUCK, etc.

Batten A thin strip of wood used in making or stiffening light frames and as a supporting piece.
Bevel An edge fully formed at an angle other than 90° to the face side.
Bodying The second stage of french polishing, using a rubber.
Buff To rub with an absorbent, soft cloth by hand or machine in the final stages of polishing.
Burr edge A wire edge such as that left on a tool after grinding or the finish on a hardboard edge after planing.
Burr, of a tree An irregular outgrowth on a tree caused by injury to the tree, often yielding a highly ornamental FIGURE.

Carcass The main frame of a construction such as a cabinet.
Carpentry The structural use of wood in the building trade.
Chamfer That part of an edge that is angled.
Chuck A device for holding wood for turning, or for gripping a bit in a hand brace or a drill bit in a hand drill or power drill.
Clamp A device for temporarily squeezing or drawing a frame together until glue has set.
Collet A collar or sleeve that grips a cylindrical object when compressed around it.
Countersink To shape a screw-hole to allow the head of a countersunk screw to finish flush with the wood surface.
Cramp see Clamp.

Dado A GROOVE cut across the wood grain. When the end of a second board is fitted into the dado, a HOUSING joint is formed.
Datum line A reference surface from which all measurements and angles are made. See FACE EDGE and FACE SIDE.
Dowel A cylindrical length of hardwood; a wooden pin or peg used in jointing.
Durability (seasoning) The length of time over which wood remains stable.

Edge The narrow surface at right angles to the sides. In this book, where it has been necessary to distinguish between the various edges of a board, the edges that run along the grain are referred to as side edges and the other two as ends.
End grain The grain shown on a cross-cut surface; a transverse section through a tree.
Escutcheon An ornamental plate surrounding a keyhole or a door or drawer handle.

Face edge Edge planed square to the FACE SIDE from which all other measurements are made.
Face mark A mark on the face side that reaches over to the face edge to distinguish them from the other surfaces during working.
Faceplate A circular metal plate with a threaded hub that fits to the HEADSTOCK SPINDLE of a lathe. Screw holes allow a work-piece to be mounted for turning.
Face side The wide surface chosen to be exposed on the finished work. Planed square to the FACE EDGE, all other measurements are made from it.
Fibres The strengthening tissues in wood.
Figure The surface appearance of the wood caused by inherent colouring substances and the arrangement of the wood tissues.

Gauge To score or mark with the spur of a gauge; a marking gauge.
Grain The arrangement and direction of the wood tissues. Wood may be worked in one of four ways: with the grain, meaning in the direction of the grain; across the grain, meaning at right angles to the grain; against the grain, meaning in the opposite direction to the grain; and along the grain, meaning up and down the grain.
Groove A channel worked along the GRAIN.

Haunch A shortened portion of a TENON to keep the joint locked at the corner.
Headstock The part of a lathe housing the mechanism that transmits the driving power.
Headstock spindle The rotating shaft protruding from a lathe HEADSTOCK to which FACEPLATES, CHUCKS and drive centres may be fitted.
Hone To sharpen a tool edge on a stone.
Housing A GROOVE cut across the grain to house the end of a board.

In-cannel Where the blade of a gouge has a grinding BEVEL on the inside.
'In winding' A defect in which a board is twisted along its length as a result of faulty drying or storage.

Jig A device for holding wood or a tool enabling work to be done quickly and accurately.
Joinery Fine woodwork in the building trade.

Kerf The cut made in wood by a saw blade.
Keying The reinforcement of a MITRED corner with 2mm (⅛in) three-ply or VENEER.
Kiln-dried Timber seasoned artificially and quickly in an environment where temperature and humidity are controlled.

Laminate Thin strips of wood glued together to form (usually) curved components.
Length The measurement along the wood grain.

Mitre joint A joint in which the junction bissects the angle of the mating pieces, usually at 45°.
Mortise A rectangular hole. On a workbench, a bench dog fits into a mortise. On a joint, a tenon fits into a mortise.
Moulding A shaped wooden edge used as decoration. It can be integral (stuck) or planted on in strip form with pins and glue.
Muntin The dividing piece of wood between two STILES or two panels, to provide extra support to the frame or drawer bottom.

Out-cannel Where the blade of a gouge has a grinding BEVEL on the outside.
Ogee A moulding consisting of concave and convex arcs.

Panel A thin infilling board in a frame.
Pare To trim or cut lightly; remove wood little by little.
Pilot hole A small hole drilled into wood to act as a guide for a large drill bit; it is usually made with a bradawl or a small drill bit.
Ply A single thin sheet of VENEER. An odd number of plies laid and bonded at right angles to the adjacent ply or plies is known as three-ply, five-ply or multi-ply, according to the number of plies.
PVA Polyvinyl acetate. It is the basis of many cold glues.

Quarter-sawn Logs first cut longitudinally into quarters, then cut into boards.
Quirk stick A small piece of wood shaped to remove excess wood filler and glue.

Rail A horizontal piece of wood between two vertical components.
Rebate A right-angled recess or step along the edge of a piece of wood.
Resin glue A chemical, vegetable or mineral glue, usually in two parts, resin and hardener, mixed together before use.

Rod A full-size model or sectional drawing showing constructional detail.

Scratch bead Beading formed by a scraping tool such as a scratch stock.
Shank, of a bit That part of a bit or drill held in the jaws of a brace or hand drill.
Shank, of a screw That part of a screw between the head and the first thread.
Shoulder The END-GRAIN surface perpendicular to the TENON.
Spigot A peg or peg-like protrusion, usually integral with the work, that enters a mating socket for locating or pivoting.
Stile The vertical sides in the frame of a door or a window.
Stopped Not cut through; when a REBATE, HOUSING or CHAMFER does not run to the end of the work.
Strop A leather strip dressed with a fine abrasive; to perfect a cutting edge by rubbing it on a strop.
Sweep The curved cross-section of a gouge.

Tang, of a bit That part of a bit that fits into the CHUCK of a brace.
Tang, of a chisel The pointed end of a chisel blade that drives into the wooden handle to hold the two parts together.
Template A shape or pattern cut to act as a guide in the repeat work on a design.
Tenon A reduced section on the end of a piece of wood that fits into a cavity or recess of the same size called a MORTISE.
Thickness The sectional measurement between the two wide surfaces.
Through From end to end; when a REBATE, HOUSING or CHAMFER runs the length of the work; joints such as some MORTISE and TENONS and dovetails that pass through the work.

Undercut To cut inside the line of the vertical.
Underside The opposite side to the FACE SIDE.

Veneer A thin layer of wood, usually having a decorative figure, bonded to a backing of less attractive but stable wood or manufactured board material. Any one of the layers in plywood.

Waney edge The natural edge of a tree trunk that has been retained after conversion.
Warping A general term used for cupping, bowing, 'IN WINDING' and diamonding in wood. It can be caused by underseasoning or careless storage.
Width The measurement across the GRAIN.

Index

Page numbers in **bold** refer to illustrations and tables.

Picture acknowledgments

Special Photography by **Laura Wickenden**: 3, 8 /9, 22 /3, 94 /5, 152 /3, 160 /1, 162, 164, 166, 168, 170, 172.

7 **John Plimmer** 10/11 *Microphotographs*: **Building Research Establishment, Princes Risborough**, *Wood photographs*: Octopus Publishing Group Limited/**Michael Busselle**, 12/13 Octopus Publishing Group Limited/**Frances Eveleigh** 15 Left **Canadian Pacific** 15 Right **Ernest Scott** 16 Octopus Publishing Group Limited/**Michael Busselle**